LEARN, TEACH...
SUCCEED...

With **REA's PRAXIS II® Elementary Education (0011)**
test prep, you'll be in a class all your own.

WE'D LIKE TO HEAR FROM YOU!

Visit **www.rea.com** to send us your comments
or email us at **info@rea.com**

Research & Education Association

The Best Teachers' Test Preparation for the

PRAXIS II®

Elementary Education:

Curriculum, Instruction, and Assessment (0011)

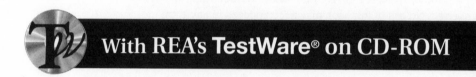

With REA's **TestWare®** on CD-ROM

Shannon Grey, Ed.D.
Associate Professor
Princeton University, Princeton, N.J.

Anita Price Davis, Ed.D.
Professor Emerita
Converse College, Spartanburg, S.C.

For updates to the test or this book visit:
www.rea.com/praxis/eled0011.htm

Planet Friendly Publishing
✔ Made in the United States
✔ Printed on Recycled Paper
Text: 10%   Cover: 10%
Learn more: www.greenedition.org

GREEN EDITION

At REA we're committed to producing books in an Earth-friendly manner and to helping our customers make greener choices.

Manufacturing books in the United States ensures compliance with strict environmental laws and eliminates the need for international freight shipping, a major contributor to global air pollution.

And printing on recycled paper helps minimize our consumption of trees, water and fossil fuels. This book was printed on paper made with **10% post-consumer waste**. According to Environmental Defense's Paper Calculator, by using this innovative paper instead of conventional papers, we achieved the following environmental benefits:

Trees Saved: 7 • Air Emissions Eliminated: 1,352 pounds
Water Saved: 1,255 gallons • Solid Waste Eliminated: 399 pounds

For more information on our environmental practices, please visit us online at **www.rea.com/green**

Research & Education Association
61 Ethel Road West
Piscataway, New Jersey 08854
E-mail: info@rea.com

The Best Teachers' Test Preparation for the Praxis II® Elementary Education: Curriculum, Instruction, and Assessment 0011 with TestWare® on CD-ROM

Published 2011

Copyright © 2009 by Research & Education Association, Inc.

Printed in the United States of America

Library of Congress Control Number 2008932814

ISBN-13: 978-0-7386-0401-5
ISBN-10: 0-7386-0401-1

Windows® is a registered trademark of Microsoft Corporation

The competencies presented in this book were created and implemented by Educational Testing Service. For individual state requirements, consult your state education agency. For further information visit the PRAXIS website at www.ets.org/praxis.

REA® and TestWare® are registered trademarks of Research & Education Association, Inc.

G10-0101

About Research & Education Association

Founded in 1959, Research & Education Association is dedicated to publishing the finest and most effective educational materials—including software, study guides, and test preps—for students in middle school, high school, college, graduate school, and beyond.

REA's Test Preparation series includes books and software for all academic levels in almost all disciplines. Research & Education Association publishes test preps for students who have not yet entered high school, as well as for high school students preparing to enter college. Students from countries around the world seeking to attend college in the United States will find the assistance they need in REA's publications. For college students seeking advanced degrees, REA publishes test preps for many major graduate school admission examinations in a wide variety of disciplines, including engineering, law, and medicine. Students at every level, in every field, with every ambition can find what they are looking for among REA's publications.

REA's practice tests are always based upon the most recently administered exams and include every type of question that you can expect on the actual exams.

REA's publications and educational materials are highly regarded and continually receive an unprecedented amount of praise from professionals, instructors, librarians, parents, and students. Our authors are as diverse as the fields represented in the books we publish. They are well-known in their respective disciplines and serve on the faculties of prestigious high schools, colleges, and universities throughout the United States and Canada.

Today, REA's wide-ranging catalog is a leading resource for teachers, students, and professionals.

We invite you to visit us at *www.rea.com* to find out how "REA is making the world smarter."

Acknowledgments

We would like to thank Larry Kling, Vice President, Editorial, for his editorial direction; Pam Weston, Publisher, for setting the quality standards for production integrity and managing the publication to completion; John Cording, Vice President, Technology, for coordinating the design, development, and testing of REA's TestWare®; Alice Leonard, Senior Editor, and Kathleen Casey, Senior Editor, for project management and preflight editorial review; Diane Goldschmidt, Senior Editor, for post-production quality assurance; Heena Patel, Technology Project Manager, for software testing efforts; Christine Saul, Graphic Artist, for cover design; and Rachel DiMatteo, Graphic Artist, for book design.

We also gratefully acknowledge Caroline Duffy for copyediting, Kathy Caratozzolo for typesetting, Ellen Gong for proofreading, and Stephanie Reymann for indexing the manuscript.

About the Authors

Dr. Shannon Grey has had a successful career in education for over sixteen years. Dr. Grey graduated with honors with a B.S. in Early Childhood Development from New York University. She received her Master of Education degree from Rutgers, The State University of New Jersey's Graduate School of Education, with a specialization in Elementary Language Arts. Dr. Grey earned her Ed.D. from Rutgers in the area of Sociological and Philosophical Foundations of Education, specializing in Curriculum Theory and Development.

Dr. Grey taught elementary school for thirteen years in highly acclaimed public schools. During her time as a teacher she served as a mentor for novice educators, staff developer, and chairperson for several school-based and district-wide committees. Dr. Grey was also the co-creator of a summer institute aimed at instructing students in the areas of language arts and mathematics. As a faculty lecturer, she has taught classes in teacher education at Rutgers University. Currently Dr. Grey teaches and supervises student teachers for Princeton University's Program in Teacher Preparation.

Dr. Anita Price Davis is The Charles Dana Professor Emerita of Education and was the Director of Elementary Education at Converse College, Spartanburg, South Carolina. Dr. Davis earned her B.S. and M.A. from Appalachian State University and her doctorate from Duke University. She also received a postdoctoral fellowship to Ohio State University for two additional years of study.

Dr. Davis had worked more than 36 years at Converse College, where she served as the faculty advisor for Kappa Delta Epsilon, a national education honor organization. She also worked 5 years as a public school teacher.

Dr. Davis has received wide recognition for her work, including a letter of appreciation from the U.S. Department of the Interior, inclusion in Contemporary Authors, and a citation of appreciation from the Michigan Council of the Social Studies. She has authored/coauthored 23 funded grants for Converse College. She has served as a mentor and was a two-time President of the Spartanburg County Council of the International Reading Association. The state of South Carolina twice named her an outstanding educator, and she was twice a nominee for the CASE U.S. Professor of the Year.

Dr. Davis has authored, co-authored, and edited more than 80 books. She has written two college textbooks titled Reading Instruction Essentials and Children's Literature Essentials. Dr. Davis has published several history books and is also the author of more than 80 papers, book reviews, journal articles, and encyclopedia entries.

CONTENTS

Introduction

ABOUT THIS BOOK AND TEST*ware*®

If you're looking to secure certification as an elementary teacher, you'll find that many states require the Praxis II: Elementary Education: Curriculum, Instruction, and Assessment Test (0011). Think of this book as your toolkit to pass the test.

Deciding to pursue a teaching career already speaks volumes about you. You would not have gotten to this point without being highly motivated and able to synthesize considerable amounts of information.

But, of course, it's a different matter when you have to show what you know on a test. That's where we come in. We're here to help take the mystery and anxiety out of the process. We're here to equip you not only with the nuts and bolts, but, ultimately, the confidence to succeed alongside your peers across the United States.

We've put a lot of thinking into this, and the result is a book that pulls together all the critical information you need to know to pass the Praxis Elementary Education 0011 Test.

Let us help you fill in the blanks—literally and figuratively!—while providing you with the touchstones that will allow you to do your very best come Test Day and beyond.

In this guide, REA offers our customarily in-depth, up-to-date, objective coverage, with test-specific modules devoted to targeted review and realistic practice exams complete with the kind of detail that makes a difference when you're coming down the homestretch in your preparation. Practice tests 1 and 2 for the PRAXIS 0011 are also included on the enclosed TEST*ware*® CD-ROM. We strongly recommend that you begin your preparation with the TEST*ware*® tests. The software provides timed conditions and instantaneous, accurate scoring, which makes it easier to pinpoint your strengths and weaknesses. We also include a quick-view answer key and competency-categorized progress chart to enable you to track your progress.

ABOUT THE PRAXIS SERIES

Praxis is Educational Testing Service's shorthand for Professional Assessments for Beginning Teachers. The Praxis Series is a group of teacher licensing tests that ETS developed in concert with states across the nation. There are three categories of tests in the series: Praxis I, Praxis II and Praxis III. Praxis I includes the paper-based Pre-Professional Skills Tests (PPST) and the Praxis I Computer-Based Tests (CBT). Both versions cover essentially the same subject matter. These exams measure reading, mathematics, and writing skills and are often a requirement for admission to a teacher education program. Praxis II embraces Subject Assessment/Specialty Area Tests, including the Praxis II Elementary Education series, of which the Praxis II 0011 exam is a part. The Praxis II examinations cover the subject matter that students typically study in teacher education courses—such content as human growth and development, school curriculum, methods of teaching, and other professional development courses. In most teacher-training programs, students take these tests after having completed their classroom training, the course work, and practicum. Praxis III is different from the multiple-choice and essay tests typically used for assessment purposes. With this assessment, ETS-trained observers evaluate an instructor's performance in the classroom, using nationally validated criteria. The observers may videotape the lesson, and other teaching experts may critique the resulting tapes.

The Praxis II 0011 covers the curriculum, the instruction, and the assessment of the content areas of reading and language arts, mathematics, science, and social studies. This study guide will deal with each content area (the curriculum) and with instruction and assessment in the content chapters to come. Two additional chapters vital to the Praxis II 0011 cover the subject matter areas of arts and physical education as well as general information about curriculum.

Who Takes the Test?

Most people who take the Praxis II 0011 are seeking initial licensure. You should check with your state's education agency to determine which Praxis examination(s) you should take; the ETS Praxis website (*www.ets.org/praxis/*) and registration bulletin may also help you determine the test(s) you need to take for certification. You should also consult your education program for its own test requirements. Remember that colleges and universities often require Praxis examinations for entry into programs, for graduation, and for the completion of a teacher certification program. These requirements may differ from the baseline requirements the state has for teacher certification. You will need to meet both sets of requirements.

When Should I Take the Test?

The Praxis II 0011 is a test for those who have completed or almost completed their teacher education programs. Each state establishes its own requirements for certification; some states specify the passing of other tests. Some states may require the test for initial certification; other states may require the test for beginning teachers during their first months on the job. Generally, each college and university establishes its own requirements for program admission and for graduation. Some colleges and universities require certain tests for graduation and/or for completion of a teacher education program. Check with your college and the state teacher certification agency for details.

When and Where Can I Take the Test?

ETS offers the Praxis 0011 seven times a year at a number of locations across the nation. The usual testing day is Saturday, but examinees may request an administration on an alternate day if a conflict—such as a religious obligation—exists.

How Do I Get More Information on the ETS Praxis Exams?

To receive information on upcoming administrations of the Praxis II 0011 test or any other test consult the ETS registration bulletin or website.

Contact ETS at:

Educational Testing Service
Teaching and Learning Division
P.O. Box 6051
Princeton, NJ 08541-6051
Phone: (609) 771-7395
Website: *www.ets.org/praxis*
E-mail: praxis@ets.org

Special accommodations are available for candidates who are visually impaired, hearing impaired, physically disabled, or specific learning disabled. For questions concerning disability services, contact:

ETS Disability Services: (609) 771-7780
TTY only: (609) 771-7714

Provisions are also available for examinees whose primary language is not English. The ETS registration bulletin and website include directions for those requesting such accommodations.

You can also consult ETS with regard to available test sites; reporting test scores; requesting changes in tests, centers, and dates of test; purchasing additional score reports; retaking tests; and other basic facts.

Is There a Registration Fee?

To take a Praxis examination, you must pay a registration fee, which is payable by check, money order, or with American Express, Discover, MasterCard, or Visa credit cards. In certain cases, ETS offers fee waivers. The registration bulletin and website give qualifications for receiving this benefit and describe the application process. Cash is not accepted for payment.

Can I Retake the Test?

Some states, institutions, and associations limit the number of times you can retest. Contact your state or licensing authority to confirm their retest policies.

HOW TO USE THIS BOOK AND TEST*ware*®

What Do I Study First?

To begin your studies, read over REA's subject reviews and suggestions for test taking. Take a practice test on the CD-ROM to determine your areas of weakness, and then restudy the material focusing on your specific problem areas. Studying the areas thoroughly will reinforce the basic skills you will need to do well on the exam. Make sure to follow up your diagnostic work by taking the practice exams in this book so that you will be familiar with the format and procedures involved with taking the actual test.

When Should I Start Studying?

It is never too early to start studying; the earlier you begin, the more time you will have to sharpen your skills. Do not procrastinate! Cramming is not an effective way to study because it does not allow you the time needed to learn the test material.

FORMAT OF THE TEST

The Praxis II 0011 is a two-hour exam comprised of 110 multiple-choice questions. The multiple-choice questions assess a beginning teacher's knowledge of certain job-related skills and knowledge. Four choices are available on each multiple-choice question; the options bear the letters A through D. The exam uses four types of multiple-choice questions:

1. The Roman Numeral Multiple-Choice Question

2. The "Which of the Following?" Multiple-Choice Question

3. The "Complete the Statement" Multiple-Choice Question

4. The Multiple-Choice Question with Qualifiers

The following sections describe each type of question and suggested strategies.

Roman Numeral Multiple-Choice Questions

Perhaps the most difficult of the types of multiple-choice questions is the Roman numeral question. This is because it allows for more than one correct answer. **Strategy:** Assess each answer before looking at the Roman numeral choices.

Consider the following Roman numeral multiple-choice question designed to test science content information and teaching methodology on the test:

> An experiment is planned to test the effect of microwave radiation on the success of seed germination. One hundred corn seeds will be divided into four sets of 25 each. Seeds in Group 1 will be microwaved for 1 minute, seeds in Group 2 for 2 minutes, and seeds in Group 3 for 10 minutes. Seeds in Group 4 will not be placed in the microwave. Each group of seeds will be soaked overnight and placed between the folds of water-saturated newspaper. When purchasing the seeds at the store, you find that no single packet contains enough seeds for the entire project; most contain about 30 seeds per packet.

Which of the following is an acceptable approach for testing the hypothesis?

  I. Purchase one packet from each of four different brands of seed, one packet for each test group.
  II. Purchase one packet from each of four different brands of seed, and divide the seeds from each packet equally among the four test groups.
  III. Purchase four packets of the same brand, one packet for each test group.
  IV. Purchase four packets of the same brand, and divide the seeds from each packet equally among the four test groups.

  (A) I and II only
  (B) II and IV only
  (C) III and IV only
  (D) IV only

In reviewing the questions, you should note that you may choose two answers by selecting (A), (B), or (C), while it is possible to choose only one answer by choosing answer (D).

Of course, the correct answer is (D). The experiment requires a control of all variables other than the one identified in the hypothesis: exposure to microwave radiation. Seeds from different suppliers may be different; for example, one brand may be treated with a fungicide and another not, or the fungicide used may differ from brand to brand. Item III might at first seem acceptable, but unless all the packages are from the same year and production run, the four packages may differ significantly from each other. The best solution is to divide randomly the available seeds equally among the four test groups. Item II allows the experiment to compare also the germination rates of the different brands, but only if (1) the seeds from each packet are isolated within each test group and (2) the number of seeds is large enough to create a statistically significant sample.

This question illustrates that both knowledge of scientific content (curriculum) and instruction (methods)—in addition to assessment—are important.

"Which of the Following?" Multiple-Choice Questions

In a "Which of the Following?" question, one of the answers is correct among the various choices. **Strategy:** Form a sentence by replacing the first part of the question with each of the answer choices in turn, and then determine which of the resulting sentences is correct. Consider the following example:

Which of the following is a level of Bloom's Taxonomy?

(A) Comprehension
(B) Context
(C) Accommodation
(D) Egocentrism

Using the suggested technique, one would read:

(A) Comprehension is a level of Bloom's Taxonomy.
(B) Context is a level of Bloom's Taxonomy.
(C) Accommodation is a level of Bloom's Taxonomy.
(D) Egocentrism is a level of Bloom's Taxonomy.

It is easy to see that (A) is the correct answer. *Context* refers to the framework of a passage of text; context can include the pictures that complement the text on the page as well as the words themselves. *Accommodation* refers to adjusting to the environment or the situation; accommodation is not a stage in Bloom's Taxonomy and is not an appropriate answer. *Egocentrism* refers to a worldview in which the individual or the self is the center. Egocentrism is not the correct answer; it does not relate to Bloom's Taxonomy. The best answer is (A), which is a level of Bloom's Taxonomy.

Not all "Which of the Following?" multiple-choice questions are as straightforward and simple as the previous example. Consider the following "Which of the Following?" multiple-choice question based on the passage (repeated here) that you have already read:

> An experiment is planned to test the effect of microwave radiation on the success of seed germination. One hundred corn seeds will be divided into four sets of 25 each. Seeds in Group 1 will be microwaved for 1 minute, seeds in Group 2 for 2 minutes, and seeds in Group 3 for 10 minutes. Seeds in Group 4 will not be placed in the microwave. Each group of seeds will be soaked overnight and placed between the folds of water-saturated newspaper. During the measurement of seed and root length, students note that many of the roots are not growing straight. Efforts to straighten the roots manually for measurement are only minimally successful as the roots are fragile and susceptible to breakage.

Which of the following approaches is consistent with the stated hypothesis?

(A) At the end of the experiment, straighten the roots and measure them.
(B) Use a string as a flexible measuring instrument for curved roots.
(C) Record the mass instead of length as an indicator of growth.
(D) Record only the number of seeds that have sprouted, regardless of length.

The answer to the question is (D). The hypothesis is to evaluate seed germination as a function of microwave irradiation. Recording the overall growth or length of the seed root, while interesting, is not the stated hypothesis. Choice (C) would be a good approach if the hypothesis were to relate seed growth to some variable, as it would more accurately reflect the growth of thicker or multiple roots in a way that root length might not measure.

Strategy: Underline key information as you read the question. For instance, as you read the previous question, you might underline or highlight the sentence: "An experiment is planned to test the effect of microwave radiation on the success of seed germination." This sentence will remind you of the stated hypothesis of the experiment and will prevent your having to read the entire question again. The highlighting will thus save you time; saving time is helpful when you must answer 110 questions in two hours.

Complete the Statement Multiple-Choice Questions

The "Complete the Statement" multiple-choice question consists of an incomplete statement for which you must select the answer choice that will complete the statement correctly. Here is an example:

To achieve lasting weight loss, students should

    (A) enter a commercial diet program.
    (B) combine permanent dietary changes with exercise.
    (C) cut calories to below 100 per day.
    (D) exercise for two hours a day.

The above question relates to health, a curriculum area on the Praxis II 0011 which addresses information that the average person needs to know. The best answer to the question is (B). Permanent dietary changes and exercise are the only way to produce lasting weight loss. Commercial diets, choice (A), do not always include a program of exercise but rather concentrate on diet. Radically reducing calorie intake, choice (C), will cause the body to go into starvation mode and slow down digestion to conserve energy. Two hours of daily exercise, choice (D), is not practical, and without controlling calorie intake, it would be ineffective.

Multiple-Choice Questions with Qualifiers

Some of the multiple-choice questions may contain qualifiers — words like *not, least,* and *except*. These added words make the test questions more difficult because rather than having to choose the best answer, as is usually the case, you now must actually select the opposite. **Strategy:** Circle the qualifier. It is easy to forget to select the negative; circling the qualifier in the question stem is a flag. This will serve as a reminder as you are reading the question and especially if you must re-read or check the answer at a later time. Now consider this question with a qualifier:

> Dance can be a mirror of culture. Which of the following is not an illustration of this statement?
>
> (A) Women in the Cook Islands dance with their feet together and sway while the men take a wide stance and flap their knees.
> (B) Movement basics include body, space, time, and relationship.
> (C) In Africa, the birth of a child is an occasion for a dance that asks for divine blessings.
> (D) The court dancers of Bali study for many years to achieve the balance, beauty, and serenity of their dance.

The answer that does not illustrate that dance is a mirror of culture is (B); it is, therefore, the correct answer to the question. The statement, "Movement basics include body, space, time, and relationship" is a true statement but it describes only the dimensions of dance movement; in no way does it speak to how dance reflects the culture of which it is part.

You should spend approximately one minute on each multiple-choice question on each of the practice tests—and on the real exams, of course. The reviews in this book will help you sharpen the basic skills needed to approach the exam and offer you strategies for attacking the questions. By using the reviews in conjunction with the practice tests, you will better prepare yourself for the actual tests.

You have learned through your course work and your practical experience in schools most of what you need to know to answer the questions on the test. In your education classes, you gained the expertise to make important decisions about situations you will face as a teacher; in your content courses, you should have acquired the knowledge you will need to teach specific content. The reviews in this book will help you fit the information you have acquired into its specific testable category. Reviewing your class notes and textbooks along with systematic use of this book will give you an excellent springboard for passing the Praxis II 0011.

SCORING THE TEST

The number of raw points awarded on the Praxis II 0011 is based on the number of correct answers given. Most Praxis examinations vary by edition, which means that each test has several variations that contain different questions. The different questions are intended to measure the same general types of knowledge or skills. However, there is no way to guarantee that the questions on all editions of the test will have the same degree of difficulty. To avoid penalizing test takers who answer more difficult questions, the initial scores are adjusted for difficulty by using a statistical process known as equating. To avoid confusion between the *adjusted* and *unadjusted scores*, ETS reports the *adjusted scores* on a score scale that makes them clearly different from the *unadjusted scores*. *Unadjusted scores* or "raw scores" are simply the number of questions answered correctly. *Adjusted scores*, which are equated to the scale ETS uses for reporting the scores, are called "scaled scores." For each edition of a Praxis test, a "raw-to-scale conversion table" is used to translate raw to scaled scores. The easier the questions are on a test edition, the more questions must be answered correctly to earn a given scaled score.

The college or university in which you are enrolled may set passing scores for the completion of your teacher education program and for graduation. Be sure to check the requirements in the catalogues or bulletins. You will also want to talk with your advisor. The passing scores for the Praxis II tests vary from state to state. To find out which of the Praxis II tests your state requires and what your state's set passing score is, contact your state's education department directly.

Score Reporting

When Will I Receive My Examinee Score Report and in What Form Will It Be?

ETS mails test-score reports six weeks after the test date. There is an exception for computer-based tests and for the Praxis I examinations. Score reports will list your current score and the highest score you have earned on each test you have taken over the last 10 years.

Along with your score report, ETS will provide you with a booklet that offers details on your scores. For each test date, you may request that ETS send a copy of your scores to as many as three score recipients, provided that each institution or agency is eligible to receive the scores.

STUDYING FOR THE PRAXIS II 0011

It is critical to your success that you study effectively. Throughout this guide you will find *Praxis Pointers* that will give you tips for successful test taking. The following are a few tips to help get you going:

- Choose a time and place for studying that works best for you. Some people set aside a certain number of hours every morning to study; others may choose to study at night before retiring. Only you know what is most effective for you.

- Use your time wisely and be consistent. Work out a study routine and stick to it; don't let your personal schedule interfere. Remember, seven weeks of studying, is a modest investment to put you on your chosen path.

- Don't cram the night before the test. You may have heard many amazing tales about effective cramming, but don't kid yourself: most of them are false, and the rest are about exceptional people who, by definition, aren't like most of us.

- When you take the practice tests, try to make your testing conditions as much like the actual test as possible. Turn off your television, radio, and telephone. Sit down at a quiet table free from distraction.

- As you complete the practice test, score your test and thoroughly review the explanations to the questions you answered incorrectly.

- Take notes on material you will want to go over again or research further.

- Keep track of your scores. By doing so, you will be able to gauge your progress and discover your strengths and weaknesses. You should carefully study the material relevant to your areas of difficulty. This will build your test-taking skills and your confidence!

STUDY SCHEDULE

The following study course schedule allows for thorough preparation to pass the Praxis II 0011. This is a suggested seven-week course of study. However, you can condense this schedule if you have less time to study or expand it if you have more time for preparation. You may decide to use your weekends for study and preparation and go about your other business during the week. You may even want to record information and listen to your mp3 player or tape as you travel in your car. However you decide to study, be sure to adhere to the structured schedule you devise.

WEEK	ACTIVITY
1	After reading the first chapter to understand the format and content of this exam, take the first practice test on CD-ROM. Our computerized tests are drawn from the tests we present in our book and provides a scored report which includes a progress chart indicating the percentage right in each category, pinpointing your strengths and weaknesses. The instantaneous, accurate scoring allows you to customize your review process. Make sure you simulate real exam conditions when you take the test.
2	Review the explanations for the questions you missed, and review the appropriate chapter sections. Useful study techniques include highlighting key terms and information, taking notes as you review each section, and putting new terms and information on note cards to help retain the information.
3 and 4	Reread all your note cards, refresh your understanding of the exam's subareas and skills, review your college textbooks, and read over notes you took in your college classes. This is also the time to consider any other supplementary materials suggested by your counselor or your state education agency.
5	Begin to condense your notes and findings. A structured list of important facts and concepts, based on your note cards, college textbook, course notes, and this book's review chapters will help you thoroughly review for the test. Review the answers and explanations for any questions you missed on the practice test.
6	Have someone quiz you using the note cards you created. Take the second practice test, adhering to the time limits and simulated test-day conditions.
7	Review your areas of weakness using all your study materials. This is a good time to retake the practice tests, if time allows.

THE DAY OF THE TEST

Before the Test

- Dress comfortably in layers. You do not want to be distracted by being too hot or too cold while you are taking the test.

- Check your registration ticket to verify your arrival time.

- Plan to arrive at the test center early. This will allow you to collect your thoughts and relax before the test; your early arrival will also spare you the anguish that comes with being late.

- Make sure to bring your admission ticket with you and two forms of identification, one of which must contain a recent photograph, your name, and your signature (e.g., a driver's license). You will not gain entry to the test center without proper identification.

- Bring several sharpened No. 2 pencils with erasers for the multiple-choice section; pens if you are taking another test that might have essay or constructed-response questions. You will not want to waste time searching for a replacement pencil or pen if you break a pencil point or run out of ink when you are trying to complete your test. The proctor will not provide pencils or pens at the test center.

- Wear a watch to the test center so you can apportion your testing time wisely. You may not, however, wear one that makes noise or that will otherwise disturb the other test takers.

- Leave all dictionaries, textbooks, notebooks, calculators, briefcases, and packages at home. You may not take these items into the test center.

- Do not eat or drink too much before the test. The proctor will not allow you to make up time you miss if you have to take a bathroom break. You will not be allowed to take materials with you, and you must secure permission before leaving the room.

During the Test

- Pace yourself. ETS administers the Praxis II 0011 in one two-hour sitting with no breaks.

- Follow all of the rules and instructions that the test proctor gives you. Proctors will enforce these procedures to maintain test security. If you do not abide by the regulations, the proctor may dismiss you from the test and notify ETS to cancel your score.

- Listen closely as the test instructor provides the directions for completing the test. Follow the directions carefully.

- Be sure to mark only one answer per multiple-choice question, erase all unwanted answers and marks completely, and fill in the answers darkly and neatly. There is no penalty for guessing at an answer, do not leave any answer ovals blank. Remember: a blank oval is just scored as wrong, but a guessed answer has a chance of being right!

Take the test! Do your best! Afterward, make notes about the multiple-choice questions you remember. You may not share this information with others, but you may find that the information proves useful on other exams that you take.

Relax! Wait for that passing score to arrive.

General Information About Curriculum, Instruction, and Assessment

2

FOUNDATIONS OF EDUCATION

When teachers truly know their students as learners and as people, they are better able to create a positive classroom environment in which all can succeed. Along with believing in each student's potential, teachers must understand the developmental levels of their students as well as their learning styles and levels of intelligence. It is also critical for teachers to be familiar with their student's home environments and greater community. This information helps teachers develop a holistic view of their students, which will assist in the planning, teaching, and assessment of content undertaken in the classroom. When teachers consider the interests, experiences, tastes, and talents of the students, they are better able to motivate learning and therefore avoid behavior problems in the classroom. Being familiar with child development theories and learning-style profiles supports this work.

Cognitive Development and Learning Theories

Teachers can use their knowledge of child development theories to understand their students on a deeper level. There are many important figures in the realm of developmental psychology who have informed our understanding of how young children grow and learn. It is vital for teachers to be aware of the cognitive, social, and physical stages through which their students mature.

Of course, teachers of young children may have to contend with a variety of issues, but all teachers should be aware of age and maturational differences among students. One of the earlier branches of educational psychology to come to the forefront was **behaviorism**. Those who consider themselves to be behaviorists believe that behavior can be predicted and controlled. The goal was the betterment of society through the management and change of human behaviors. One of the leading figures in behavioral psychology was **B. F. Skinner** whose work centered on studying stimulus and response, paired with reinforcement. Behaviorism received much criticism for its failure to adequately account for language development or differences among learners. As behaviorism fell from favor, developmental psychology and the proponents of the theories associated with this branch of learning became prominent.

Jean Piaget identified four stages of cognitive development starting at birth and progressing to young adulthood. Stage one, the **sensorimotor period** (birth to 2 years), describes the infant maturing from simple reflexes to organized behaviors. Stage two, the **preoperational period** (ages 2 to 7), describes the child moving from motor- or physical-based responses to the use of symbols in an increasingly complex manner. Stage three, the **concrete operational period** (ages 7 to 11), describes the child's acquisition of logic capacities that allow for additional cognitive functions. Stage four, the **formal operational period** (ages 11 to 15), describes the child moving into adolescence and developing the ability to think hypothetically.

Piaget, whose ideas on cognitive development have greatly influenced American education, thought that children younger than eight years of age (because of their egocentric thought) were unable to view situations from the perspective of another individual. Thus, Piaget concluded that children under the age of eight made decisions about right and wrong on the basis of how much harm was caused. For example, children might say that a child who ate two forbidden cookies was less guilty than the child who ate six forbidden cookies. Children over the age of eight, however, were able to take into consideration whether the individual acted purposely or accidentally. For example, a child who broke a toy by accident was not as guilty of misbehavior as the child who broke the toy on purpose. Researchers who have tested Piaget's ideas have found that children younger than age eight are able to engage in moral reasoning at much more complex levels than Piaget thought possible.

Erik Erikson, one of the most influential theorists in the area of social concern, based his work on Sigmund Freud's discoveries in the area of psychosexual development. Erikson elaborated on the basic concepts by delineating a set of eight psychosocial stages. The third and fourth stages apply to preschool and elementary school-age children. Stage three (ages 3 to 5) is characterized as **Initiative vs. Guilt**. This preschool stage starts with signs of initiated behaviors, the development of the conscience, and sexual identity. Stage four (ages 6 to 12) is characterized as **Industry vs. Inferiority**. This school-age stage shows the development of self-worth and maturity of skills.

Another key figure in developmental psychology is **Lev Vygotsky**. His learning theories remain relevant to today's learners and classrooms. Vygotsky wrote of the origins of thought and speech. His rationale explains that when these elements come together, around age two, thinking becomes verbal and speech becomes logical. According to Vygotsky, language lays the foundation of thought. The **zone of proximal development** is the theory for which Vygotsky is most widely known. This zone is defined as the distance between a child's independent ability or developmental level to solve problems and his or her potential to problem-solve with the guidance of an adult or higher-level peer. This theory dictates that theoretically a child can accomplish more advanced tasks when he works collaboratively with a more able person. This supports the argument for cooperative learning, guided inquiry, modeling, explanations, leading questions, and positive reinforcement. Vygotsky argued that social interactions such as these, as well as exposure to cultural aspects, support learning. Communication in various forms is highly valued by this theory, specifically outward and internalized speech. Both are connected to thinking and problem solving.

The term *standards*, when used with regard to behavior, evokes issues of right and wrong, sometimes referred to as *ethical or moral decisions*. With regard to moral development, teachers should be familiar with the concepts of **Lawrence Kohlberg**. Kohlberg (1984), following the example of Piaget, developed a scenario to quiz children and teens. Kohlberg told a story about a man whose wife was so seriously ill that she would die without medication, yet her husband had no money to buy her medicine. After trying various legal means to get the medicine, her husband considered stealing it. Kohlberg asked if it was wrong or right to steal the drug and to explain why it was either wrong or right. Kohlberg did not evaluate whether the respondent said it was wrong or right to steal the drug; he was interested in the reasons given to justify the actions. On the basis of the responses he received, Kohlberg proposed six stages of moral development.

Stage 1, punishment and obedience, describes children who simply follow the rules so as to escape punishment. If kindergarten-age children, for example, are told not to talk or they'll lose their chance to go outside for recess, they will not want to lose their play-ground privileges, and so they will not talk.

On the other hand, **stage 2**, individualism and change, refers to children who follow the rules not only to escape punishment but also to receive a reward or benefit for their good behavior. This stage generally applies to older primary grade children.

Kohlberg's **stage 3** encompasses mutual interpersonal expectations and interpersonal conformity; at this stage, children want to please the people who are important to them. Junior high students, for example, may behave in a manner that gains the approval of their peers or their idols.

At **stage 4**, Kohlberg said, adolescents become oriented to conscience, and they recognize the importance of established social order. Teens at this stage obey the rules unless those rules contradict higher social responsibilities. In other words, most high school students realize that rules are necessary, and they will obey most rules if the rules reflect basic social values, such as honesty, mutual respect, courtesy, and so forth.

Post-conventional morality was the term Kohlberg gave to stages 5 and 6. At **stage 5**, individuals recognize the importance of both individual rights and social contracts but believe that people should generally abide by the rules to bring the greatest good to the majority. Kohlberg believed that about one-fifth of adolescents reach stage 5. Therefore, Kohlberg would have expected that few high school students would be operating at this level.

Finally, Kohlberg would not have expected high school students to reach **stage 6**; he believed that very few individuals ever reach this stage. The person in stage 6 recognizes principles of justice. Those at this stage believe that individuals should obey most rules because most rules reflect just principles; however, if rules violate ethical principles, individuals have a greater obligation to follow their conscience even if that means breaking the rules. Social reformers, such as Martin Luther King, Jr., would be examples of those who have attained stage 6 of moral reasoning.

Kohlberg's theory describes the progression of children's moral reasoning from school entry at kindergarten (stage 1) to graduation from high school (stages 4 and 5, for some). Kohlberg's theory is widely taught and applied in school settings but not without controversy. Some have contended that Kohlberg's theory is limited and biased because of his research techniques (getting reactions to a scenario) and because a study of white, middle-class males under the age of 17 was the basis of his theory. Many would say that his ideas have limited application to other ethnic groups, socioeconomic groups, or females.

One theorist interested in applying Kohlberg's theory to women is **Carol Gilligan**, a student of Kohlberg's, who developed an alternative theory of moral development in women. Gilligan (1982) found that women, unlike the men at Kohlberg's stages 5 and 6, tend to value caring and compassion for others above abstract, rational principles. Therefore, when women make decisions, they base their conclusions on how their choices and actions will affect others. Gilligan posited that women pass through three levels of moral reasoning, although, as in Kohlberg's theory of development, not all reach the third level. At the first level, the individual has concerns only about herself. At the second level, the individual sacrifices her own interests for the sake of others. Finally, at the third level, the individual synthesizes responsibilities to both herself and to others.

Jerome Bruner is the theorist associated with **constructivism**. According to constructivist theory, learning is an active process, which involves the learner constructing new concepts based on prior knowledge. It is the learner who employs cognitive structures to process information, create and test hypotheses, and draw conclusions. This means that schema or brain structures that have been created through learning experiences and discoveries are accessed in new situations. New information is processed through this system of mental models, which allows the learner to make connections, organize thoughts, and construct meaning. Bruner contends that instruction should consider the following: (1) natural learner tendencies, (2) the organization of knowledge for ease of learning, (3) effective sequencing of content, and (4) appropriate rewards and punishments. Constructivist theory supports a spiral curriculum that includes the scaffolding of skills.

Effective teachers may want to consider the implications of these theories for the behavior of students in their classes, in particular, how students will respond to rules of behavior. These theories are a valuable resource for assessing student behavior.

The Role of the Learner

Jaime Escalante, called "America's greatest teacher" (Barry et al., 198–99) and the subject of the motion picture *Stand and Deliver*, tells a story about having two students named Johnny in his class. He says that one, "good Johnny," was a dedicated and responsible student, courteous, polite, and high achieving. The other Johnny, "bad Johnny," seldom came to class, and when he did, he created discipline problems. "Bad Johnny" wouldn't listen, wouldn't do his work, and wouldn't cooperate.

On the night of the annual open house, a very nice woman came to Mr. Escalante's classroom and introduced herself, saying, "I am Johnny's mother." Mr. Escalante assumed she was "good Johnny's" mother. He said, "Oh, I am so glad to meet you. You must be very proud of your son. He is an exceptional student, and I am pleased to have him in my class."

The next day, "bad Johnny" came to class. After class, he approached Mr. Escalante and asked, "Hey, why did you tell my mother those things last night? No one has ever said anything like that about me." It was then that Mr. Escalante realized his mistake. He did not admit his error to Johnny, and the strangest thing happened next. "Bad Johnny" stopped being bad. He started coming to class. He started doing his work. He started making good grades. Mr. Escalante concludes his story by saying, "I ended up with two 'good Johnnys' in my class."

This anecdote emphasizes an important aspect of teaching: teacher perception is ultimately significant. Students may be what their teachers think them to be. What's more, students may become what their teachers believe them to be. Teachers report that when they treat their students as responsible young adults, most students rise to the occasion. (Barry et al., 198–99).

Learning Styles and Personality Types

Information about learning styles and personality types essential to effective teaching can also shed light on how individuals make ethical and moral decisions. Research based on the typological theories of Carl Jung, as published in his 1921 book *Psychological Types* (Baynes 1923), indicates that people fit into four dichotomous categories: thinking/feeling, sensing/intuition, judging/perception, and extrovert/introvert. During World War II Katharine Cook Briggs and her daughter, Isabel Briggs Myers, developed personality indicators based on Jung's typologies. Today researchers continue to find strong support for the indicators' construct validity, internal consistency, and test-retest reliability. In general, the indicators have been found to meet or exceed the reliability of other psychological instruments. In fact, psychological type has been shown to affect how students learn, how teachers teach, how leaders lead, and how everyone works and communicates (Elias and Stewart 1991; Foster and Horner 1988).

Jung identified two pairs of psychological functions: the two Perceiving functions, Sensing and iNtuition (thus spelled in Myers-Briggs jargon); and the two Judging functions, Thinking and Feeling. Although each person uses one of these four functions more dominantly and proficiently than the other three, all four functions are used at different times depending on the circumstances. Researchers believe the population is fairly evenly distributed between people who make decisions based on rational, logical, and objective data—thinking types—and those who make decisions based on feelings—feeling types. Slightly more males than females are thinking types. The feeling half of the population tends to make decisions based on how those decisions may affect others, avoiding conflict and promoting harmony; slightly more females than males are feeling types.

Most people (approximately 76 percent) are the sensing type, those who learn through sensory experiences; they are linear learners who enjoy facts and details. They like sequential organization and memory tasks. They often work slowly and methodically and take great care to finish each project before beginning another one. On the other hand, the minority (approximately 24 percent) are the intuitive type. This type learns not through experience but by insight and inspiration. Facts and details bore these students, who prefer global concepts and theories. They dislike memory work. Generally, they are quick to grasp ideas and catch on to the gist of things; this means they can be disruptive because they have already learned their lesson or finished their assignment. While they generally perform well on tests, they also daydream and lose interest quickly in the things that they deem uninteresting or dull. They like to do several things at once and find it tedious to have to slow down or wait for others to finish.

The learning styles of the students should influence the decisions teachers make regarding curriculum, instruction, and assessment. **Learning style inventories** can be used to determine the types of learners in a particular classroom. Traditionally learners have fit into three categories, referred to collectively as VAK: those who learn best through **visual** (V) means, those who learn best through **auditory** (A) means, and those who do best with **kinesthetic** (K) means. Recently **reading and writing** (R) have been added as a learning style, expanding the acronym to VARK. Through informal observations and through the use of inventories (formal and informal), teachers should determine the learning styles of their students. A learning style inventory consists of several questions aimed at determining through which mode individual students learn best.

Teachers who use a variety of instructional techniques that tap into the different learning styles have a greater chance of reaching a diverse group of students. Models, charts, pictures, demonstrations, notes, overheads, movies, and presentations all cater to **visual** learners. **Auditory** learners benefit from lectures, choral chants, repetition, mnemonic devices, presentations, think-pair-shares, and other listening-based methods. Those who are **kinesthetic** tend to work best with manipulatives, tools, models, clay, paint, role playing, games, and other physical activities. Students who learn best through **reading and writing** activities enjoy literature-based tasks such as those that involve a variety of texts, such as reading and/or writing journals, newspapers, letters, and poetry. Learning styles describe the way students approach learning, as well as the types of learning experiences in which they feel most comfortable.

In addition to learning styles, teachers should be familiar with Harvard University Professor Howard Gardner's **theory of multiple intelligences**. In 1983, Gardner published *Frames of Mind: The Theory of Multiple Intelligences*, in which he unveiled his theory that human minds maintain seven intelligences. His extensive research indicates that individuals possess all of the intelligences to varying degrees. Similar to learning styles, multiple intelligence theory maintains that students learn best when instruction taps into their strengths. *Intelligences* refer to ways in which an individual's mind constructs meaning and tackles problems. In the decades that have followed, Gardner has determined an eighth intelligence that meets his criteria, with the potential of more to be added. Currently, the list includes linguistic, logical/mathematical, spatial, bodily kinesthetic, musical, interpersonal, intrapersonal, and naturalist. Each intelligence represents a cognitive strength. While all human beings possess potential in each of the eight areas, as with fingerprints, no two people have the same intelligence profile. Educative experiences can help people develop strengths in all areas of the mind.

Teachers who incorporate an understanding of the eight intelligences into their lesson planning will facilitate student learning by providing a variety of educational experiences. Knowing the student's intellectual strengths will help teachers create potential pathways for learning. Teachers can reach students by presenting material that taps into their more developed intelligences. The following list provides a key word explanation and examples of activities or items that address the different intelligences:

1. Linguistic (words): reading, writing, oral presentations, plays, speeches

2. Logical/mathematical (numbers): puzzles, calculations, estimations

3. Spatial (objects/pictures): geometry, graphing, building, model making

4. Bodily kinesthetic (movements): dance, sports, manipulating, role playing

5. Musical (sounds): music, choral chants, patterns, songs, instruments

6. Interpersonal (others): cooperative learning, sharing, interviewing

7. Intrapersonal (self): journals, reflections, self-portraits, narrative writing

8. Naturalist (nature): living things, nature walks, field trips, class pets

CURRICULUM

Standards

Since the early 1990s, there has been a movement to develop state and national education standards. Elementary teachers need to be aware of the standards developed by the state in which they are teaching. State standards detail the learning objectives for students at each grade level and for each curriculum area: language arts, mathematics, science, social studies (social sciences), technology, fine arts, physical education, and health. These standards provide not only benchmarks for student learning but also direct information regarding the skills and knowledge students need to acquire in school. This information is essential for planning lessons and units, as well as for assessing student work.

Curriculum Planning

There are many different approaches to curriculum planning; however, becoming acquainted with the standards established by your state is a crucial first step. Next, a teacher must outline the objectives or the big ideas that will address these standards. Some standards can be attended to through one or two lessons, some through an entire unit of study, while others may be touched on for months or even years of schooling. Each lesson a teacher implements may include several standards and reach across multiple curriculum areas. It is vital that teachers are familiar with the developmental levels of the students they teach in order to provide appropriate materials and instruction. Knowing the learning styles, interests, and capabilities of your students assists in the planning process.

Standards, Objectives, and Sequencing

The education departments of the various states and the professional organizations for each subject have set curriculum standards for the curriculum for each of the grade levels and subjects; school districts also set objectives that guide the teachers in their instructional planning. Teachers, too, must set objectives for their classes.

The name most frequently associated with objectives is Robert F. Mager. He defines an *objective* as "being an intent that a statement communicates to the reader" (Mager 1962, 3). The statement describes a proposed change in behavior. An objective, then, describes the behavior or outcome that the educator wants the learner to demonstrate. There are three types of objectives: **cognitive** (that have to do with thinking and learning), **affective** (that have to do with valuing and feelings), and **psychomotor** (that have to do with skills). The cognitive objectives particularly must be open to few interpretations. The outcomes must be observable. This means that some words are more acceptable than others in a behavioral objective. Ideally, the objective will give the criteria for success. The following are some examples:

- The student will be able to list three out of four of the seasons.

- The student will be able to locate the state capital on a map of the state.

- The student will be able to solve 7 out of 10 addition problems correctly.

A complete cognitive behavioral objective will also include the condition under which the students will achieve the criteria and the behavioral outcome desired. The following are examples of some objectives with the condition and the criteria for success:

- In a five-minute time period, the student will be able to solve 50 one-digit addition facts correctly.

- Given a map of their state, all the third-grade students will be able to locate their state capital correctly.

- Given a calendar, the students will be able to locate today's date accurately.

Planning

The effective teacher realizes that having an interesting, carefully planned curriculum is one of the best ways to bring about student learning, promote desired student behavior, and prevent most discipline problems. The teacher knows how to plan and conduct lessons in a variety of learning environments that lead to student outcomes consistent with state and district standards.

Table 2-1. Unobservable (Unacceptable) and Observable (Acceptable) Words for Behavioral Objectives

Unobservable Words; Words and Phrases Open to Many Interpretations	Observable Words; Words and Phrases Open to Fewer Interpretations
To appreciate	To construct
To appreciate fully	To define
To comprehend	To demonstrate
To enjoy	To differentiate
To grasp the significance of	To draw
To know	To identify
To understand	To list
To understand fully	To locate on a map
	To match
	To recite
	To solve
	To underline
	To write

- The teacher determines instructional long-term goals and short-term objectives appropriate to student needs.

- The teacher identifies activities that support the knowledge, skills, and attitudes students must learn in a given subject area.

- The teacher identifies materials based on instructional objectives and student learning needs and performance levels.

As outlined above, traditional lesson planning starts with determining the standards and objectives; then developing the student and teacher actions that will meet these goals; and last, creating ways to assess student learning. In recent years, with the increased emphasis on student achievement, educators have begun to broaden their perspectives on instruction and assessment. Some school districts have adopted Grant Wiggins's and Jay McTighe's "backwards" approach to lesson planning, as assessment has become more imperative. In their book *Understanding by Design* (2005), they explain that teachers should start by thinking about the end, or the desired outcome, of the learning experiences. Teachers need to consider the following questions: What do you want students to know or understand? What standards-based skills and content are essential for students to acquire? Next, according to this model, teachers should think about how this learning can be assessed. How will student learning be determined? What evidence will be assembled? Last, teachers should think about the types of instructional methods that will facilitate student learning. What experiences will inspire student interest, motivation, and success? In this framework, teachers establish understandings and objectives or big ideas, develop tools that will assess whether students have developed the understandings and have met objectives, and create lessons/activities that will facilitate student learning.

Teachers often have autonomy in determining how and when standards, skills, and content knowledge are focused on within their classroom. Other times the sequence of the curriculum is established by grade-level or subject-area teams of teachers, by supervisors or other school administrators, or by district-level curriculum coordinators. Certain areas such as mathematics, history, literacy skills, foreign or second language, and some science and technology need to be learned sequentially, which will determine the timeline for instruction. Teachers ought to be aware of the standards and benchmarks students were expected to meet in previous years, as well as the materials the students are familiar with. This will aid in the selection of appropriate goals, objectives, resources, and instructional strategies.

Higher-order Thinking Skills

Teachers ought to take into account higher-order or critical-thinking skills in addition to state standards and district benchmarks. Every decision a teacher makes, from the literature and math manipulatives to the questions asked, impacts student learning. It is critical that teachers set objectives and pose questions that require students to think and respond in a variety of ways. A teacher might encourage higher-level thinking skills in the classroom through activities like mapping and webbing; study plans; puzzles, riddles, and "think alouds"; and programs like *Tactics for Thinking*. Teachers often refer to Bloom's Taxonomy when setting objectives and developing instruction.

Benjamin Bloom describes six levels of comprehension in his taxonomy (Bloom 1956). The teacher may wish to develop questions at each level to increase critical thinking and problem solving, develop a series of questions for thought and discussion, or prepare a test or other form of assessment.

Bloom's Taxonomy

Knowledge level: Students give back the information that is on the page.

Comprehension level: Students show that they can give the meaning of terms, idioms, figurative language, and other elements of written material.

Application level: After reading a story about how a class raised money for playground equipment, the students discuss some ways that they might improve their own playground.

Analysis level: Students examine the parts or components of a passage. For example, students might examine a menu and locate food groups, or they might identify terms in a word problem to determine the operations they should use.

Synthesis level: Students move from specifics to generalities. For instance, the class might develop a solution to the overcrowding problem suggested in a story, or students might construct a platform for the main character to use if she should run for class officer in the school described in another story.

Evaluation level: Students judge if a passage is fact or opinion, true or false, biased or unbiased.

Metacognition

A vital component of critical thinking is **metacognition**, which can be defined as knowledge of thought. Metacognition or "thinking about thinking" involves an awareness of cognitive functioning and learning processes. Students should be instructed to consider the strategies and thought processes they utilize while solving problems and approaching tasks. Becoming aware of how one learns helps to build critical-thinking skills. Activities such as journals, logs, and assignments that require explanations encourage students to develop metacognition.

Puzzles, Riddles, and "Think Alouds"

Students can practice their thinking skills by solving puzzles and riddles alone, in small groups, or as a class with the teacher helping in the modeling process. Here are some puzzles that encourage students to think:

Table 2-2. Bloom's Taxonomy

Level of Question	Student Capability	Questioning Verbs
Level 1: Knowledge	Remembers, recalls learned (or memorized) information	*define, describe, enumerate, identify, label, list, match, name, read, record, reproduce, select, state, view*
Level 2: Comprehension	Understands the meaning of information and is able to restate in own words	*cite, classify, convert, describe, discuss, estimate, explain, generalize, give examples, make sense out of, paraphrase, restate (in own words), summarize, trace, understand*
Level 3: Application	Uses the information in new situations	*act, administer, articulate, assess, chart, collect, compute, construct, contribute, control, determine, develop, discover, establish, extend, implement, include, inform, instruct, operationalize, participate, predict, prepare, preserve, produce, project, provide, relate, report, show, solve, teach, transfer, use, utilize*
Level 4: Analysis	Breaks down information into component parts; examines parts for divergent thinking and inferences	*break down, correlate, diagram, differentiate, discriminate, distinguish, focus, illustrate, infer, limit, outline, point out, prioritize, recognize, separate, subdivide*
Level 5: Synthesis	Creates something new by divergently or creatively using information	*adapt, anticipate, categorize, collaborate, combine, communicate, compare, compile, compose, contrast, create, design, devise, express, facilitate, formulate, generate, incorporate, individualize, initiate, integrate, intervene, model, modify, negotiate, plan, progress, rearrange, reconstruct, reinforce, reorganize, revise, structure, substitute, validate*
Level 6: Evaluation	Judges on the basis of informed criteria	*appraise, compare and contrast, conclude, criticize, critique, decide, defend, interpret, judge, justify, reframe, support*

1. A truck heading to Chicago is loaded with ice cream. At a tunnel in a mountain, a sign announces the height of the tunnel is 12 feet, 3 inches. The truck driver knows the truck is 12 feet, 4 inches. To get to Chicago, the trucker would have to make a 75-mile detour to avoid the tunnel. The trucker knows that the ice cream will melt in another hour. How can the truck driver get through the tunnel?

2. Twelve elementary school teachers meet at a party. If each teacher shakes hands with every other teacher, how many handshakes will occur at the party?

3. "As I was going to St. Ives, I met a man with seven wives. Each wife had seven sacks. Each sack had seven cats. Each cat had seven kittens. Sacks, cats, kits, wives. How many were going to St. Ives?" (This is an old nursery rhyme.)

Tactics for Thinking

Developed by Robert J. Marzano and Daisy E. Arredondo (1986) for the South Carolina schools, Tactics for Thinking implements the teaching of thinking skills for kindergarten through grade 12. The program asserts that thinking-skills development should be part of the classroom and teacher directed. Components include elaboration, synthesizing, goal seeking, and deep processing.

Goals

All successful teachers begin the term with a clear idea of what they expect students to learn in a given course. Establishing long-range goals for a course—goals that are age appropriate and reflect student ability and needs—help to clarify the knowledge and skills that teachers and students will work toward during the school year.

The local board of education can establish long-range goals as can knowledgeable curriculum specialists, a single teacher, or a group of teachers. Stated in clear, concise language, these goals define the knowledge that students will achieve or the skills that they will acquire through specific instructional activities. For example, a language arts instructor might state the following long-range goals for high school students:

- The student is able to identify major American poets and authors of the twentieth century.

- The student is able to write narrative, informative, and persuasive essays. The student is able to properly cite research references.

- The student is able to identify important themes in literature.

- The student is able to identify with multicultural perspectives on the American experience.

After developing a list of potential goals for a course, the teacher should evaluate those goals against the following criteria:

Importance: The resulting learning must be significant and relevant enough for students to want to achieve it.

Instruction: Appropriate classroom activities must be able to support the learning of the stated goal.

Evaluation: Students must be able to demonstrate the achievement of the goal.

Suitability: The goal must be challenging, as well as reachable, for all students.

Importance of Goals

There are many ways to evaluate the importance of selected goals. Teachers can judge goals on the basis of whether the stated outcome is necessary to gain advanced knowledge of a particular field of study, as in the following goals: Students will memorize the letters of the alphabet; students will master the use of punctuation. Goals can be evaluated on the basis of whether their achievement will lead students to become better citizens, as in this goal: Students will apply their knowledge of the constitution to judge a contemporary court case. Goals can also be judged on the basis of whether their achievement will lead students to become well-adapted members of society or competitive in the workforce, as in the following: Students will be able to demonstrate their ability to use the Internet to locate information. Finally, goals can be selected on the basis of whether their achievement will help prepare students for college admissions standards.

One-minute Goal Setting

Kenneth Blanchard and Spencer Johnson (1982), the authors of *The One Minute Manager*, a best-selling book for those wanting to achieve success, describe one-minute goal setting as (1) deciding on goals, (2) identifying what good behaviors are, (3) writing out goals, (4) reading and rereading goals, (5) reviewing goals every day, and (6) determining if behaviors match goals. This list is applicable to the classroom teacher who needs to decide on behavioral goals and identify behaviors both expected and unacceptable.

Outcome-oriented Learning

Effective teachers plan carefully so that outcome-oriented activities will produce students who are self-directed learners, in group or individual environments. Effective teachers know how to plan so that the curriculum guides, lesson plans, actual lessons, tests, and assessments are correlated. They plan in advance, explain the unit's goals and objectives to the students, then choose activities that will help the class reach the desired outcomes.

In outcome-oriented learning, teachers define outcomes, or what they want students to know, do, and be when they complete a required course of study. The teachers set high but realistic goals and objectives for their students and plan instructional activities that will assist students in achieving these goals. The key to effective outcome-oriented planning is to consider the desired outcomes and determine the teacher and student behaviors that will improve the probability that students will achieve the outcomes.

Outcome-based planning starts with the end product—what must the students learn or accomplish in a particular course or grade level. For example, a third-grade math teacher may decide that one final outcome of the math class is for the students to be able to complete 100 basic addition facts in five minutes with 100 percent accuracy. He or she then works "backward" to determine prerequisite knowledge and skills students need to have to accomplish this outcome. By continuing to ask these questions about each set of prerequisites, the teacher finds a starting point for the subject or course and develops goals and objectives. The outcomes should be important enough for the teacher to require them of all students. An outcome-oriented system means that the teacher supplies the students with sufficient time and practice to acquire the knowledge and skills. It also means that the teacher takes into account students' various learning styles and time required for learning, and makes adaptations by providing a variety of educational opportunities.

INSTRUCTION

To ensure that students achieve the stated goal, teachers must choose appropriate classroom activities to support learning. When students have completed these activities, they should be able to demonstrate successfully the knowledge or skills that they have achieved. Teachers who utilize a variety of instructional methods, resources, and strategies are most effective in helping students reach their goals. Instruction should involve learning activities, classroom rules and routines, and physical and social-emotional environments all designed to meet the needs of the students.

Learning Activities

Classroom tasks can and should be structured in a variety of ways. Teachers make decisions on how to organize student learning activities based on students' levels of intelligence, styles, abilities, prior knowledge, group dynamics, and other factors. Some content can be addressed in a whole class setting, while other concepts are best taught through individual, partner, or small-group work. For instance, skills and/or topics in mathematics and literacy may be new for most students and require direct teaching. This situation lends itself to large-group instruction. In science, experiments are often best attempted through lab partnerships. Students work together to measure, mix, observe, and draw conclusions. Many topics in the area of social studies lend themselves to small-group tasks. For instance, students might work in groups of five to create a big book of facts on the state they are studying.

PRAXIS Pointer

> **Read all of the answers for the multiple-choice questions. You may think you have found the correct response but do not assume it is. Read through each choice to be sure that you are not making a mistake by jumping to conclusions.**

Groups should always be thoughtfully and intentionally made. They should change throughout the year to provide students with the opportunity to work with all of their classmates. **Heterogeneous** groups include students who represent different abilities and needs. **Homogeneous** groups consist of students who are most similar in their skills and perhaps, interests. Teachers need to use their professional judgment, knowledge of the students, and understanding of the curriculum in order to choose what types of groups are appropriate and when to use them.

Many group-based tasks are considered **cooperative learning**. This popular strategy combines individual accountability with group expectations. Some group work may involve students fulfilling specific roles or jobs depending on how it is structured by the teacher. The **think-pair-share** and **jigsaw** are two of the most common cooperative learning arrangements. Students turn to a partner to discuss a question or concept in the think-pair-share model. This technique can be used for any learning situation in any content area. It boosts students' confidence to be able to confirm or test their ideas with a peer before sharing with the larger class. This model does not involve much preparation or time. Some other cooperative learning strategies, such as jigsaws, depend on a great deal of organization and time. This model requires the teacher to provide different articles, for instance, to groups of students in the class. The students need to be prepared to discuss this article first, with others who have read the same one. Next, this *expert group* then meets to determine teaching points and main ideas that represent the most important aspects of their reading. Each expert is then grouped with classmates who each read different articles. The students teach each other the readings, and all students are held accountable for all of the information explored.

Suitability

All goals for a given course must be achievable for the entire class, while leaving room to challenge students to master new skills. To determine if long-range goals are appropriate, teachers can refer to a number of resources, including student files, which may include the results of basic skills tests, reading level evaluations, and writing samples.

The teacher has knowledge of strategies to create and sustain a safe, efficient, supportive learning environment.

- The teacher evaluates the appropriateness of the physical environment for facilitating student learning and promoting safety.

- The teacher identifies a repertoire of techniques for establishing smooth, efficient, and well-paced routines.

- The teacher identifies strategies to involve students in establishing rules and standards for behavior.

- The teacher identifies emergency procedures for student and campus safety.

Physical Environment

While certain physical aspects of the classroom cannot be changed (size, shape, number of windows, type of lighting, etc.), others can be. Windows can have shades or blinds that distribute light correctly and permit darkening the room for video or computer viewing. If the light switches do not allow some of the lights to remain on, sometimes schools will change the wiring system. If not, teachers can use a lamp to provide minimum lighting for monitoring students during videos or films. Schools often schedule maintenance, such as painting and floor cleaning, during the summer. Often school administrators will accede to teachers' requests for a specific color of paint, given sufficient time for planning.

All classrooms should have a bulletin board used by the teacher and by the students. The effective teacher has plans for changing the board according to units of study. Space should be reserved for display of students' work and projects, either on the bulletin board, the wall, or in the hallway. (Secondary teachers who need creative ideas can visit elementary classrooms.)

Bare walls can be depressing; however, covering the wall with too many posters can be visually distracting. Posters with sayings that promote cooperation, study skills, and content ideas should be displayed, but teachers should change them several times during the school year because students will ignore the displays when they become too familiar.

Most classrooms have movable desks, which allow for varied seating arrangements. If students are accustomed to sitting in rows, this is sometimes a good way to start the year. Harry K. Wong (2005) describes his method of assigning seats on the first day of school, which is to assign each desk a column and row number, then give students assignment cards as they come into the room. Another method is to put seating assignments on an overhead, visible when students enter the room. Once students are comfortable with classroom rules and procedures, the teacher can explain to students how to quickly move their desks into different formations for special activities, then return them to their original positions in the last 60 seconds of class.

The best place for the teacher's desk is often at the back of a room, so there are few barriers between the teacher and the students and between the students and the chalkboards. This arrangement encourages the teacher to walk around the classroom for better monitoring of students.

Social and Emotional Climate

The effective teacher maintains a climate that promotes the lifelong pursuit of learning. One way to do this is to have students practice research skills that will be helpful throughout life. All subject areas can promote the skills of searching for information to answer a question, filtering it to determine what is appropriate, and using what is helpful to solve a problem.

The effective teacher also facilitates a positive social and emotional atmosphere and promotes a risk-taking environment for students. The teacher should set up classroom rules and guidelines for how he or she will treat students, how students will treat him or her, and how students will treat each other; students should be a part of developing the rules. In part, this means that the teacher does not ridicule or put down students or tolerate such behavior among the students. It also means that the teacher has an accepting attitude toward student ideas, especially when the idea is not what he or she was expecting to hear. Sometimes students can invent excellent ideas that are not always clear until they are asked to explain how they arrived at them.

Students should feel free to answer and ask any questions that are relevant to the class, without fear of sarcasm or ridicule. Teachers should always avoid sarcasm. Sometimes teachers consider sarcasm to be mere teasing, but because some students often interpret it negatively, effective teachers avoid all types and levels of sarcasm.

Academic Learning Time

The effective teacher maximizes the amount of time spent for instruction. A teacher who loses 5 minutes at the beginning of class and 5 minutes at the end of class wastes 10 minutes a day that could have been spent on educational activities. Ten minutes may not seem like a lot of time to lose. However, this is equivalent to a whole period a week, four classes a month, and 25 periods a year.

Academic learning time is the amount of allocated time that students spend in an activity at the appropriate level of difficulty with the appropriate level of success. The appropriate level of difficulty is one that challenges students without frustrating them. Students who have typically been lower achievers need a higher rate of success than those who have typically been higher achievers. One way to increase academic learning time is to teach procedures to students so they will make transitions quickly. Another way to increase academic learning time is to have materials and resources ready for quick distribution and use. In addition, teachers can give students a time limit for a transition or an activity. To encourage time on task and to prevent off-task behavior and discipline problems, time limits for group work should be slightly shorter than the amount students need. It is also essential for the teacher to have additional activities planned should the class finish activities sooner than anticipated. As students complete group work, they should have other group or individual activities so they can work up until the last minute before the end of class.

Procedures for Learning Success

One of the most challenging and important synthesizing activities of the teaching professional is determining how to match what needs to be taught with the specifications of those who need to learn it. The successful teacher spends considerable time becoming familiar with required instructional objectives, curriculum, and texts; the teacher should do this well in advance of the start of the school year. In addition to general knowledge about the intellectual and social developmental levels of students, the particular needs that characterize any specific group of students, including their individual learning styles, are more apparent to the teacher after the first few days and weeks of school. The effective teacher must be organized enough to choose and sequence learning activities before the school year begins but flexible enough to adapt these activities after becoming acquainted with the special needs and learning styles of specific students.

There are several steps the teacher should follow to ensure success for student learning:

- Know and start teaching at the proper level of the students.

- Share learning objectives with students—and the processes chosen to attain them.

- Prepare for the successive steps in the learning process—from instruction, through guidance and support, to feedback.

- Choose relatively small steps in which to progress, and include regular assessments of these progressions.

- Distinguish between the learning a student can do independently and that which is best facilitated and monitored by the teacher; choose methods appropriate to content and skills. Include a variety of activities and methods that appeal to the full range of student learning styles, intelligence levels, interests, and preferences.

Organizing Activities

Instructional objectives necessitate that the skill or knowledge to be taught should be valuable on its own or should clearly lead to something else that is valuable. When the class begins, the teacher should share these long-range objectives with students as part of the teacher's planned "idea scaffolding" to acknowledge learning as a mutual enterprise. Sharing these objectives is the first important learning activity because this serves as the basis for the communal task of "making sense" of the learning in progress. Because teachers are expected to be professionally prepared to recognize the cognitive and social levels of students, they may need to review the generally accepted theories of Jean Piaget, Erik Erikson, and other research theorists to recall specific characteristics appropriate to various developmental levels. Familiarity with the learning objectives and material to be mastered and the level of the students enables the teacher to choose and develop a wide range of appropriate activities and tentatively to sequence them in ways that facilitate learning.

Careful, incremental goal setting allows for considerable flexibility in pace and methods and leads to further valuable sequencing of strategies. For example, a variety of activities may enhance close reading: the teacher may model close reading of a very short story; the teacher may assign small-group work with close reading of paragraphs in which one student identifies an important detail, and another student suggests its relevance to the details; the teacher can show the class an overhead color-marking of important descriptive words from one page of a short story or poem; students can work on individual in-class color-marking for the next page, followed by a group discussion of student results; the teacher can assign homework to color-mark a short story or poem; and students can work on group assignments graphing elements of literary text.

A perceptive teacher's growing awareness of individual student learning styles can enhance preliminary planning for any specific group of students. Because students do not fall precisely into theoretical stages, activities must reflect a range of developmental levels and learning styles. This includes concrete as well as abstract dimensions, opportunities for instruction by the teacher, and exploration and discovery by individual students and groups. Once the teacher launches the learning enterprise, the teacher's continued instruction, support, regular assessment, and feedback help maximize the potential of learning opportunities.

Wait Time for Questions

Students need adequate time to respond to questions. Teachers must not allow outbursts or unsolicited choral responses of answers to their questions. Allowing students to answer questions without first being specifically called on for their response generates a faction of students who are always answering the questions. In addition, providing a wait time—or an appropriate time to think about the answer—of three to five seconds is necessary for students to formulate their responses. The proper way to ask a question is to (1) ask the question, (2) provide adequate wait time, (3) call on the student, and (4) tell the student if the response was correct. If it is correct, it is appropriate to give specific praise. However, overuse of specific praise devalues the praise mechanism within the classroom. Students who constantly receive praise do not know when to be proud of their good answers. The only time a teacher should call a student's name *before* asking the question is when the teacher needs to bring a student back into the discussion for disciplinary reasons. Then, it is appropriate to call the name first to ensure that the student is aware of the question being asked. This technique not only brings back a disruptive or off-task student but also gives the student a nonverbal message that his or her attention is necessary.

Effective Use of Time

Idle hands generate a variety of discipline issues. The teacher should keep a steady pace throughout the entire class from the beginning of the lesson to the independent practice or homework time. A mere minute wasted each day adds up to well over three hours of lost instruction during a single year. Smooth transitions from topic to topic, class to class, and subject to subject are necessary so there is no wasted time, a minimal amount of interruptions, and almost nonexistent downtime.

Organizing Instruction

First, a teacher should have prepared all materials and be ready to go before beginning any classroom lesson. When class begins, the teacher should immediately start with an initiating or motivational activity that has the students working and interested from the beginning. This activity could begin with a "hook" that draws student interest, states the objective for the lesson, or reviews concepts that will help lead to lesson success. During this time, the teacher may choose to take attendance or complete other required administrative activities. The teacher should use a smooth transition into the instructional part of the lesson and follow it by a short assessment, also referred to as a *guided practice activity* that determines the students' level of understanding. Last, the closure of the lesson should remind the students of the key components of the lesson.

The transition from initiation to lesson presentation to closure follows the rules for giving a good speech. First, the teacher tells the students what he or she is going to say (motivational hook); second, the teacher tells the students (instructional section); and last, the teacher reviews what was just taught (closure). Keep in mind that the instructional section can use a variety of approaches including a guided discovery lesson, a free exploration lesson, cooperative projects, or a teacher-directed lesson. Instructional variety is a surefire way of maintaining student interest and improving achievement. Good instruction may include providing clear directions, asking open-ended questions, addressing questions, modeling approaches, encouraging discourse, and assessing student understanding to monitor their progress and to provide them feedback. The conclusion of most lessons will have students practicing the skills they learned in class. This momentum ensures a smooth transition and a natural routine that encourage learning, provide a consistent pattern that students will anticipate, and assist the teacher in moving smoothly from one activity to another. Routines help students anticipate the next move. However, varied routines help in minimizing the boredom that can exist within a regulated, highly routine environment.

One experienced teacher of upper elementary students has suggested the following guidelines for teachers in managing their classes:

• Let students have input whenever you can, and when you cannot, let them think they are giving input.

- Listen to students; they have surprising insights and viewpoints.

- Be consistent with expectations and consequences.

- Do not make exceptions to school rules, even if you do not agree with them.

- Do not correct or reprimand a student in front of a class. Quickly establish that your classroom is a safe place and can be a fun place, but that disrespect for learning, others, or property is not appropriate and there will be no warnings.

- Do not begin teaching until everyone is ready to learn.

- Do consult with colleagues and administrators for advice.

- Make sure that students know their rights and their responsibilities.

Technology in Instruction

The effective teacher has knowledge of strategies for the implementation of technology in the teaching and learning processes:

- The teacher identifies appropriate software to prepare materials, deliver instruction, assess student achievement, and manage classroom tasks.

- The teacher identifies appropriate classroom procedures for student use of available technology.

- The teacher identifies appropriate policies and procedures for the safe and ethical use of the Internet, networks, and other electronic media.

- The teacher identifies strategies for instructing students in the use of search techniques, the evaluation of data collected, and the preparation of presentations.

Educational Technology in the Primary Classroom

Technology is an important part of the world and, therefore, must be an important part of the educational environment. Students should be exposed as early as possible to computer literacy so that they will be prepared for a technologically advanced society. Teachers can use appropriate software to meet content standards and curriculum goals. Teachers must be able to integrate their existing curriculum to meet these standards.

Classroom Management

Teachers who understand the differences among the learners and their ways of thinking, whether it is in regard to information processing or moral decision making, can use this information to establish standards for classroom behavior. Standards should reflect community values and norms and should take into consideration students' ethnicity (that is, what language they speak at home), socioeconomic status, and religious beliefs. These factors are important when formulating a dress code, determining how to address authority figures, defining the use of appropriate language, examining interactions between males and females, or developing school safety procedures. An important part of the teacher's role is to educate the students about school policies and/or district and state policies with regard to these issues.

What are common values across cultural, ethnic, religious, and social strata? Honesty, mutual respect, consideration, and courtesy are among those virtues that have widespread acceptance. Students (and their parents) should know about standards for attendance, grades, and student behavior. Students should know how to dress for school, how to address their teachers and other school employees, and what is appropriate language for school (limiting the use of slang or vulgarities). They should know rules for turning in homework, for making up missed assignments, and for handing in work late (if it is accepted). They should know what they can and cannot bring to school (certain kinds of materials and tools). They should know what will happen if they break the rules.

Psychological research on behavior modification and reducing aggression shows that modeling acceptable and nonaggressive behaviors is more effective than catharsis and punishment. Teachers are most effective when they follow the rules and exemplify the standards of conduct themselves. Teachers who are courteous, prompt, enthusiastic, in control, patient, and organized provide examples for students through their own behavior. Teachers should (1) make reasonable efforts to protect students from conditions that would harm learning or mental and physical health and safety; (2) not restrain students from independent action in pursuit of learning; (3) not deny students' access to diverse points of view; (4) not intentionally suppress or distort information regarding students' academic program; (5) not expose a student to unnecessary embarrassment or disparagement; (6) not violate or deny students' legal rights; (7) not harass or discriminate against students on the basis of race, color, religion, sex, age, national or ethnic origin, political beliefs, marital status, handicapping condition, sexual orientation, or social and family background; (8) make reasonable efforts to assure that students are protected from harassment and discrimination; (9) not exploit a relationship with a student for personal gain or advantage; and (10) keep information in confidence or as required by law. Teachers who honor this code will be modeling the appropriate standards of behavior for their students. In addition to modeling appropriate behaviors, another effective way of treating misbehavior (that is, more effective than catharsis and punishment) is the use of incompatible responses. Effective teachers learn how to employ these responses. Some studies even suggest that teachers use open body language (arms open, not crossed) and positive facial expressions (smiling) to diffuse student anger.

"With It"-ness in the Classroom

Teachers must be "with it" in a classroom to prevent misbehavior that will interrupt the flow of learning. The level of "with it"-ness must extend beyond the obvious events of the classroom. A teacher needs to understand the dynamics behind the actions that occur in the classroom, and then proceed accordingly.

Many factors influence student behavior. Young children will generally follow the rules of the classroom out of a desire to please their teachers. Misbehavior that occurs in a classroom may be the result of a conflict that is occurring elsewhere. Teachers should be aware that these conflicts can occur between peers, between students and the teacher, or as a result of events in the student's family or out-of-classroom experiences.

The goal of "with it"-ness is to prevent misconduct in the classroom. Through everyday interactions, the teacher develops a sense of an individual student's normal behavior and general mental state. The "with it" teacher also develops a sense of the relations between the students in a class and within the school. Noticing the beginning of a conflict between individuals in a class enables the "with it" teacher to mediate the students to a resolution that avoids the disruption of class time. The teacher should explain well and clearly display the desired behavior for the students in a classroom. Posted rules provide a constant guide and reminder of classroom rules. Teachers can also use these displays as a reference when discussing expected behavior, either individually or with the class as a whole.

Teachers should self-monitor their interactions with misbehaving students. Children may act out if they feel they are threatened, disliked, or treated unfairly. A "with it" teacher knows which particular students are causing the class disruption and works to curb this behavior without punishing the class as a whole. The teacher's response to the behavior or the teacher's allowing the misbehavior to persist can disrupt the learning momentum.

Both the individual student and the class as a whole are affected by how the teacher handles classroom misconduct. The effective approach is when the teacher compliments the positive behavior modeled by other students in the classroom, rather than individually reprimanding student misbehavior. If certain students are not properly addressing the task at hand, the teacher can say, "I like the way Glen is working in his math book" or "Belinda, I like the way you are quietly raising your hand and waiting your turn." By doing so, the teacher is reinforcing the desired behavior for the class without directly addressing and calling attention to the misbehavior. The individual student has an opportunity to monitor his or her own behavior, and class momentum is not lost.

Teachers can also guide a student toward appropriate behavior by stating the student's name or explaining on what task he or she should currently be working. Nonverbal cues include walking toward the student, making eye contact, or gently touching the student's desk or shoulder. These techniques will not disrupt the flow of the classroom. Teachers must clearly voice their expectations without yelling or becoming angry. Quiet and controlled reprimands are very effective. Maintaining control without involving punitive measures lowers the tension in the entire classroom. Students should not feel uncomfortable because the teacher is angry. This is especially important when teachers are working with small groups or when working on simultaneous tasks. Individualized instruction should not suffer when the teacher must reprimand another student. When a teacher demonstrates "with it"-ness, students do not feel that they have an opportunity to misbehave just because the teacher is not focusing attention directly on them.

Management through Motivation

Good teachers recognize their role in keeping students interested, on-task, and involved in learning experiences. Many off-task and disruptive behaviors can be avoided through proactive and thoughtful lesson planning. Instruction that engages the students in active learning that is meaningful and purposeful helps to maintain order in the classroom. When students are truly engaged in the content and actively participating in class activities, they are less likely to be disruptive. Students who are motivated to learn find value in what they are doing, thus they aim to succeed. It is important that teachers use resources, materials, and activities that are appropriate to the student's developmental levels. One strategy for increasing student motivation is incorporating a variety of instructional strategies that address the different learning styles (kinesthetic, auditory, visual, reading and writing) and intelligences (linguistic, mathematical, musical, spatial, naturalist, interpersonal, intrapersonal). Another strategy is to connect lessons to authentic or "real world" situations and problems that students can relate to. Differentiating instruction in order to meet the needs and interests of the individual students is an effective method to keep students actively learning. Efficient classroom management involves using your knowledge of the interests, concerns, tastes, and talents of your students in your lesson planning.

"One-minute Praise"

Blanchard and Johnson (1982) offer a "one-minute praise" method by which they encourage catching people (in this case, students) doing something right. Blanchard and Johnson suggest that teachers should praise people immediately and tell them what they did right. In applying this principle to students, the teacher would tell students how he or she feels about their behavior, how it has helped others in class, and how it has helped the success of the class. The teacher would stop for a moment after the praise to let the student feel good about the praise. Finally, the teacher would encourage the student to continue behaving in this manner, shaking hands with the student.

Likewise, the one-minute reprimand could also be useful. However, the teacher should reprimand the student after class, avoiding interruptions to a lesson whenever possible. Specifically, the teacher should tell the student what was done wrong. After correcting the student, the teacher should stop and let the student think about the situation for a moment. Then, the teacher should shake hands with the student and remind the student that he or she is important as a person, even though his or her behavior was inappropriate. It is important to distinguish between the individual student (who deserves respect) and the individual's actions (which may be disrespectful and/or unacceptable).

As final advice, Blanchard and Johnson admonish, "When it's over, it's over." After correcting the student, the teacher should not harbor a grudge or ill-will toward the student or dwell on the infraction but move on to the next task at hand. The authors conclude their book by stating, "Goals begin behaviors, [*sic*] Consequences maintain behaviors." (Blanchard and Johnson [1982] as cited by Barry et al., 283–84).

Other Practices to Encourage Good Classroom Behaviors

Some other practices that may encourage good classroom behaviors are monitoring, low-key interventions, "I" messages, and positive teaching.

Briefly, *monitoring* refers to the teacher's walking around the room to monitor what students are doing. After a teacher gives an assignment, he or she should wait a few minutes to give students time to get started, then move around the room, and check to make sure that all students have begun their work. The teacher can also give individualized instruction as needed. The teacher's presence can perhaps motivate the students who are not working. The teacher should not interrupt the class during monitoring but should use a quiet voice to show personal attention.

Low-key interventions are quiet and calm. Effective teachers are careful that students are not rewarded for misbehavior by becoming the focus of attention. By being proactive, teachers have anticipated problems before they occur. When correcting misbehaving students, the teachers are inconspicuous, making sure not to distract others in the class. When they lecture, effective teachers know to frequently mention students by name to bring the students' attention back to class.

"I" messages are an effective communication technique for the classroom. The message begins with the word *I* and conveys feelings. For example, a teacher might say, "I am very frustrated about the way you are ignoring instruction. When you talk while I am talking, I have to stop teaching and that is very frustrating."

Positive discipline refers to the use of language to express what the teacher wants instead of the things that students cannot do. Instead of saying, "No fighting," a teacher might say, "Settle conflicts using your words." Taking a positive approach with language also means praising students frequently. An effective teacher is quick to praise students for their good behavior and to use smiles, positive body language, and laudatory words.

Classroom Misbehavior

Teachers should maintain a system of classroom rules, consequences, and rewards to guide students toward proper classroom behavior; the goal of the teacher is keeping students engaged and on task. Inevitably, students will misbehave and test the techniques and procedures that teachers use to guide students back on task. Some students will not respond to the effective teacher's standard procedures. If a student continues to misbehave frequently or in a disturbing manner, the effective teacher observes the student with the intent of determining if any external influences are causing the misbehavior that may require additional intervention from the student's teacher and family.

When under stress, students may be inclined to act out or to behave differently for the duration of the stress-inducing event. Students may react to events in the classroom or in their homes in a manner that violates the established policies of the classroom. For example, nervousness caused by a test or a school play audition may cause a student to speak out of turn or appear skittish. The loss of a loved one may cause a student to become depressed. Such behaviors are normal reactions to stress. However, teachers must pay attention to these situations and observe if the misbehavior occurs for an extended period of time. Unusual and/or aggressive student behavior may indicate that the student is suffering from severe emotional distress. Teachers must be careful to note the frequency, duration, and intensity of the student's misconduct.

Teachers should note frequent, atypical behaviors, such as lying, stealing, and fighting. The teacher should attempt to determine the motivation behind the behavior. Is the child lying to avoid a reprimand? Is the student telling false stories to hide feelings of insecurity? Does the student cry during a particular subject or at random moments during the school day? These are some of the many questions the teacher needs to consider.

Misbehaving may be a sign that a student is losing control of his or her actions and is looking for help. The role of the teacher in these situations is to help determine if the student is acting out as a reaction to a particular issue or if there is a deeper emotional problem. Some students may require various forms of therapy to treat the emotional disturbances that cause the misbehavior. Therapy can examine the possibilities of a more severe cause for the student's behavior.

If concerned that a student is suffering from emotional stress, the teacher should contact, and remain in constant discussion with, the student's parents. It is particularly important in these situations to establish an open dialogue with the student's family to facilitate the student's treatment. Parents and teachers working together will be able to provide important and unique insights into the student's situation.

School professionals are another valuable resource for advice, assistance, and support when dealing with students' emotional disturbances. Guidance counselors, school psychiatrists, and other specialists are able to aid in the counseling of these students and make recommendations for the parents and teacher. Together with the student's family, these professionals may develop or recommend a particular program or therapy for treatment.

When working with a class of students with emotional disorders, the teacher might have to be flexible. While the goal of any management system is to prevent misbehavior, the teacher must be prepared to provide an area or opportunity for the student to regain control if an emotional episode occurs.

Teachers should also be aware that drug therapy is often a form of treatment. Prescribed by medical doctors, the drug treatments that are available can help students gain independence from their disorder. However, these drugs treat the symptoms rather than the cause of the disorder, and can have severe side effects. No one should take drug treatments lightly; adults should make sure to monitor the use of the drugs.

Rules and the Student's Role in Decision Making

Some educational experts have suggested that standards and rules are most effective if students play a role in formulating them. This does not mean that students make all the rules; it means that they can contribute ideas. Stephen Covey, author of the best-selling *The Seven Habits of Highly Effective People* (1989), suggests that people who desire to be effective or successful should be proactive. He explains that being *proactive* means anticipating everything that can go awry before it does; teachers should think about what could go wrong in class concerning a student's conduct and be prepared in case it ever happens. Of course, a teacher may not be able to predict everything that a student may attempt, but trying to analyze many possibilities may provide a teacher some level of comfort in dealing with misbehaviors. Covey also uses the term *proactive* to stress the importance of self-direction, not only for teachers but also for students.

Allowing students to have a voice in establishing standards and formulating codes provides the students with an excellent opportunity to exercise their problem-solving skills and critical-thinking abilities. Although one key purpose of education is graduating students who are responsible citizens capable of participating thoughtfully in a democratic society, educational practices have had a tendency to foster dependency, passivity, and a "tell me what to think and do" complacency. Older students especially can benefit from participating in the decision-making process.

PRAXIS Pointer

By eliminating even one answer choice, you increase your odds of answering correctly. You will have a 1:3 chance of choosing the correct answer. Without elimination, you would have only 1:4 chances.

Many of the principles of total quality management (TQM)—a technique American industries and businesses have used to attain greater success, efficiency, and effectiveness—have been successfully applied to American education. One of the key ingredients of TQM is information sharing so that all partners in an endeavor are aware of goals and objectives. If education is the endeavor, then applying TQM principles means that teachers and students, parents and principals, and other supporting players are all partners in the endeavor. Following TQM principles also means that if all partners have information concerning goals and objectives, then they can form a team to work cooperatively with greater efficiency and effectiveness to achieve goals and objectives.

These ideas require teachers to share authority with students and allow students a voice in decision making. For some teachers, learning to share control with students may be difficult. Helping students to make some of their own decisions will conflict with some teachers' training and with their own ideas and expectations about being in charge; however, the many benefits of shared decision making, already described, are worth the struggle to adjust.

Although this may not sound like the perfect classroom to every teacher, Covey (1989) describes what is, for him, the most exciting learning experience:

> As a teacher, I have come to believe that many great classes teeter on the very edge of chaos. . . . There are times when neither the teacher nor the student knows for sure what's going to happen. In the beginning, there is a safe environment that enables people to be open, to learn, and to listen to each other's ideas. Then comes the brainstorming, where the spirit of evaluation is subordinated to the spirit of creativity, imagining, and intellectual networking. Then an absolutely unusual phenomenon begins to take place. The excitement transforms the entire class.

Covey describes a dynamic classroom, not one in stasis; however, there are important requirements for the classroom. First, the students have to feel safe, safe not only from physical harm but also from mental harm—from mockery, intimidation, unfair criticisms, threats—from teachers, or, especially, classmates. These features describe a classroom where mutual respect and trust exists between teacher and students and among the students themselves.

ASSESSMENT

Assessing Learners

Assessment is a continuum of informal to formal means. The purpose of both formal and informal assessments in the classroom is to improve the instruction and the learning of the students—all the students. It is important for the teacher to analyze and interpret the information gathered through informal and formal means and to use test results professionally to help all students in the classroom to learn to the best of their ability.

Both formative and summative evaluations are part of effective teaching. **Formative evaluation** occurs during the process of learning when the teacher or the students monitor progress in obtaining outcomes and while it is still possible to modify instruction. **Summative evaluation** occurs at the end of a specific time or course of study. Usually, a summative evaluation applies a single grade to represent a student's performance.

Informal Assessment

The teacher may make **observations** for individual or group work. This method is very suitable for skills or for effective learning. Usually, the teacher makes a **checklist** of competencies, skills, or requirements and then uses the list to check off the ones a student or group displays. A teacher wishing to emphasize interviewing skills could devise a checklist that includes personal appearance, mannerisms, confidence, and addressing the questions asked. A teacher who wants to emphasize careful listening might observe a discussion while using a checklist that includes paying attention, not interrupting, summarizing the ideas of other members of the group, and asking questions of others.

Advantages of checklists include the potential for capturing behavior—such as shooting free throws on the basketball court, following the correct sequence of steps in a science experiment, or incorporating important elements in a speech in class—that a paper-and-pencil test cannot accurately measure. One characteristic of a checklist that is both an advantage and a disadvantage is its structure, which provides consistency but inflexibility. An open-ended comment section at the end of a checklist can overcome this disadvantage.

Informal checks are a beneficial strategy for determining student understanding and progress. These are observations aimed at quickly and informally obtaining information about the students. Teachers visit students during individual seatwork or small-group work times to check their class work and to speak about concepts taught. There should be a system in place for keeping track of information gathered. Data collection tools include clipboards, index cards, notebooks, name cards, and sticky notes.

Formal Assessment

Formal measures may include teacher-made tests, district exams, and standardized tests. The effective teacher uses a **variety of formal assessment techniques**. Ideally, instructors should develop their teacher-made assessment instruments at the same time that they are planning goals and outcomes, rather than after the completion of the lessons. Carefully planned objectives and assessment instruments serve as lesson development guides for the teacher. Paper-and-pencil tests are the most common method for evaluating student progress.

Classroom Tests

Teacher-made Tests

Teachers should develop assessments at the same time that they plan goals and outcomes; teachers should not wait to prepare assessments until after they have taught all the lessons. Carefully planned objectives and assessment instruments serve as lesson development guides for the teacher.

Paper-and-pencil tests are the most common method for evaluation of student progress. Among the various types of questions are multiple-choice, true/false, matching, fill-in-the-blank, short answer, and essay questions. The first five types tend to test students' knowledge or comprehension levels; teachers can, however, with some forethought develop objective tests that cover all levels of Bloom's Taxonomy. Essays may test at the lower levels also, but they can be suitable for assessing learning at higher levels. **Projects, papers, and portfolios** (authentic assessments) can assess higher-level thinking skills.

To test students' recall of factual information, a short objective test (with multiple-choice, true/false, matching, fill-in-the blank questions) might be most effective and efficient. Students can answer the first three types of questions on machine-scorable scan sheets for quick and accurate scoring. Again, the teacher does not have to limit the objective test questions to the lower levels of knowledge and can even provide an opportunity for an explanation of answers.

To test students' ability to analyze an event, compare and contrast two concepts, make predictions about an experiment, or evaluate a character's actions, an **essay** question may provide the best opportunity for the students to show what they can do. The teacher should make the question explicit enough for students to know exactly what is expected. For example, "Explain the results of World War II" is too broad; students do not know the teacher's expectations. A more explicit question is, "Explain the three results of World War II that you think had the most impact on participating nations. Explain the criteria you used in selecting these results."

Advantages of an essay include the opportunity for students to be creative in their answers and to explain their responses, and the potential to test for higher-level thinking skills. Disadvantages of essay questions include the time needed for students to formulate meaningful responses, language difficulties of some students, and the time needed for teachers to evaluate the essays.

Consistency in evaluating essays can also be a problem for some teachers, but an outline of the acceptable answers—a scoring **rubric**—can help a teacher avoid inconsistency. Teachers who write specific questions and know what they are looking for are more likely to be consistent in grading. Also, if there are several essay questions, the effective teacher grades all student responses to the first question, then moves on to all responses to the second, and so on.

Teachers must consider fundamental professional and technical factors to construct effective classroom tests. One of the first factors to recognize is that test construction is as creative, challenging, and important as any aspect of teaching. The planning and background that contribute to effective teaching are incomplete unless evaluation of student performance provides accurate feedback to the teacher and the student about the learning process.

Good tests are the product of careful planning, creative thinking, hard work, and technical knowledge about the various methods of measuring student knowledge and performance. Classroom tests that accomplish their purpose are the result of the development of a pool of items and refinement of those items based on feedback and constant revision. It is through this process that evaluation of students becomes valid and reliable.

Tests serve as a valuable instructional aid because they help determine pupil progress and also provide feedback to teachers regarding their own effectiveness. Student misunderstandings and problems that the tests reveal can help the teacher understand areas of special concern in providing instruction. This information also becomes the basis for the remediation of students and the revision of teaching procedures. Consequently, the construction, administration, and proper scoring of classroom tests are among the most important activities in teaching.

Performance-based Assessment

Some states and districts are moving toward performance-based tests, which assess students on how well they perform certain tasks. Students must use higher-level thinking skills to apply, analyze, synthesize, and evaluate ideas and data. For example, a biology performance-based assessment might require students to read a problem, design and carry out a laboratory experiment, and then write summaries of their findings. The performance-based assessment would evaluate both the processes students used and the output they produced. An English performance-based test might ask students to first read a selection of literature and then write a critical analysis. A mathematics performance-based test might state a general problem, require students to invent one or more methods of solving the problem, use one of the methods to arrive at a solution, and write the solution and an explanation of the processes they used.

Performance-based assessment allows students to be creative in solutions to problems or questions, and it requires them to use higher-level skills. Students work on content-related problems and use skills that are useful in various contexts. There are weaknesses, however. This type of assessment can be time-consuming. Performance-based assessment often requires multiple resources, which can be expensive. Teachers must receive training in applying the test. Nonetheless, many schools consider performance-based testing to be a more authentic measure of student achievement than are traditional tests.

Authentic Assessments

Paper-and-pencil tests and essay tests are not the only methods of assessment. Other assessments include projects, observations, checklists, anecdotal records, portfolios, self-assessments, and peer assessments. Although these types of assessments often take more time and effort to plan and administer, they can often provide a more authentic measurement of student progress.

Projects are common in almost all subject areas. Projects promote student control of learning experiences and provide opportunities for research into various topics and the chance to use visuals, graphics, videos, or multimedia presentations in place of, or in addition to, written reports. Projects also promote student self-assessment because students must evaluate their progress at each step of the project. Many schools have subject-specific fairs for which students plan and develop projects to display. Projects for a history fair, for example, can incorporate part of economics and other areas of the social sciences.

Effective teachers must make clear the requirements and the criteria for evaluation of projects before students begin work. Teachers must also assist students in selecting projects that are feasible, for which the school has learning resources, and that do not require an exorbitant investment of time and expense.

The advantages of projects are that students can use visuals, graphics, art, or even music; students can be creative in their topics and research; and the projects can appeal to various learning styles. The primary disadvantage is difficulty with grading, although this can be overcome by devising a checklist for required elements and a rating scale for quality.

Anecdotal records are helpful in some instances, such as capturing the process a group of students uses to solve a problem. This formative data can be useful during feedback to the group. Students can also write explanations of the procedures they use for their projects. One advantage of an anecdotal record is that it can include all relevant information. Disadvantages include the amount of time necessary to complete the record and the difficulty in assigning a grade. If the anecdotal record is solely for feedback, no grade is necessary.

Portfolios are collections of students' best work and can be useful in any subject area in which the teacher wants students to take more responsibility for planning, carrying out, and organizing their own learning. Like a portfolio that an artist, model, or performer creates, a student portfolio provides a succinct picture of the child's achievements over a certain period. Portfolios may contain essays or articles written on paper, videotapes, multimedia presentations on computer disks, or a combination. Teachers often use portfolios as a means of collecting the best samples of student writing over an entire year, and some teachers pass on the portfolios to the next teacher to help in student assessment.

Teachers should provide or assist students in developing guidelines for what materials should go in their portfolios because it would be unrealistic to include every piece of work in one portfolio. Using portfolios requires the students to devise a means of evaluating their own work. A portfolio should not be a scrapbook for collecting handouts or work done by other individuals, although it can certainly include work by a group in which the student was a participant.

Some advantages of portfolios over testing are that they provide a clear picture of a student's progress, they are not affected by one inferior test grade, and they help develop students' self-assessment skills. One disadvantage is the amount of time required to teach students how to develop meaningful portfolios. However, the time is well spent if students learn valuable skills. Another concern is the amount of time teachers must spend to assess portfolios. As students become more proficient at self-assessment, however, the teacher can spend more time in coaching and advising students throughout the development of their portfolios. Another concern is that parents may not understand the grading of portfolios. The effective teacher devises a system that the students and parents understand before work on the portfolio begins.

Self-Assessment and Peer Assessment

One goal of an assessment system is to promote student self-assessment. Because most careers require employees or managers to evaluate their own productivity as well as that of others, self-assessment and peer assessment are important lifelong skills. Effective teachers use a structured approach to teach self-assessment, help students set standards at first by making recommendations about their own standards, and then have students gradually move toward developing their own criteria and applying those criteria to their work.

One method of developing self-assessment is to ask students to apply the teacher's own standards to a product. For example, a history teacher who uses a rating scale for essays might have the students use that scale on their own papers and compare their evaluations with those of the teacher. A science teacher who uses a checklist while observing an experiment might ask students to use the same checklist; students can compare their scores with the teacher's. The class can set standards for evaluating group work and individual work. Collaborative groups are effective vehicles for practicing the skills involved in self-assessment and peer assessment.

PRAXIS Pointer

Mark up your test book. Crossing out answer choices you know are inappropriate will save you time.

Criterion-Referenced Tests

In **criterion-referenced tests (CRTs)**, the teacher attempts to measure each student against certain objectives or criteria. CRTs allow the possibility that all students can score 100 percent because they understand the concepts being tested. Teacher-made tests should be criterion-referenced because the teacher should develop them to measure the achievement of predetermined outcomes for the course. If teachers have properly prepared lessons based on the outcomes and if students have mastered the outcomes, then scores should be high. This type of test is noncompetitive because students are not in competition with each other for a high score, and there is no limit to the number of students who can score well. Some commercially developed tests are criterion-referenced; however, most are norm-referenced.

Norm-Referenced Tests.   The purpose of a **norm-referenced test (NRT)** is to compare the performance of groups of students. This type of test is competitive because a limited number of students can score well. A plot of large numbers of NRT scores resembles a **bell-shaped curve**, with most scores clustering around the center and a few scores at each end. The **midpoint** is an average of data; therefore, by definition, half the population will score above average and half below average. The bell-shaped curve is a mathematical description of the results of tossing coins. As such, it represents the chance or normal distribution of skills, knowledge, or events across the general population. A survey of the height of sixth-grade boys will result in an average height, with half the boys above average and half below. There will be a very small number with heights far above average and a very small number with heights far below average; most heights will cluster around the average.

A **percentile score** (not to be confused with a percentage) is a way of reporting a student's NRT score; the percentile score indicates the percentage of the population whose scores fall at or below the student's score. For example, a group score at the eightieth percentile means that the group scored as well as or better than 80 percent of the students who took the test. A student with a score at the fiftieth percentile has an average score. Percentile scores rank students from highest to lowest. By themselves, percentile scores do not indicate how well the student has mastered the content objectives. **Raw scores** indicate how many questions the student answered correctly and are, therefore, useful in computing a percentage score.

A national test for biology would include objectives for the widest possible biology curriculum, for the broadest use of the test. Reported **normed scores** would enable schools to compare the performance of their students with the performance of students whom the test developers used as its norm group. The test would likely include more objectives than are in a particular school's curriculum; therefore, that school's students might score low in comparison to the norm group. A teacher must be very careful in selecting a norm-referenced test and should look for one with objectives that are the most congruent with the school's curriculum.

The teacher must also consider the test **reliability**, or whether the instrument will give consistent results with repeated measurements. A reliable bathroom scale, for example, will give almost identical weights for the same person measured three times in a morning. An unreliable scale, however, may give weights that differ by six pounds. A teacher evaluates test reliability over time by giving the same, or almost the same, test to different groups of students. However, because many factors can affect reliability, teachers must be careful in evaluating test reliability.

Another aspect of a test that the teacher must carefully assess is the test's **validity**, or whether the test actually measures what it is supposed to measure. If students score low on a test because they could not understand the questions, the test is not valid because it measures reading ability instead of content knowledge. If students score low because the test covered material that was not taught, the test is not valid for that situation. A teacher assesses the validity of his or her own tests by examining the questions to see whether they measure what was planned and taught in the classroom. A test must be reliable before it can be valid. However, measurements can be consistent without being valid. A scale can indicate identical weights for three weigh-ins of the same person during one morning but actually be 15 pounds in error. A history test may produce similar results each time the teacher administers it, but the test may not be a valid measure of what the teacher taught and what the students learned.

Tests should be both reliable and valid. If the test does not measure consistently, it cannot be accurate. If it does not measure what it is supposed to measure, then its reliability does not matter. Commercial test producers perform various statistical measures of the reliability and validity of their tests and provide the results in the test administrator's booklet. In addition, the tests should be **objective** so that any bias of the person scoring the test cannot enter into the grading.

The school districts and state may prescribe **standardized tests** as a means of formal assessment. These formal tests should meet the criteria of objectivity, reliability, and validity. Any grouping within the classroom should involve more than just the score on one standardized test. The teacher may wish to use the tests that frequently accompany the reading textbooks or basal readers as another means of assessment; if the tests include scores from previous administrations, the teacher can determine how the student's performance compares with that of others who have taken the same test.

The use of criterion-referenced, norm-referenced, performance-based, classroom, and authentic assessments is essential to giving the child, the teacher, and the parents a complete picture of the child and the child's progress. The range of informal and formal assessments is necessary and appropriate regardless of the content area. It is essential to note that assessment comes before, during, and after instruction. Pre-assessment is as important as post-assessment.

REFERENCES

Barry, Leasha M., Betty J. Bennett, Lois Christensen, Alicia Mendoza, Enrique Ortiz, Migdalia Pagan, Sally Robison, and Otilia Salmón. *The Best Teachers' Test Preparation for the FTCE: General Knowledge.* Piscataway, NJ: Research and Education Association, 2005.

Bennett, William. *What Works: Research about Teaching and Learning.* Washington, DC: U.S. Department of Education, 1987.

Blanchard, Kenneth H. and Spencer Johnson. *The One Minute Manager.* New York: Morrow, 1982.

Bloom, Benjamin, Max D. Engelhart, Edward J. Furst, Walker H. Hill, and David R. Krathwohl. *Taxonomy of Educational Objectives: The Classification of Educational Goals. Handbook I: Cognitive Domain.* New York: Longmans, Green, 1956.

Bruner, J. *Toward a Theory of Instruction.* Cambridge, MA: Harvard University Press, 1966.

Carbo, Marie. "Reading Styles and Whole Language." *Schools of Thought II.* Video. Bloomington, IN: Phi Delta Kappa, 1993.

———. "Teaching Reading with Talking Books" *Reading Teacher* 32:3 (December 1978): 267–73.

Clay, M. M. "Emergent Reading Behavior." PhD diss., University of Auckland, New Zealand, 1966.

———. *Reading: The Patterning of Complex Behavior.* Auckland, New Zealand: Heinemann Educational Books, 1979.

Clymer, Theodore. "The Utility of Phonic Generalizations in the Primary Grades." *The Reading Teacher* 16 (January 1963): 252–58.

Combs, Martha. *Readers and Writers in Primary Grades: A Balanced and Integrated Approach.* Upper Saddle River, NJ: Pearson, 2006.

Commission on Reading. *Becoming a Nation of Readers.* Washington, DC: U.S. Department of Education, September 1986.

Cook, Jimmie E. and Gregory J. Nolan. "Treating Auditory Perception Problems: The NIM Helps." *Academic Therapy* 15:4 (March 1980), 473–81.

Covey, Stephen R. *The Seven Habits of Highly Effective People: Restoring the Character Ethic.* New York: Simon and Schuster, 1989.

Davis, Anita P., and Thomas R. McDaniel. "Essential Vocabulary Words." *Reading Teacher* 52:3 (November 1998), 308–09.

Davis, Anita P., and Katharine Preston. *Discoveries.* Hillsborough, ID: Butte Publications, 1996.

Davis, Anita Price. *Reading Instruction Essentials.* 3rd ed. Boston: American Press, 2004.

Dolch, Edward William. "Dolch Sight Word List." Champaign, IL: Garrard Press, 1960.

Elias, J. A., and Stewart, B. R. The effects of similarity and dissimilarity of student and teacher personality type on student grades. *The Marketing Educator,* 17 (1991): 42–51.

Erikson, Erik H. *Childhood and Society.* New York: Norton 1950.

Finn, Patrick J. *Helping Children Learn to Read.* New York: Longman, 1990.

Flesch, Rudolf. *Why Johnny Can't Read—And What You Can Do About It.* New York: Harper and Row, 1955.

Foster, R. M., and Horner, J. T. National profile of agricultural teacher educators and state supervisors of vocational agriculture by MBTI preference type. *Journal of the American Association of Teacher Educators in Agriculture* 29(3) (1988), 20–27.

Fry, Edward. "Fry's Readability Graph: Clarifications, Validity and Extension to Level 17." *Journal of Reading* 21:3 (December 1977): 242–52.

———. "The New Instant Word Lists." *Reading Teacher* 34:3 (December 1980): 264–89.

Gardner, H. *Frames of Mind: The Theory of Multiple Intelligences.* New York: Basic Books, 1983.

Gentry, J. R. "Learning to Spell Developmentally." *Reading Teacher* 34:4 (January 1981): 378–81.

Gilligan, Carol. *In A Different Voice: Psychological Theory and Women's Development.* Cambridge, MA: Harvard University Press, 1982.

Goudvis, Anne, and Stephanie Harvey. *Strategies That Work.* Portland, ME: Stenhouse Publishers, 2000.

Gunning, Thomas G. *Creating Reading Instruction for All Children.* Boston: Allyn and Bacon, 1996.

Heckleman, R. G. "A Neurological-Impress Method of Remedial-reading Instruction." *Academic Therapy* IV (Summer 1969): 277–82.

Hollingsworth, Paul. "An Experimental Approach to the Impress Method of Teaching Reading." *Reading Teacher* 31 (March, 1978): 624–26.

Huck, Charlotte S. and Doris Young Kuhn. *Children's Literature in the Elementary School.* New York: Holt, Rinehart and Winston, 1968. First published 1961 by Holt, Rinehart and Winston.

"IRA Takes a Stand on Phonics." (Vol. 14:5) *Reading Today* (April/May 1997), 1–4.

Jung, C. G. *Psychologischen Typen.* Zurich: Rascher Verlag. Translated by H. G. Baynes, 1923. First published in 1921.

Jung, C. G. (1971). *Psychological types* (Collected works of C. G. Jung, volume 6). (3rd ed.). Princeton, NJ: Princeton University Press, 1971. First appeared in German in 1921.

Karlin, Robert. *Teaching Elementary Reading.* New York: Harcourt Brace Jovanovich, 1971.

Klein, Marvin L. *The Development of Writing in Children Pre-K through Grade 8.* Englewood Cliffs, Prentice-Hall, NJ, 1985.

Kohlberg, Lawrence with Rita DeVries [et. al] *Child psychology and childhood education: a cognitive-developmental view.* New York: Longview. 1984.

Lawrence, G. D. *People types and tiger stripes: A practical guide to learning styles* (2nd ed.). Gainesville, FL: Center for Application of Psychological Type. 1985.

Mager, Robert F. *Preparing Instructional Objectives.* Palo Alto, CA: Fearon Publishers, 1962.

Marzano, Robert J., and Daisy E. Arredondo. *Tactics for Thinking.* Aurora, CO: Mid-Continent Regional Education Laboratories, 1986.

Michaelis, John U., and Jesus Garcia. *Social Studies for Children: A Guide to Basic Instruction.* Boston: Allyn and Bacon, 1996.

Myers, Isabel Briggs, *Gifts Differing: Understanding Personality Type.* Mountain View, CA: Davies-Black Publishing, 1980. Reprint edition May 1, 1995.

Noyce, Ruth M., and James F. Christie. *Integrating Reading and Writing Instruction in Grades K–8.* Boston: Allyn and Bacon, 1989.

Piaget, J. *The Origins of Intelligence in Children.* New York: Norton and Company, 1963. First published 1936.

Piaget, J. *Intelligence and Affectivity: Their Relationship during Child Development.* Palo Alto, CA: Annual Review, 1981. First published 1954.

Richardson, Judy S., and Raymond F. Morgan. *Reading to Learn in the Content Areas.* Belmont, CA: Wadsworth, 1990.

Routman, Regie. *Conversations: Strategies for Teaching, Learning, and Evaluation.* Portsmouth, NH: Heinemann, 2000.

Routman, Regie. *Invitations: Changing Teachers and Learners.* Portsmouth, NH: Heinemann, 1994.

Routman, Regie. *Writing Essentials.* Portsmouth, NH: Heinemann, 2005.

Skinner, B. F. *The Behavior of Organisms: An Experimental Analysis.* New York: Appleton-Century, 1938.

Southern Regional Education Board Health and Human Services Commission. *Getting Schools Ready for Children: The Other Side of the Readiness Goal.* Atlanta, GA: Southern Regional Education Board, 1994.

SREB. *See* Southern Regional Education Board.

Tompkins, Gail E. *Literacy for the 21st Century: A Balanced Approach*. 4th ed. Upper Saddle River, NJ: Pearson, 2006.

Trelease, Jim. *The Read-Aloud Handbook.* New York: Penguin Books, 1985.

Tsuchiya, Yukio. *Faithful Elephants: A True Story of Animals, People, and War*. Boston: Houghton Mifflin, 1988.

"Using a Neurological Impress Activity." No author. *www.sil.org/lingualinks/literacy-program/UsingANeurologicalImpressActiv.htm*

Vacca, Richard T., and Jo Anne L. Vacca. *Content Area Reading*. 3rd ed. Glenview, IL: Scott Foresman, 1989.

Vygotsky, Lev. *Thought and Language.* Edited and translated by Eugenia Hanfmann and Gertrude Vakar. Cambridge, MA: The M.I.T. Press, 1962. First published 1934.

Wiggins, Grant, and Jay McTighe. *Understanding by Design, Expanded 2nd Edition*. Alexandria, VA: Association for Supervision and Curriculum Development, 2005.

Wong, Harry K. and Rosemary T. Wong. *First Days of School: How to be an Effective Teacher.* Mountain View, CA: Harry K. Wong Publications, 2005.

Language Arts Pedagogy

3

The language arts include all the subjects related to communication. The school curriculum often gives most attention to reading, writing, literature, and spelling; listening and speaking are other essential parts of the language arts curriculum. A balanced language arts curriculum addresses each topic. Ideally, reading, writing, spelling, listening, speaking, and even literature are integrated into other content areas.

LITERACY: THE SCOPE AND SEQUENCE OF LEARNING TO READ

Marie M. Clay (1966) coined the term *emergent literacy* in her unpublished doctoral dissertation, *Emergent Reading Behavior* (University of Auckland, New Zealand). She defined *emergent literacy* as the stage during which children begin to receive formal instruction in reading and writing and the point at which educators and adults expect them to begin developing an understanding of print.

Today, educators use the term to describe the gradual development of literacy behavior, or the stage in which students begin learning about print. Educators usually associate emergent literacy with children from birth to about age five. During the emergent literacy period, children gain an understanding of print as a means of conveying information. It is essential that they develop an interest in reading and writing in this stage (Tompkins 2006).

Some educators suggest that reading readiness or emergent literacy is a **transitional period** during which a child changes from a nonreader to a beginning reader; others suggest that reading readiness/emergent literacy is a stage (Clay 1979). The Health and Human Services Commission of the Southern Regional Education Board (SREB 1994) cautions that children go through emergent literacy at individual rates. Some **transmission educators** suggest that if a child is not ready to read, the teacher should get the child ready. Others declare that the teacher should not begin formal reading instruction until the child is ready. Most reading-readiness advocates take the position that there are certain crucial factors that a teacher or parent should consider in deciding if a child is ready to read (Davis 2004).

Concepts of Print

An important part of emergent literacy is the skill of identifying print concepts, which involves being able to identify the parts of a book, indicate the directionality of print, and recognize the connection between spoken and written words.

Parts of Books

Clay (1985) developed a formal procedure for sampling a child's reading vocabulary and determining the extent of a child's print-related concepts. For instance, her assessment checks whether a child can find the title of a book, show where to start reading the book, and locate the last page or end of the book. These components considered essential before children can begin to read may differ from those typically considered essential, such as discriminating between sounds and finding likenesses and differences in print (Finn 1990; Davis 2004). A teacher or parent might hand a book to a child with the back of the book facing the child and in a horizontal position. The adult would then ask questions such as "Where is the name of the book?" "Where does the story start?" "If the book has the words *the end*, where might I find those words?" (Davis 2004).

Directionality of Print

Another part of the skill of identifying concepts of print is being able to indicate the directionality of print. The reader in American society must start at the left side of the page and read to the right. This skill is not an inborn skill but rather one acquired through observation or through direct instruction. Some societies do not write from left to right. For instance, in ancient Greek society, writing followed the same pattern as a person would use when plowing: the reader would start at the top of the page and read to the right until the end of the line, turn, drop down a line, read that line to the left, turn, drop down a line, read that line to the right, and so on. Other languages, such as Hebrew, require the reader to begin at the right and read to the left. Japanese writing is generally vertical (Davis 2004).

To teach left-to-right direction, the teacher can place strips of masking tape on the child's desk, study center, or table area. One strip goes where the left side of the book or writing paper would be and one strip where the right side of the book or writing paper would be. The child colors the left side green and the right side red. The teacher helps the child use this device as a clue to remember on which side to begin reading or writing and reminds the child that *green* means "go" and *red* means "stop." Ideally, the teacher should use similar strips on the chalkboard or poster paper to model writing from left to right (Davis 2004).

Children can also remember on which side to begin reading by holding up their hands with their thumbs parallel to the floor. The left hand makes the shape of the letter *L*, for "left," the side on which to begin reading; the right hand does not make the *L* shape. Another way a teacher can help children who are having trouble distinguishing left from right, or on which side to begin reading and writing, is to point to sentences while reading from a big book or writing on the board; observing the teacher do this can help children master print directionality. Books that are 18 × 12 inches or larger are designed for this purpose and are effective with groups of children. Teachers or parents can also model directionality by passing their hands or fingers under the words or sentences as they read aloud. In fact, reading aloud is an essential activity in the school and at home throughout the school years. (Davis 2004).

Teachers can use games such as Simon Says or songs such as "The Hokey Pokey" to give children practice in the skills of distinguishing left from right. In another instructional game, each child holds a paper plate as if it were a steering wheel, and the teacher calls out directions such as "Turn the wheel to the left" and "Turn your car to the right." As the children "drive" their cars, the teacher observes whether they are turning the wheel in the correct direction (Davis 2004).

Voice-to-Print Match

Being able to recognize the connection between the spoken word and the written word is important to developing reading and writing skills. During the emergent literacy period, children should begin to understand that the printed word is just speech written down. Shared reading (discussed in more detail in the next section, "Identifying Strategies for Developing Concepts of Print") can help children gain this understanding. As the adult reads aloud, the children join in with words, phrases, repetitions, and sentences they recognize. They begin to make the connection between the printed word and the spoken word and between phonemes and graphemes. **Phonemes** are the speech sounds; **graphemes** are the written symbols for the speech sounds. These voice-to-print relationships are important to reading (Davis 2004).

Strategies for Developing Concepts of Print

Emergent literacy research cautions that in preschool and kindergarten programs, teachers should avoid isolated, abstract instruction and tedious drills. Teachers should avoid programs that tend to ignore and repeat what the children already know. Programs that focus on skills and ignore experiences often place little importance on reading as a pleasurable activity and ignore early writing—important components of whole language (Noyce and Christie 1989).

Developmentally Appropriate Classrooms, Materials, and Curriculum

The SREB (1994) states that the classroom, materials, and curriculum should be developmentally appropriate. **Developmentally appropriate** is a concept with two dimensions: individual appropriateness and age appropriateness. **Individual appropriateness** recognizes that each child is unique. Ideally, schools and teachers respect and accommodate individual differences, which include growth, interest, and styles. **Age appropriateness** implies that there are sequences of growth and change during the first nine years that a teacher must consider when developing the classroom environment and experiences. In general, the age-appropriate skills considered necessary for reading—during the reading-readiness period and beyond—are visual discrimination, auditory discrimination, and left-to-right direction (Davis 2004).

Reading Aloud

The U.S. Department of Education recognizes that "parents are their children's first and most influential teachers" (Bennett 1987, 5). The department further notes "what parents do to help their children learn is more important to academic success than how well-off the family is" (7). After reviewing many studies, the department reports:

> The best way for parents [and other adults] to help their children become better readers is to read to them—even when they [the children] are very young. Children benefit most from reading aloud when they discuss the stories, learn to identify letters and words, and talk about the meaning of words. (7)

The department also finds that:

> children whose parents simply read to them perform as well as those whose parents use workbooks or have had training in reading. . . . Kindergarten children who know a lot about written language usually have parents who believe that reading is important and who seize every opportunity to act on that conviction by reading to their children. (7)

Jim Trelease (1985) reinforces that parents and teachers should read aloud regularly to children. The reasons Trelease cites for reading aloud include "to reassure, to entertain, to inform or explain, to arouse curiosity, and to inspire" (68). Trelease also explains that reading aloud to a child can strengthen writing, reading, and speaking skills and the child's entire civilizing process. Another important reason for reading to children while they are young is that at that age, children want to imitate what they hear and see adults do. In his book, *The Read-Aloud Handbook*, Trelease suggests stories and books ideal for reading aloud. The SREB (1994) recommends that schools help parents to become actively involved in their children's education and that schools adopt formal policies to improve communication between parents (or caregivers) and schools.

Shared Reading

At the emergent literacy level, the students and the teacher "share" the tasks involved in reading and writing. Teachers are practicing "shared reading" when they read big books (18 × 12 inches) to their students. Parents are practicing shared reading when they read aloud to their children. At this early stage, the adult is doing most of the reading, but the child follows as the adult reads and chimes in for the reading of familiar words, repeated words, and/or repeated phrases. An upper-grade teacher can also use shared reading when students are reading a difficult book that they may not fully comprehend if they were to read independently; the teacher can read portions aloud, and the students can follow along and read silently (Tompkins 2006).

In 1969, R. G. Heckleman developed his **neurological-impress method (NIM)**, an approach that adults had probably been using with children for generations. He advocates that the teacher sit slightly behind the reader; the teacher and the learner hold (share) the book jointly and read aloud together whenever possible. The teacher should slide a finger along each line and follow the words as the two say the words together. Heckleman reports significant gains in children with whom the method was used. LinguaLinks notes that the method can help (1) develop fluency in reading; (2) impress the words into the memory of the learner; (3) foster correct phrasing, intonation, fluency, mechanics, and pronunciation; (4) build the learner's confidence; (5) provide immediate success and feedback; and (6) provide a pleasant reading experience ("Using a Neurological Impress Activity," *www.sil.org/lingualinks/literacy/implementaliteracyprogram/usinganeurological impressactiv.htm*). Jimmie Cook and his colleagues (1980) also report on page 473, "The NIM Helps." In 1978, Paul Hollingsworth suggested using a wireless system to make it possible to use the NIM with several students at one time. Marie Carbo (1978) suggests using "talking books" or the recorded book to teach reading. Her method is like NIM, except the child has a recording instead of a one-on-one tutor during the reading. Heckleman, however, emphasizes that human contact is essential to the enjoyment and success of the NIM plan.

Environmental Print

Our environment is rich with words. People see signs advertising everything from fast foods to fast cars. Television shows display many words, and newspapers and magazines depend on words to sell their products and to communicate their messages. Around swimming pools, playgrounds, recreation centers, and movie theaters are printed signs and cautions to help ensure the safety of customers and users. Becoming aware of these environmental words is important to children. They should begin to notice and try to recognize these important words at an early age. Noting the signs and words around them will help children feel comfortable with words and make them aware of the importance of reading in our society.

Anita P. Davis and Thomas R. McDaniel (1998) identify words that they consider essential for physical safety, social acceptability, and the avoidance of embarrassment. Some of these "essential words" are *exit, danger, high voltage, stop, beware, keep out,* and *no trespassing*. Being able to read these words is vital. Davis and McDaniel advocate that teachers and adults help children notice and master these words in their environment.

Edward Dolch (1960) identifies the most frequently used vocabulary words from preprimer level to grade 3. Listing the words by grade in the Dolch Word List, the author recommends teaching them to primary children to develop their reading vocabulary. Because Dolch advocates teaching the beginning reader to read the words quickly and to "pop" them off immediately, many teachers call the words the "popper words."

Language Experience Approach

The language experience approach (LEA) attempts to facilitate students' language development through the use of experiences, rather than with printed material alone. After an event or experience in which the learners in the class participate, the students make a written record of it as a group (with the help of the teacher). In this way, each student can see that

- what I say, I can write

- what I can write, I can read

- what others write, I can read

The LEA can be a part of many levels of teaching. Even high school classes often have the teacher at the board recording information that the class offers about something read or experienced as a group.

Like Clay (1966), Martha Combs (2006) recognizes the first stage in literacy as the emerging stage but also notes two other stages of development in literacy. Combs's three stages are

Emerging literacy stage: Children in this stage are making the transition from speaking to writing and reading—with support from others. Reading might involve predictable books; these books will be at the child's frustration reading level initially, but as the children practice, the books are at the instructional level of the children—and eventually at their independent level. Shared reading and interactive writings, which the children compose and the teachers record, provide practice and build confidence.

Developing stage: Children in the developing stage are becoming more independent in their reading, their writing, and their speaking. These children are usually on a middle-first to late-second-grade level. Their texts should include many decodable words—these are words that follow a regular pattern and have a predictable sound: *man*, *tip*, *me*. The children can practice their decoding skills as they read and gain confidence; they are progressing with their handwriting skills and are becoming more independent in spelling words they need in writing.

Transitional reading stage: Children who are transitional readers usually have an instructional reading level of second grade or beyond. Ideally, these children should spend much of their time with independent-level and instructional-level materials. Their instructors are still there to help them, but the children are able to refine their old skills and practice new skills.

STRATEGIES FOR TEACHING WORD RECOGNITION AND LANGUAGE ACQUISITION

It is important for teachers, schools, and parents to remember that reading should always be a pleasurable activity. It is best to avoid programs that (1) focus entirely on skills with no connections to reading actual books, (2) ignore the experiences of the children, and (3) repeat what the students already know. Programs that are totally skills based, nonpleasurable, and unrelated to authentic materials and that neglect the child's needs are nonmotivating (Noyce and Christie 1989). As noted earlier, the programs for teaching word recognition and language acquisition should be developmentally appropriate, individually appropriate, and age appropriate (SREB 1994).

Phonological Awareness

Increased phonological awareness occurs as children learn to associate the roughly 44 speech sounds in the English language with their visual representation. Children learn to pronounce these 44 sounds as they begin to talk. Because the English language has only 26 letters, it obviously is not a phonetic language; that is, there is no one-to-one correspondence between letters and sounds. The 26 letters are combined in many different ways to reproduce the needed sounds.

When they try to write, children in the early grades create **invented spellings** by applying their understanding of spelling rules. As children progress through the grades, their spellings usually become more conventional.

J. R. Gentry (1981) identifies the stages that students go through in their spelling development. These stages are particularly evident in the writing of students in a whole language classroom. The stages include the **pre-communication stage**, when the student randomly uses letters; the **pre-phonetic stage**, when the student begins to use some letters correctly; the **phonetic stage**, when the student spells the words the way that they sound; the **transitional stage**, during which the student uses both correct spelling and phonetic spelling; and the **correct spelling stage**, when the student spells words correctly (Davis 2004).

> *PRAXIS Pointer*
>
> **Do not leave an answer blank. It is better to guess than to leave an answer space blank.**

Phonics

The most commonly used method of teaching reading in the United States from colonial times through the 1920s was the phonics method. Other reading methods—the sight word method, modified alphabet approach, and the whole language approach, for example—came into being after the 1920s. However, phonics is still an important part of reading instruction in the United States.

The phonics method of teaching reading emphasizes the association between the grapheme (the written symbol) and the phoneme (the speech sound). The phonics method attempts to relate spelling rules to the process.

William Holmes McGuffey and Rudolf Flesch were proponents of the phonics method. McGuffey produced his series of reading books in 1836. The readers used phonics while teaching morals to students; it was a cultural force, not just a reading textbook. By 1920, sales of McGuffey readers had reached 122 million. In 1955, Flesch wrote *Why Johnny Can't Read—And What You Can Do About It* to warn parents that the reason many children could not read was that the schools were not using the phonics approach.

Phonics is, of course, a skills-based approach. There are several **advantages of the phonics method** that are readily apparent. One important advantage of the phonics method is that it gives children tools for decoding, or figuring out, how to read and pronounce words that they do not know immediately. Because the phonics approach involves phoneme–grapheme associations, auditory learners—those who learn best through the sense of sound—often prefer to read using phonics. Auditory learners can usually hear a sound and associate it easily with its printed symbol. Using phonics with auditory learners is an evident advantage. A third advantage of this method with its emphasis on sound–symbol relationships is that phonics readers can often transfer their skills to spelling. Spelling involves associating sounds with letters; it is the opposite of phonics, which associates symbols with sounds. A final advantage is that phonics readers are often good spellers (Davis 2004).

At its January 1997 meeting, the board of directors of the International Reading Association (IRA) passed a position statement titled "The Role of Phonics in Reading Instruction." The key assertions were that phonics is an important aspect in beginning reading instruction, primary teachers value and teach phonics, and effective phonics is integrated into the total language arts program (IRA takes a stand on phonics, 1997).

There are, however, **disadvantages to the phonics method**. A major disadvantage of phonics is that visual learners may not read well by this method. A second disadvantage of the method is that the rules do not hold true all the time. In his now-classic study, Theodore Clymer (1963) reports that he found few phonics generalizations that held true in more than 50 percent of the cases in the primary grades. Four years later, however, Mildred Hart Bailey (1967) found in her study of phonics rules that 27 of the 45 generalizations identified by Clymer held true in 75 percent of the words appearing most often in reading materials for grades 1 through 6.

A third disadvantage of the phonics method is that some students are confused when they learn a phonics rule and then encounter frequent exceptions; inconsistencies pose a problem for them. Some educators, though not all, note a fourth disadvantage to the phonics method: they believe that there is no basis for the view that there are subskills, such as phonics, that students need to read; they see the skills as mythical (Davis 2004).

To help children learn phonics, many teachers find certain techniques for teaching the method helpful. Students should have opportunities to practice the phonics rules and generalizations in context; instructors should make every effort to illustrate the transfer of the phonics rules and generalizations to everyday materials and to other subjects. Analytic phonics (using phonics in context with actual materials), as opposed to synthetic phonics (phonics taught in isolation from meaningful books and materials, often using worksheets), seems to be the more helpful technique. Teachers can introduce a phonics rule or generalization as it appears, but such an incidental approach does not ensure that all students meet and practice the most frequently encountered phonics rules. A structured, systematic, sequential program of phonics helps ensure that readers have at their disposal an arsenal of skills to decode new words and spell the words correctly. Such a plan of presenting the rules and regulations of phonics can help eliminate gaps in students' word-attack skills (Davis 2004).

Marie Carbo (1993), nationally known for her work with reading styles, recognizes the importance of making available phonics instruction in any reading program. She particularly warns, "A good whole language program does include phonics." In *Becoming a Nation of Readers*, the Commission on Reading (1986) stresses that phonics is an essential strategy for beginning reading. Teachers should use a systematic approach and present the skills in meaningful sentences, passages, and materials, not just as words in isolation.

A word of caution for teachers of phonics is that in the beginning, students may read slowly. When students begin to commit high-frequency words to memory, however, reading speed and, in turn, comprehension will increase (Davis 2004). The young child begins recognizing letters and their sounds. These skills will help the child with reading and spelling. Another technique that will help the child in attacking unknown words is analyzing the structure of the words, or structural analysis (Davis 2004).

Word Structure

Breaking a word into its parts, or syllables, is called **structural analysis**. By dividing a word into its syllables and sounding out these smaller parts, students are often able to pronounce longer, unknown words that they previously did not recognize. There are many rules for dividing words into syllables; some of these rules often hold true, but some of the rules do not. As mentioned earlier, Bailey (1967) found in her study of phonics rules that 27 of 45 syllabication rules hold true in 75 percent of the words a child frequently encounters in grades 1 through 6.

Children do not work with all the rules for structural analysis in the early years. Usually, children work mainly with adding word endings to words that are already a part of their sight vocabulary or word families. Some of the endings that children encounter first are the suffixes *-ed*, *-s*, *-es*, and *-ing* (Davis 2004). Fry (1980) says that six suffixes cause a large percentage of the variants: *-ed*, *-s*, *-er*, *-ly*, *-est*, and *-ing*.

However, all the words a beginning reader sees may not be those in the list of sight words the child already knows. Although some texts try to limit the new words a beginning reader (children in kindergarten through grade 3) meets at a given time (**controlled vocabulary**), most children do not experience such a protected environment. Young children are constantly encountering new words. It is important, therefore, for the child to have some word-attack skills such as structural analysis to decipher new, unknown words. Separating the prefix and/or the suffix from the root word is an example of structural analysis. After separating these word parts, the child may be able to sound out the word. Examples include *un-tie*, *re-peat*, and *sing-ing* (Davis 2004).

Another important rule for separating words into parts is the **compound word rule**. With this rule, the child divides a compound word into its parts. The child and the teacher can work together to sound out each part. Examples include *cow-boy* and *foot-ball* (Davis 2004).

Two essential rules for structural analysis are the **v/cv and the vc/cv rules**. Teachers introduce these rules and encourage the students in the later stages of reading development to employ these attack skills. To use the rules successfully, the child must first determine if each letter in a word is a vowel (v) or a consonant (c). The child can write the label over each letter in the word. Looking for the v/cv or vc/cv pattern, the child separates the word at the appropriate place. Examples of the v/cv rule are *o-ven* and *bo-dy*. Examples of the vc/cv rule are *sum-mer* and *ig-loo* (Davis 2004).

Some rules of structural analysis, such as the following, are complex, useful, and best for older readers (Davis 2004):

1. When *-le* comes at the end of the word and a consonant comes before it, the consonant goes with the *-le*, as in the word *pur-ple* and *bub-ble*. (An exception to this rule is when the word contains a *ck*, one would not separate the *c* and the *k*, as in the word *pick-le*.)

2. The suffix *-ed* forms a separate syllable if *d* or *t* comes before the *-ed*, as in *skidd-ed* and *mist-ed*.

Context Clues

As children progress in their skills and confidence, teachers might encourage them to use picture clues and previously read materials to predict what word would make sense.

To help children make their predictions, the teacher can give them a clue, like the first sound of the word. Another way a teacher can provide context clues is to mask words or portions of words with a "magic window"—a sturdy piece of cardboard with a small rectangle cut out of the center. This allows the teacher to single out a letter or syllable for the children to consider. The teacher can also cover up words or parts of words on a transparency sheet on the overhead projector (Combs 2006).

The technique of using all the language cueing systems together is important to comprehension. The following are the three major types of language cues:

Syntactic cues: Attention to syntax can increase **comprehension**, or understanding. These cues include grammatical hints; the order of words; word endings; and the way the words function, or work, in a phrase, sentence, or passage.

Semantic cues: Semantics can include "hints" within the sentence and from the entire passage or text that help the reader determine the meaning. Semantic cues, then, are meaning clues.

Phonemes and graphemes: The phonemes (sounds) and graphemes (written letters) are crucial to reading and writing. A child who does not know the word *phone* but knows that the letters *ph* often sound like the letter *f* and knows that the sound of a *phone* is a ring may be able to figure out the word in the sentence *I heard the phone ring*.

Again, through demonstration, invitation, and discussion, the teacher can help children confirm or correct as they read, monitor understanding during the reading process, and review and retain information after the reading is complete (Davis 2004).

Views about reading and the stages vary from source to source. Most sources agree that it is imperative that teachers **scaffold**, or support, children of all ages. Scaffolding involves demonstrating, guiding, and teaching; the amount of support the teacher provides should depend on the instructional support needed and the individual child. Five stages that mark scaffolding are—moving from greatest to the least as students assume more and more responsibility—the modeled, shared, interactive, guided, and independent levels of support (Tompkins 2006).

Reading Strategies

Looking at strategies used by proficient readers helps teachers make skillful choices of activities to maximize student learning in subject area instruction. Anne Goudvis and Stephanie Harvey (2000) offer the following list:

Activating prior knowledge: Readers pay more attention when they relate to the text. Readers naturally bring their prior knowledge and experience to reading, but they comprehend better when they think about the connections they make between the text, their lives, and the larger world.

Predicting or asking questions: Questioning is the strategy that keeps readers engaged. When readers ask questions, even before they read, they clarify understanding and forge ahead to make meaning. Asking questions is at the heart of thoughtful reading.

Visualizing: Active readers create visual images based on the words they read in the text. These created pictures enhance their understanding.

Drawing inferences: Inferring is when the readers take what they know, garner clues from the text, and think ahead to make a judgment, discern a theme, or speculate about what is to come.

Determining important ideas: Thoughtful readers grasp essential ideas and important information when reading. Readers must differentiate between less important ideas and key ideas that are central to the meaning of the text.

Synthesizing information: Synthesizing involves combining new information with existing knowledge to form an original idea or interpretation. Reviewing, sorting, and sifting important information can lead to new insights that change the way readers think.

Repairing understanding: If confusion disrupts meaning, readers need to stop and clarify their understanding. Readers may use a variety of strategies to "fix up" comprehension when meaning goes awry.

Confirming: As students read and after they read, they can confirm the predictions they originally made. There is no wrong answer. One can confirm negatively or positively. Determining whether a prediction is correct is a goal.

Using parts of a book: Students should use book parts—such as charts, diagrams, indexes, and the table of contents—to improve their understanding of the reading content.

Reflecting: An important strategy is for students to think about, or reflect on, what they have just read. Reflection can be simply thinking, or it can be more formal, such as a discussion or writing in a journal.

While providing instruction in a subject area, the teacher needs to determine if the reading material is at the students' level of reading mastery. If not, the teacher needs to make accommodations either in the material itself or in the manner of presentation.

Teaching the Strategies

An instructor can teach reading strategies explicitly to students in a carefully orchestrated manner. First, the teacher should model the strategy, explain it, and describe how to apply the strategy successfully. It helps if the teacher "thinks aloud" while modeling the strategy for students. Second, the teacher should practice the strategy with the students. It is important to scaffold the students' attempts and support their thinking by giving feedback during conferencing and classroom discussion. In this case, it helps if the students "think aloud" while practicing the strategy. Third, the teacher should encourage the students to apply the strategy and should give them regular feedback. Fourth, once the students clearly understand the strategy, they should apply it on their own in new reading situations. While monitoring students' understanding of the subject matter, the teacher should become aware of students' thinking as they read and as they detect obstacles and confusions that derail their understanding. The teacher can suggest, teach, or implement strategies to help students repair meaning when it breaks down.

Comprehension and Strategies To Teach It

Reading is more than calling words. Reading must result in *comprehension*, or understanding. Comprehension skills include the ability to identify supporting details and facts, the main idea or essential message, the author's purpose, fact and opinion, point of view, inference, and conclusion. To help students develop these skills, teachers can consistently emphasize meaning in the classroom and should focus on the four levels of comprehension: literal, interpretive, critical, and creative.

The **literal level of comprehension**, the lowest level of understanding, involves **reading the lines**, or reading and understanding exactly what is on the page. Students may give back **facts** or **details** directly from the passages as they read. For example, a teacher works with students as they make their own play dough and use the recipe to practice **authentic reading** (Davis 2004). The teacher might question the students on the literal level as they mix their ingredients. Here are some sample questions:

Factual question: How much salt do you add to the mixture?

Sequence question: What is the first step in making the play dough?

Contrast question: Do you add more or less salt than you did flour?

PRAXIS Pointer

Read the question before studying graphs, maps or tables. Then read the graph with the question in mind.

The **interpretive level of comprehension**, the second level of understanding, requires students to **read between the lines**. At this level, students must explain figurative language, define terms, and answer interpretive or inferential questions. **Inferential questions** require the students to **infer**, or figure out, the answers. Asking students to figure out the **author's purpose**, the **main idea** or **essential message**, the **point of view**, and the **conclusion** are examples of inferential questions. Inferential questions may require students to draw conclusions, generalize, derive meaning from the language, speculate, anticipate, predict, and summarize. All such questions are from the interpretive level.

Here are some examples of interpretive questions the teacher could ask at the cooking center while students are making play dough:

Contrast: How is the dry measuring cup different from the liquid measuring cup? Why are they different?

Deriving meaning: What does the term *blend* mean?

Purpose: What is the purpose of making play dough at home? Why would you want to make play dough instead of buying it?

Cause and effect: Why do the directions say to store the play dough in a covered, airtight container?

The **critical level of comprehension** requires a high level of understanding. The students must judge the passage they have read. The critical level is one of the two highest of the levels of understanding; it requires students to **read beyond the lines**. Having students determine whether a passage is true or false, deciding whether a statement is a fact or opinion, detecting propaganda, or judging the qualifications of the author for writing the passage are examples of using the critical level of comprehension. Here are some examples of questions the teacher could ask students as they make play dough to encourage their thinking and understanding at the critical and creative levels:

Checking author's reputation: The recipe for the play dough comes from a book of chemistry experiments. A chemist wrote the book. Do you think that a chemist would be a good person to write about play dough? Why, or why not?

Responding emotionally: Do you prefer to use the play dough we made in class or the Play-doh that the local stores carry?

Judging: Do you think that the recipe for play dough that is on the recipe card will work? Why, or why not?

The **creative level of comprehension** is at the highest level of understanding. As with the critical level of comprehension, the student must **read beyond the lines**. The student must often make judgments about other actions to take. Answers may vary among the students. The teacher must take care not to stifle creativity by saying one action is better than another. For instance, a teacher might suggest that after making a batch of cookies, a student finds that the baked cookies do not fit in the cookie jar; the teacher asks the students, "What can we do?" Answers might include, "Donate the extras to the first graders," "Give some to the teacher," "Share with my little sister," "Put them in a plastic storage bag." All these answers are creative; the teacher should not judge one as better than another.

Checking for Understanding

Teachers need to be explicit about teaching students to be aware, to check for understanding, and to use reading comprehension strategies to make meaning. To monitor and repair students' understanding, teachers should explicitly teach them to do the following (Goudvis and Harvey 2000):

- Track their thinking through coding with sticky notes, writing, or discussion.

- Notice when they lose focus.

- Stop and go back to clarify thinking.

- Reread to enhance understanding.

- Read ahead to clarify meaning.

- Identify and articulate what is confusing or puzzling about the text.

- Recognize that all of their questions have value. (There is no such thing as a stupid question.)

- Develop the disposition to question the text or author.

- Think critically about the text and be willing to disagree with its information or logic.

- Match the problem with the strategy that will best solve it.

Depending on the situation, instructors may use these strategies across the curriculum in any subject area. In addition, the effective teacher can use graphic organizers such as these:

Double-entry journals: The student enters direct quotes from the text (with page number) in the left column and enters "thinking options"—such as "This is important because," "I am confused because," "I think this means"—in the right column.

Venn diagrams: Venn diagrams consist of two overlapping concentric circles in which the student compares two items or concepts by placing specific criteria or critical attributes for one in the left circle, for the other in the right circle, and attributes or characteristics that are shared by the two in the overlapping section in the center.

Webs or maps: The student charts out a concept or section of text in a graphic outline. The web or map begins with the title or concept often written in the middle of the page and branches out in web fashion; students will note specific bits of information on the branches or strings of the web. Arrows or lines in other formats can make connections from one bit of information to another. The map or web helps the student to think about the reading passage and illustrate its structure; the student is able with the map/web to make a passage more concrete and develop a visual representation of the book or reading section. (Davis, 2004)

Fishbone organizer: This type of graphic can help the reader to illustrate cause and effect. A reader viewing the fishbone chart can immediately see the cause and the direct result of the cause.

Fishbone Map

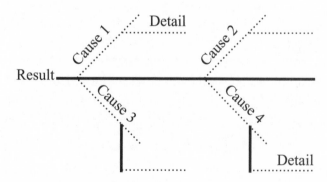

ASSESSING COMPREHENSION

A frequent device for assessing comprehension is the use of oral or written questions. A question may be **convergent**, which indicates that only one answer is correct, or **divergent**, which indicates that more than one answer is correct. Most tests, however, include a combination of question types.

Another device for checking comprehension is a **cloze test**, a passage with omitted words the test taker must supply. The test maker must decide whether to require the test taker to supply the exact word or to accept synonyms. Passing scores reflect which type of answer is acceptable. If meaning is the intent of the exercise, the teacher might accept synonyms and not demand the surface-level constructs, or the exact word.

The speed at which a student reads helps determine comprehension, *up to a point*. The faster a student reads, the better that student comprehends, *up to a point*. The slow reader who must analyze each word does not comprehend as well as the fast reader. It is possible, however, to read too fast. Most students have had the experience of having to reread materials. For example, a student reading a physics chapter in preparation for a test might read more slowly than when reading a novel but not slowly enough to note every important detail.

A teacher might ask students to read a passage and record their reading times. Then the teacher might give the students a quiz on the passage. After scoring the quizzes, the teacher could meet with each student to discuss the student's reading speed and its relation to the quiz grade. For students who received low quiz scores, the teacher could assign another passage and attempt to have the student slow down, or perhaps even accelerate, the speed of reading.

Mapping and Webbing

Story mapping or webbing helps students think about a reading passage and its structure. Some typical devices in good narrative fiction and that might be useful on a story map include setting, stylistic devices, characters, and plot. A class reading Wilson Rawls's *Where the Red Fern Grows* (1961/1976) created the story map shown in Figure 3.1 on the next page.

Study Plans

The teacher might acquaint students with several plans to help them read content materials. Many of these plans already exist, and the teacher and the students can simply select the plan(s) that works best for them with various subjects. Students may use **mnemonic devices**, or memory-related devices, to help them remember the steps in reading a chapter effectively. Students often use plans like the following survey-question-read-recite-review (SQ3R) plan when reading text in content areas:

**Figure 3-1
Story Map**

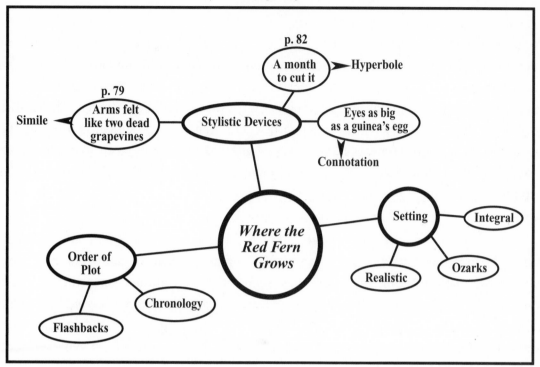

Survey: Before reading a passage or an entire section of the text, the student should look over the assigned page or chapter and consider some questions. Are there illustrations, charts, or diagrams? What are some of the chapter headings? Are some words in bold type?

Question: The student may wish to devise some questions that the chapter will probably answer. If an assigned chapter has questions at the end, the student can look over the questions before reading the chapter; the questions serve as a guide to the text.

Read: The student now reads the passage to answer the questions at the end of the chapter or to answer the questions that the student developed before reading the chapter.

Recite: The student attempts to answer orally or in writing the student-developed questions or the questions at the end of the chapter.

Review: The student reviews the material to "double-check" the answers given in writing or orally at the previous step.

Richard Vacca and Jo Ann Vacca (1989) express doubt that most students actually use a study plan. Even though an instructor may try to teach the "formula" for reading and studying a passage by having a class memorize the steps, practice the procedure several times, and view the formulas as a lifelong activity, Vacca and Vacca contend that a study system "evolves gradually within each learner" and that the SQ3R plan is difficult even for junior high school students (227). They suggest that students need to become "text smart" and learn to preview, skim for the main idea, and organize information through mapping or outlining.

Other reading authorities disagree. Judy S. Richardson and Raymond F. Morgan (1990) suggest that students can use the SQ3R plan by fifth or sixth grade. Thomas G. Gunning (1996) reminds teachers that SQ3R has been around since the 1930s; he describes the method as "a widely used and effective study strategy incorporating five steps" (319). John U. Michaelis and Jesus Garcia (1996) suggest that students can create their own self-directed reading strategies. They cite the purpose-read-organize-vocabulary-evaluate (PROVE) strategy as an example:

Purpose: Establish a purpose or set up questions to guide your reading.

Read: Read the passage to try to achieve the purpose or answer the questions.

Organize: Outline; place details under main ideas.

Vocabulary: Note any new vocabulary or concepts that you master.

Evaluate: Evaluate to determine if you achieved your purpose.

Vocabulary in Context and Concept Vocabulary

Vocabulary instruction is important to the teaching of the language arts—and other subjects. Teachers identify important vocabulary words in their units and often single out these words for study.

Vocabulary study is more than memorizing definitions, however. Effective teachers employ many strategies to increase the vocabulary of their students. They post new words on the word wall as reminders of the new vocabulary words. The teachers develop lessons about idioms, the use of dictionaries and glossaries, multiple meanings of words, antonyms, synonyms, homonyms, figurative meanings, word parts, and other word-study techniques.

Effective instruction includes making connections to the background of the students. Repetition, meaningful use, and encouraging independent reading also work to enhance vocabulary development (Tompkins 2006, 196–213). Combs (2006) reminds the educator that children seem to acquire vocabulary when the adult provides explanations of the new words encountered in context. To enhance the learning, the children should have ample opportunities to review and use that knowledge—especially in other contexts. Shared reading especially aids in vocabulary development (190).

Types of Children's Literature

Literary genres include poetry, prose, novels, short stories, plays or drama, and personal narratives or essays.

Poetry

Poetry is a genre that is difficult to define for children, except as "not prose." Poetry is the use of words to capture something: a sight, a feeling, or perhaps a sound. Poetry needs to be chosen carefully for a child, as poetry ought to elicit from the child a response that connects with the experience of the poem. All children need poetry in their lives. Poetry needs to be celebrated and enjoyed as part of the classroom experience, and a literacy-rich classroom will always include a collection of poetry to read, reread, savor, and enjoy. Some children enjoy the discipline of writing in a poetic format. Reggie Routman has published a series of slim books about teaching children to write poems on their own.

Poetry is perhaps the oldest art and has been a part of people's lives through the centuries. Like the ancient listeners who thrilled to Homer's poetry and the tribes who chanted invocations to their gods, both children and adults in today's generation listen to song lyrics and find themselves, sometimes despite themselves, repeating certain rhythmic lines. An advertisement that listeners chuckle over—or say they hate—has a way of repeating itself as listeners use the catchy phrase or snappy repetition. Both lyricists and advertisers cleverly use language and play on people's ability to pick up on a repeated sound or engaging rhythm or inner rhyme—a part of poetry. Children love poetry: nursery rhymes, ball-game rhythms, jump-rope patterns. Even with no idea of the meaning of the words (e.g., "Little Miss Muffet sat on a tuffet"), a child can respond to their sounds and the pattern they form.

Prose

Prose is another literary type. Students are sometimes confused as to what exactly prose is. Basically, prose is not poetry. Prose is what people write and speak most of the time in everyday intercourse: unmetered, unrhymed language. This does not mean, however, that prose does not have its own rhythms; language, whether written or spoken, has cadence and balance. Certainly prose can have instances of rhyme or assonance, alliteration, or onomatopoeia. Language is, after all, phonic. Furthermore, prose may be either fiction or nonfiction. A novel (or short story) is fiction; an autobiography is nonfiction. Whereas a novel (or short story) may have some autobiographical elements, an autobiography is, from most readers' point of view, entirely factual.

Textbooks are generally nonfiction prose. Reading textbooks (**basals**) may contain both fiction and nonfiction, poetry and prose.

The **narrative** is a common style of prose that can be fiction or nonfiction. A narrative tells a story or gives an account of an incident or a series of incidents. The account may be autobiographical to make a point, as in George Orwell's essay "Shooting an Elephant."

Narrative fictional children's literature is either traditional or modern in form. **Traditional literature** is composed of ancient stories, and it has a set form. People have passed these stories down through the centuries by word of mouth. Later, others, like Joel Chandler Harris, the Grimm Brothers, and Charles Perrault, recorded the stories for future generations. **Modern literature**, on the other hand, is, as the name suggests, much more recent; its categories can overlap some of the categories of traditional literature and can include additional forms of literature.

Making Sure the Text or Reading Material Is on the Student's Level

To match the reading level of the text to the reading level of the student, the instructor can use a cloze test. A **cloze test** is a reading comprehension test in which the student must supply words that have purposely been omitted from the text. A teacher can create a cloze test by using a selection from the textbook or other material and omitting every *n*th word; the student then must fill in the blanks. The teacher may adjust the percentage of words that the student must fill in correctly on the basis of whether there is an accompanying word bank and whether the teacher will accept synonyms or only the exact words. This test will help to determine if the text is on the student's instructional level, independent level, or frustration level.

Table 3-1. Cloze Test Scoring Guide

Percentage Correct	Reading Level	Difficulty
Above 60%	Independent reading level	This material is easy enough that a child could read it without help.
40%–60%	Instructional reading level	This material is of such a level that a child must have the help of a teacher to complete it successfully.
Below 40%	Frustration reading level	This material is too difficult for the student. Often the child will begin to make excuses to stop the exercise. The child may begin biting his/her nails, twisting her/his hair, fidgeting, and perhaps even asking to go to the bathroom or to get water. The teacher should probably not make the child use material on this level.

Pre-reading Strategies

The teacher may guide the student in prereading instruction. The teacher and class together may set up a know-want-learned (K-W-L) chart. The chart may list what they already *know* about the topic or the story, what they *want* to know and find out as they read, and—after the reading—what they have *learned*.

To ensure that the students master the material, the teacher may even develop **process guides** to help the students as they read. In a process guide, the teacher develops specific helps for a section of the text that the students are going to read and that the teacher believes might cause some problems for specific students. A teacher might include in a process guide to a particular chapter the following information:

• A list of key terms for the students to identify as they read

• A list of key people for the students to identify as they read

- A list of new vocabulary for the students to identify as they read

- A guide to relational words in the passages

- Questions to call the readers' attention to graphic aids in the passage

It is true that process guides are time-consuming to develop, but because schools use most texts and other reading materials for more than one year, the teacher may be able to reuse them from year to year if there are sections of the text that continue to be applicable to the subject and to the students of later years. After the teacher calls the students' attention to certain features of the text and how to read it, the students may be able to develop process guides for themselves or for the person whom they tutor; preparing the guides may serve as a learning/organizing experience (Davis 2000; Karlin 1971).

An important part of helping the students read effectively is helping them to be aware of the **patterns of organization** of various books, the **text structure**, and the use of **book parts**. Because book parts and organization may vary, particularly from one content area to another, the effective teacher will develop methods and/or materials to introduce the students to the texts that they will be using. The teacher will make sure that students know the purpose of bold font, the index, the side heads, the contents page, and so on.

Before, during, and after instructional input, the students preview, rehearse, or apply what they've learned. In **guided practice**, the teacher watches carefully to make sure that students realize what they are to observe during their reading and that they have grasped the material correctly. Because the teacher is on hand to assess student responses, he or she is able to provide correction or additional input if necessary. During independent practice, students work independently. At the end of each lesson (or at the end of the class), the teacher or students summarize or review what has been learned (Davis 2004).

WRITING: ITS STAGES, PROCESS, AND ASSESSMENT

For years, educators believed that reading preceded writing in the development of literacy. This belief has recently changed.

Stages in Writing Development

Emerging literacy research indicates that learning to write is an important part in a child's learning to read. As children begin to name letters and read print, they also begin to write letters and words. Writing development seems to occur at about the same time as reading development—not afterward, as traditional reading readiness assumed. Whole language seeks to integrate the language arts rather than sequencing them. Just as change has marked educators' beliefs about reading instruction and the way that reading develops, change has also marked the methods and philosophies behind the teaching of writing in the schools.

Children seem to progress through certain stages in their writing. Although many authorities have examined the stages in writing development, Alexander Luria presents the most thoroughly elaborated model (Klein 1985; Davis 2004). He cautions, however, that the stages are not entirely a function of age. Luria explains that it is not uncommon to find children from three to six years old who are the same age but are two to three stages apart in their writing. He also notes that children do not advance systematically through the stages. At times, a child may regress or "zigzag." At other times, the child may appear to remain at one level without progression or regression. Here is a summary of Luria's stages in writing:

> *PRAXIS Pointer*
>
> **Work quickly and steadily. You have two hours to complete the test. Avoid focusing on any one problem too long. Taking the practice tests in this book will help you learn to budget your precious time.**

Stage 1: The undifferentiated stage from ages three to five is a period that Luria defines as a prewriting or preinstrumental period. The child does not distinguish between marks written on a page. The marks (writing) seem merely random to the child and do not help the child recall information.

Stage 2: The differentiated stage from about age four is when the child intentionally builds a relationship between sounds and written expression. For instance, the child represents short words or short phrases with shorter marks and longer words, phrases, or sentences with longer marks. The child might use dark marks to help remember a sentence such as *The sky was dark*. Making such marks is an example of mnemonics, or associating symbols with information.

Stage 3: The pictographic stage from ages four to six is the period that Robert Klein (1985, 66) says is "the most important stage in the development of the child's perception of writing-as-a-conceptual-act."

The Writing Process

Teachers in the early 1970s were very concerned with spelling and punctuation in students' papers. The teacher did all the "correcting" and watched carefully for grammatical, spelling, and punctuation errors. In the late 1970s, writing "experts" denounced students' compositions as being too dull. The schools began to foster creative writing and encouraged teachers to provide opportunities for creative writing each week. However, many teachers began to view the creative writing as lacking in structure. **Process writing** has since become the buzzword in writing. With process writing, students engage in several activities (Noyce and Christie 1989):

Prewriting stage: During the first stage in the writing process, the students begin to collect information for the writing that they will do.

Composing or writing stage: The classroom resembles a laboratory. Students may consult with one another and use various books and materials to construct their papers. At this stage, the student-writers do not worry about spelling and mechanics. This is the drafting stage. Some students will use invented spelling as they try to apply their understanding of spelling rules. The students may later edit and revise the words, but on first writing their drafts, they can simply record the word quickly and go on to the next word in the sentence.

Revising stage: Writers polish and improve their compositions.

Editing/evaluation/postwriting stage: Students read and correct their own writing and the works of others. The teacher does not have to do all the evaluating. Students use the dictionary, the thesaurus, their peers, and even the spell-check program on the classroom computers.

Rewriting stage: After their self-evaluations and after their classmates and teachers share praise and constructive criticisms, including spelling and punctuation corrections, the students rewrite their compositions.

In some classes, the students publish their own works and even have an **author's chair** from which the writers can tell some things about themselves, discuss their writing process, and read their compositions aloud (Noyce and Christie 1989). This is often called the **publishing stage**. Writing that is published in the classroom can be as informal as a final draft handwritten by a student or as formal as a book bound by a school's publishing center. Teachers do not necessarily have their students take each piece of writing to the publishing stage. According to research, the most effective writing process includes at least the prewriting, composing, revising, and editing/evaluation/postwriting stages (Bennett 1987).

SPEECH

Conventions of Standard American English

The way you speak can vary depending on whom you are speaking to—just as what you wear can vary depending on whom you are going to see. More commonly, language varies according to geographic region, ethnic group, social class, and educational level. The language usually used in U.S. schools is Standard American English. This formal language (dialect) is the language in texts, newspapers, magazines, and the news programs on television.

There are several other forms of the English language spoken in the United States besides Standard American English. These variations include the forms spoken in Appalachia, in urban ghettos, and by Mexican Americans, particularly in the Southwest. In all these variations, the syntax, phonology, and semantics differ from Standard American English. When instructing students who do not speak the standard dialect, teachers should not try to replace the culture or the language with Standard American English; the goal of school is to add Standard American English to students' language registers (Tompkins 2006).

Writing Standard American English requires the use of certain mechanics or conventions. Using the conventions in capitalization, punctuation, spellings, and formatting, among others, is a courtesy to readers of the written language (Tompkins 2006). With the language experience approach (LEA)—as previously discussed in this chapter—the teacher attempts to facilitate the students' language development through the use of experiences, rather than printed material alone. After the class participates in an experience or event, the students, as a group, record what happened (often with the help of the teacher). The teacher writes exactly what the students say—even if they do not use Standard American English. The idea is to enable each student to see that

- what I say, I can write

- what I can write, I can read

- what others write, I can read (Davis 2004)

The teacher may talk at this time about alternative ways to say what the students do not say in Standard American English. Elementary-age children in particular need direct instruction in order to develop proper speaking habits. This includes using an appropriate tone and volume of voice depending on the audience and situation. Students should be provided with opportunities to express their thoughts, share their writing, or discuss content in small- and large-group contexts. The teacher should model desired speaking behaviors, in addition to informing students of expectations and norms. Young children should practice making eye contact while speaking with others. Along with speaking skills, students should be encouraged to develop strong listening skills. This includes looking at the speaker, listening quietly, and responding in a positive manner. Speaking and listening skills are integral aspects of language arts instruction.

ASSESSMENT TO IMPROVE INSTRUCTION AND ENHANCE LEARNING

Informal Assessment

Evaluation does not have to be expensive and purchased to be useful to the teacher and student alike. Clay (1985) developed a procedure for sampling the child's reading vocabulary and determining the extent of a child's print-related concepts. Her assessment checks whether children can find the title, show where to start reading a book, and locate the last page or the end of the book. As such, Clay's procedure is an informal way of **determining a child's readiness for reading** (Davis 2004).

Teachers can gain much valuable information by simply observing their students at work. Many school districts use a type of inventory/report card to inform adults in the home of the progress that the kindergartner or first grader is making. Long-time teachers usually develop, through trial and error, their own means of assessing the skills of students in their classes. Almost every book on teaching reading contains its own informal tests. The SREB's Health and Human Services Commission (1994) cautions that assessment should be **ongoing** and **natural**. The commission has determined that **continual observation of the physical, social, emotional, and cognitive domains of students** by both parents and teachers is the most meaningful approach to assessing young children. To obtain a meaningful, complete view of a young child, the commission endorses portfolios of a child's progress and performance inventories rather than standardized test results. Similarly, letter grades and numeric grades are less likely to give a complete picture than narrative reports on the young child.

Teachers can also develop their own informal reading inventories. The purpose of these assessments is to collect meaningful information about what students can and cannot do. A **running record** is a way to assess students' word-identification skills and fluency in oral reading. As the teacher listens to a student read a page, the teacher uses a copy of the page to mark each word the child mispronounces: the teacher writes the incorrect word over the printed word, draws a line through each word the child skips, and draws an arrow under repeated words.

✳ After determining the words that the child did not read successfully, the teacher can analyze the missed words to determine the reason that the child missed them. This assessment of missed words is **miscue analysis**. The teacher is looking for a pattern in the student's mistakes so that the teacher can provide help to the student.

Edward Fry developed in 1957 a list of "instant words." In 1980, he developed "The New Instant Word List." He explains that the words on the list are the most frequently used words in the English language. He says these words are the ones that young readers need to know. He explains that half of the words in the language are composed of the first 100 words (and their variants) in his list. Using this list is a way to assess how well the students are reading the words instantly (Davis 2004).

Fry also developed a **readability graph**. This mathematical equation gives the relationship between two variables: the number of sentences per 100 words and the number of syllables per 100 words. The result of graphing this information is the grade level of the book (Davis 2004).

Asking a child to **retell** a story is another type of informal assessment. The ability to retell a story is an informal type of assessment that is useful to the teacher, parent, and—eventually—the child. Informal assessment measures can also include observations, journals, written drafts, and conversations.

REFERENCES

Bailey, Mildred Hart. "The Utility of Phonic Generalizations in Grades One Through Six." *Reading Teacher* 20:5 (February 1967): 413–18.

Bennett, William. *What Works: Research about Teaching and Learning.* Washington, DC: U.S. Department of Education, 1987.

Blanchard, Kenneth H, and Spenser Johnson. *The One Minute Manager.* New York: Morrow, 1982.

Bloom, Benjamin, Max D. Engelhart, Edward J. Furst, Walker H. Hill, and David R. Krathwohl. *Taxonomy of Educational Objectives: The Classification of Educational Goals. Handbook I: Cognitive Domain.* New York: Longmans, Green, 1956.

Bruner, J. *Toward a Theory of Instruction.* Cambridge, MA: Harvard University Press. 1966.

Carbo, Marie. "Reading Styles and Whole Language." *Schools of Thought II.* Video. Bloomington, IN: Phi Delta Kappa, 1993.

————. "Teaching Reading with Talking Books" *Reading Teacher* 32:3 (December 1978): 267–73.

Chase, Richard. *Jack Tales.* New York: Houghton Mifflin, 1943.

————. *Grandfather Tales.* New York: Houghton Mifflin, 1948.

Clay, M. M. "Emergent Reading Behavior." PhD diss., University of Auckland, New Zealand, 1966.

————. *Reading: The Patterning of Complex Behavior.* Auckland, New Zealand: Heinemann Educational Books, 1979.

Clymer, Theodore. "The Utility of Phonic Generalizations in the Primary Grades." *The Reading Teacher* 16 (January 1963): 252–58.

Combs, Martha. *Readers and Writers in Primary Grades: A Balanced and Integrated Approach.* Upper Saddle River, NJ: Pearson, 2006.

Commission on Reading. *Becoming a Nation of Readers.* Washington, DC: U.S. Department of Education, September 1986.

Cook, Jimmie E. and Gregory J. Nolan. "Treating Auditory Perception Problems: The NIM Helps." *Academic Therapy* 15:4 (March 1980), 473–81.

Covey, Stephen R. *The Seven Habits of Highly Effective People: Restoring the Character Ethic.* New York: Simon and Shuster, 1989.

Davis, Anita P. *Children's Literature Essentials.* Boston: American Press, 2000.

Davis, Anita P., and Ed Y. Hall. *Harriet Quimby: First Lady of the Air (An Activity Book for Children).* Spartanburg, SC: Honoribus Press, 1993.

———. *Harriet Quimby: First lady of the Air (An Intermediate Biography).* Spartanburg, SC: Honoribus Press, 1998.

Davis, Anita P., and Thomas R. McDaniel. "Essential Vocabulary Words." *Reading Teacher* 52:3 (November 1998), pages 308-9.

Davis, Anita P., and Katharine Preston. *Discoveries.* Hillsborough, ID: Butte Publications, 1996.

Davis, Anita Price. *Reading Instruction Essentials.* 3rd ed. Boston: American Press, 2004.

Dolch, Edward William. "Dolch Sight Word List." Champaign, IL: Garrard Press, 1960.

Finn, Patrick J. *Helping Children Learn to Read.* New York: Longman, 1990.

Flesch, Rudolf. *Why Johnny Can't Read—And What You Can Do About It.* New York: Harper and Row, 1955.

Fry, Edward. "Fry's Readability Graph: Clarifications, Validity and Extension to Level 17." *Journal of Reading* 21:3 (December 1977): 242–252.

———. "The New Instant Word Lists." *Reading Teacher* 34:3 (December 1980): 264–89.

Gentry, J. R. "Learning to Spell Developmentally." *Reading Teacher* 34:4 (January 1981): 378–81.

Goudvis, Anne, and Stephanie Harvey. *Strategies That Work.* Portland, ME: Stenhouse Publishers, 2000.

Gunning, Thomas G. *Creating Reading Instruction for All Children.* Boston: Allyn and Bacon, 1996.

Heckleman, R. G. "A Neurological-Impress Method of Remedial-reading Instruction." *Academic Therapy* IV (Summer 1969): 277–82.

Hollingsworth, Paul. "An Experimental Approach to the Impress Method of Teaching Reading," *Reading Teacher* 31 (March, 1978): 624–26.

Huck, Charlotte S. and Doris Young Kuhn. *Children's Literature in the Elementary School.* New York: Holt, Rinehart and Winston, 1968. First published 1961 by Holt, Rinehart and Winston.

"IRA Takes a Stand on Phonics." (Vol. 14:5) *Reading Today* (April/May 1997), 1–4.

Karlin, Robert. *Teaching Elementary Reading.* New York: Harcourt Brace Jovanovich, 1971.

Klein, Marvin L. *The Development of Writing in Children Pre-K through Grade 8.* Englewood Cliffs, NJ: Prentice-Hall, 1985.

Mager, Robert F. *Preparing Instructional Objectives.* Palo Alto, California: Fearon Publishers, 1962.

Marzano, Robert J., and Daisy E. Arredondo. *Tactics for Thinking.* Aurora, CO: Mid-Continent Regional Education Laboratories, 1986.

Michaelis, John U., and Jesus Garcia. *Social Studies for Children: A Guide to Basic Instruction.* Boston: Allyn and Bacon, 1996.

Noyce, Ruth M., and James F. Christie. *Integrating Reading and Writing Instruction in Grades K–8.* Boston: Allyn and Bacon, 1989.

Rawls, Wilson. *Where the Red Fern Grows.* New York: Bantam, 1976. First published 1961. by Doubleday, Garden City, New York.

Richardson, Judy S., and Raymond F. Morgan. *Reading to Learn in the Content Areas.* Belmont, CA: Wadsworth, 1990.

Routman, Regie. *Conversations: Strategies for Teaching, Learning, and Evaluation.* Portsmouth, NH: Heinemann, 2000.

Routman, Regie. *Invitations: Changing Teachers and Learners.* Portsmouth, NH: Heinemann, 1994.

Routman, Regie. *Writing Essentials.* Portsmouth, NH: Heinemann, 2005.

SREB. *See* Southern Regional Education Board Health.

Tompkins, Gail E. *Literacy for the 21st Century: A Balanced Approach.* 4th ed. Upper Saddle River, NJ: Pearson, 2006.

Trelease, Jim. *The Read-Aloud Handbook.* New York: Penguin Books, 1985.

"Using a Neurological Impress Activity." No author. *www.sil.org/lingualinks/literacy-program/UsingANeurologicalImpressActiv.htm*

Vacca, Richard T., and Jo Anne L. Vacca. *Content Area Reading.* 3rd ed. Glenview, IL: Scott, Foresman, 1989.

Mathematics Pedagogy

4

CRITICAL THINKING AND MATHEMATICS

Mathematics is not strictly memorization or literal-level work; thinking and reasoning skills, such as deductive reasoning, inductive reasoning, and adaptive reasoning, are essential. Students must employ upper-level skills from Bloom's Taxonomy. This requires that teachers utilize a variety of instructional techniques for the teaching of mathematics. Careful planning will help to ensure that students will practice previously taught concepts while learning new ones. This is critical for building a foundation of numeracy skills.

Deductive reasoning proceeds from general to specific. In deductive lessons, the teacher first teaches the generalizations or rules and then develops examples and elaboration to support the generalizations or rules. For example, a teacher would first instruct students on how to regroup in adding a two-place number and then have the students apply the regrouping rules in the examples they practice. Using deductive methods, teachers present material through lectures, and students teach each other through presentations. Deductive thinking often requires students to make assessments based on specific criteria that they or others develop.

The **mastery lecture** is a deductive method whereby the teacher presents information to students. New teachers are especially attuned to lecturing because that is the usual mode of instruction in college classes. An advantage of the mastery lecture is that teachers can present large amounts of information in an efficient manner; however, teachers should avoid giving students too much information through lectures. To be most effective, mastery lectures should be short, usually no more than 10 or 15 minutes, and frequently interrupted by questions to and from students. The effective teacher uses both lower- and higher-level questions during lectures.

Lectures must also be supplemented with an array of visual materials that will appeal to both visual and auditory learners. Putting words or outlines on the board or a transparency is very helpful; however, this is still basically a verbal strategy. Drawings, diagrams, cartoons, pictures, caricatures, and graphs are attention-getting visual aids for lectures. Teacher drawings need not be highly artistic, merely memorable. Often a rough or humorous sketch will be more firmly etched in students' minds than elaborate drawings. Using a very simple sketch is a better means of teaching the most critical information than is a complicated drawing. The major points stand out in a simple sketch; details can be added once students understand the basic concepts.

Teachers should also be careful to instruct students on how to take notes while listening to a speaker. Note taking is a skill that will be useful during every student's career, whether educational or professional. One way teachers can teach note-taking skills is to show students notes or an outline from the lecture they are about to hear or to write notes or an outline on the board or on a transparency while they are presenting the information. This activity requires careful planning by the teacher and will result in a more organized lecture. A well-structured lecture is especially helpful for sequential learners, who like organization. It also helps random learners develop organizational skills. A web, map, or fishbone is a more creative method of connecting important points in a lecture or a chapter. The effective teacher will use both systems and teach both to students, so they have a choice of strategies.

PRAXIS Pointer

Don't make questions more difficult than they are–there are no "trick" questions or hidden meanings.

In contrast to deductive reasoning, **inductive reasoning** proceeds from specific to general. During inductive lessons, the teacher first introduces a hypothesis or concept, and using inferences from the data, the students develop generalizations. For instance, after seeing the teacher demonstrate several times how to regroup or carry when adding two-place numbers, the students figure out the rule for themselves. With deductive thinking, the teacher gives them the rule first and then the students practice it; with inductive thinking, the students see many applications of the rule and then determine the rule themselves.

Inquiry or discovery lessons are inductive in nature. An **inquiry lesson** starts with a thought-provoking question for which students are interested in finding an explanation. After posing the question, the teacher guides students in brainstorming a list of what they already know about the topic and then categorizing the information. Students use these categories as topics for group or individual research. The lesson typically ends with students presenting their research to the class (a form of deductive learning, as discussed earlier).

A teacher who uses inquiry strategies takes the role of a facilitator who plans outcomes and provides resources for students as they work. In their role as inquirers, students must take responsibility for their own learning by planning, carrying out, and presenting research and projects.

Some advantages of inductive lessons are that they generally require higher-level thinking by both teacher and students, and they usually result in higher student motivation, interest, and retention than more passive methods. They also provide an interesting change to the teacher, who deals with the same concepts year after year. Disadvantages of inductive lessons include the need for additional preparation by the teacher, access to numerous resources, and additional time for students to conduct research.

In general, the more planning, predicting, and preparing the teacher does for an inductive lesson, the more successful the students will be. This does not mean that the teacher must use only tightly structured or rigid activities but that the effective teacher tries to predict students' responses and their reactions to them. Fortunately, teachers today do not have to purchase as many additional resources thanks to the variety of information available via the Internet, computerized bibliographic services, interlibrary loans, and compact discs (CDs). Because inductive, research-oriented units require more class time, subject-area teachers must work together to determine which concepts are essential for students to understand, which are nonessential, and which ones they can omit.

An effective teacher plays many roles in the classroom. The teacher who uses lecture is in the role of information provider. Students listening to the lecture are usually in the passive, often inattentive, role of listener. The teacher who uses cooperative strategies takes on the roles of a coach, encouraging students to work together, and a facilitator, smoothing students' way through activities and providing resources. Students in a collaborative role must learn social and group roles as well as content to accomplish learning tasks. The teacher who listens to student discussions and presentations and evaluates student papers and projects assumes the role of an audience providing constructive feedback. Students in a discussion role must prepare carefully and think seriously about the topic under discussion.

Adaptive reasoning refers to logical thinking. In mathematics, adaptive reasoning refers to the capacity to think logically about the relationships between concepts and situations. For instance, after solving a subtraction problem, the student should look at the answer to see that it is reasonable. If a child solves the problem $7 - 4$ and finds that the answer is 11, the child might think, "I only had 7 to start with, and then I took 4 away. I could not possibly end up with 11 because that is bigger than 7, not less." Adaptive thinking allows the students who disagree on an answer to check that their reasoning is valid.

The key to converting word problems into mathematical problems is attention to **reasonableness** (adaptive thinking), with the choice of operations being crucial to success. Often, individual words and phrases translate into numbers and operation symbols; making sure that the translations are reasonable is important.

Benjamin Bloom identified six levels of thinking. The fourth stage—analysis—is a vital part of solving mathematical word problems. This level requires the student to break down information into component parts and examine parts for inferences. Effective mathematics teachers, however, must examine each level of Bloom's Taxonomy as they develop objectives for their classrooms.

SCOPE AND SEQUENCE OF SKILLS

The main topics (scope) in elementary mathematics and the sequence (order) in which the school introduces the topics is essentially the same in all states. Table 4-1 details these main topics and their introduction order.

Table 4-1. Scope and Sequence of Skills

Grade Level	Numbers, Order, Values	Addition, Subtraction	Ratios, Measurement, Decimals	Fractions, Comparisons	Equations, Colors, Geometry	Multiplication, Division	Graph, Estimation, Solving
Kinder-garten	Count by 1s and 10s to 100 Count by 2s and 5s Write numbers to 10 Write families to 100 Use values of 10s and 1s place	Add single digits with no regrouping	Use dime, nickel, penny, and dollar Tell time on hour and half hour Name days of week and seasons Identify cup and quart Read inches	Recognize $\frac{1}{2}$, $\frac{1}{3}$, and $\frac{1}{4}$ Compare longer, shorter, taller, etc.	Recognize primary and secondary colors and black Recognize square, circle, and triangle Use *up*, *down*, *top*, and *next*		Identify what comes next Read pictographs and simple bar graphs
1	Count by 1s, 2s, 5s, and 10s Use place values of 1s, 10s, and 100s place	Write and give addition facts from 1 to 18 Add with regrouping in 1s place Subtract without regrouping	Name months and days Tell time on quarter hour Use nickel, dime, and quarter Identify pint and pound	Recognize $\frac{1}{2}$, $\frac{1}{3}$, $\frac{1}{4}$, $\frac{1}{5}$, $\frac{1}{6}$, $\frac{1}{8}$	Recognize circle, square, oval, diamond, triangle, and cube		Read bar graphs Identify height and length Round numbers using a number line
2	Identify even and odd numbers Use tally marks Use and explain the value of 1,000s place Determine greater than, less than, equal to Identify what comes before and after Use Roman numerals	Add with carrying in 1s, 10s, and 100s place Perform horizontal addition Solve word problems	Name months and their abbreviations Tell time on five minutes Perform operations with money, including $5, $10, and $20 bills Read a Fahrenheit thermometer Identify liquid and dry measures	Compare two numbers Read fraction words Identify fractional parts of groups and sets	Determine area, perimeter, and volume Recognize pyramid, pentagon, and hexagon	Use multiplication facts from 0 to 10	Round numbers, height, and time Read grids and line graphs

(Continued)

Table 4-1. (Continued from previous page)

Grade Level	Numbers, Order, Values	Addition, Subtraction	Ratios, Measurement, Decimals	Fractions, Comparisons	Equations, Colors, Geometry	Multiplication, Division	Graph, Estimation, Solving
3	Read word numbers to 1 million Show expanded numbers Explain the properties of 1 and 0 Use the terms *odd, tally marks, greater than* Be able to tell what comes before, what comes after Use the 1000s place Use Roman numerals	Use sum, estimating, borrowing, word problems Demonstrate carrying or regrouping in the 1s, 10s, and 100s place Use horizontal addition Solve word problems	Use Fahrenheit and Celsius temperature measurements Use tenths Add and subtract dollars and cents Be able to use months and their abbreviations Tell time with accuracy to five minutes Perform operations with money Recognize five, ten- and twenty-dollar bills Use both liquid and dry measures	Identify fractional parts of whole and sets Rename fractions Compare numbers using greater than, less than, and equal signs Use fraction words Demonstrate the use of fractional parts of groups Use sets to illustrate fractions and illustrate fractions with sets	Compute the volume of cube Recognize rays, angles, congruent shapes, and prisms Compute area and perimeter of volume, pyramid, pentagon, hexagon	Use division facts from 1 to 10 Calculate 1- and 2-digit quotients with and without remainders Use multiplication facts 0 to 10	Continue work with graphs and grids Round numbers to the 10,000 place Tell time accurately to the minute
4	Use values to 100 billion Use and recognize prime and composite Determine factors Give ordinal and cardinal numbers	Give addition properties Add and subtract numbers up to 6 digits Subtract with regrouping Subtract money	Use the terms AM and PM Explain the term *century* Compute time in various time zones Use the prefixes *milli-, centi-, deci-, deca-, hecto-, kilo* Convert fractions to decimals Perform operations on decimals and ratios Use equal ratios	Recognize fractional parts of whole and name them correctly Give word fractions Provide equivalent fractions Add and subtract fractions with like and unlike denominators	Recognize shapes and solids Use the terms *obtuse, vertex, ray, diameter, radius* Perform operations on equations	Calculate averages Use zeros in the quotient correctly Multiply 2- to 3-digit numbers	Compare and coordinate graphs

(Continued from previous page)

Grade Level	Numbers, Order, Values	Addition, Subtraction	Ratios, Measurement, Decimals	Fractions, Comparisons	Equations, Colors, Geometry	Multiplication, Division	Graph, Estimation, Solving
5	Determine prime factors Use factor trees Use exponents Equal, not equal	Apply addition properties and facts Apply addition operation with 2 to 6 digits Determine missing addends Work with equations Subtract Estimate	Use standard and metric measure Count change Solve problems with ratios and percentages Figure amount of sales tax Determine discounts	Find least common multiples Solve problems with unlike denominators Perform operations on mixed numerals Rename numbers Reduce fractions to lowest terms	Use a compass and a protractor Solve measurement problems using surface area Perform operations on fractions Recognize and use chords Classify polygons	Calculate mean, mode, and median Problem solve by choosing the proper operation Figure probability with one-variable problems Demonstrate ability to apply calculator math	Multiply 3-digit numbers Calculate averages with remainders Divide money Estimate quotients Determine division and multiplication properties
6	Round to 10s, 100s, and 1000s Use scientific notation Use the correct order of operations Use integers Calculate square roots	Continue addition and subtraction Continue to work with equations	Cross products Divide and multiply by 10, 100, 1000 Determine equal ratios Use cross products to solve for n	Determine reciprocals Divide by fractions Perform operations on fractions Divide by whole and mixed numbers	Construct a right and equilateral triangle, and a parallelogram and square Bisect an angle	Choose the proper operation Find patterns Set up budgets Apply some business math, such as figuring interest and balancing a check book.	Divide using 4-digit divisors Estimate quotients Supply missing factors

MATHEMATICAL CONCEPTS

Sets and Number Concepts

Sets

A basic mathematical concept is that of set. A **set** is a collection of things, real or imagined, related or unrelated. Students may manipulate the objects within the set in various ways.

Classifying Objects in a Set.   Classification allows the students to sort materials according to some specific criteria. A child who is not yet able to count, for example, might sort objects by whether the objects are soft or hard, by whether or not a magnet will attract them, or by other attributes.

Ordering Objects in a Set.   Students may **order** the objects or arrange them in size from smallest to largest or from largest to smallest.

Patterning Objects in a Set.   Students may try arranging the objects in a set to duplicate **a pattern that they observe**. The students may, for instance, try to replicate a color pattern with beads: red, yellow, red, yellow, and so on. Later, they may try to replicate a number pattern using magnetic numbers; the pattern may be 2, 4, 6, and so on. They may even match the correct number of pennies to the magnetic number for another type of patterning. Making a pattern of geometric shapes would be another example; for instance, square, circle, triangle, square, circle, triangle, and so on.

Comparing Objects in a Set.   Students may **compare** objects in a set to objects in another set as a help in preparing for number skills. Is there a chair for each toy bear? Does each child in the set of children in the classroom have a carton of milk? Does each carton of milk have a straw for the child to use? Later, the students will compare each object in a set with a counting number; this will give the total number of objects in the set.

Students may try pairing objects with the numbers that they have memorized through rote; this is **oral counting**. After classifying objects, a student may try counting the objects in the groups. For example, if the teacher asks, "How many objects were soft?" the answer is a number that tells how many, and the student will have to count to find the answer.

Number

Number is a concept or idea that indicates how many. Children may memorize the counting numbers from 1 to 10 and be able to count by rote before they start school. Many times, however, there is little understanding in the beginning of what number is. After the students have some idea of the value of the numbers, they may arrange the numbers from largest to smallest, or smallest to largest. Students may try counting by pairing the objects with a number on the number line; this will give a visual comparison. The set {1, 2, 3, 4, . . . } can represent counting numbers. Study the following number line. Notice that the counting numbers start with 1 and that 0 is not in the set of counting numbers.

Whole numbers are the counting numbers plus 0: {0, 1, 2, 3, . . . }. Study the following number line. Notice that 0 is a part of the set of whole numbers.

A **number** is a concept; a **numeral** is a symbol used to represent a number. The students must be able to read and to write the numerals. This skill is an important part of a student's early mathematical development. An important part of mathematical learning and of language arts learning is being able to read and to represent the numbers in words: *one, two, three,* and so on. Students may also try another way of counting: **skip counting**. They may start with 1 and count only the odd numbers: 3, 5, 7, 9, and so on. **Odd numbers** are those that cannot be evenly divided by 2. Students may also try skip counting with another beginning point; for instance, they may start with 2 and count only the even numbers: 4, 6, 8, 10, and so on. **Even numbers** are those that one can evenly divide by 2.

Base-10 Numeration System and Place Value

Our numeration system uses the Hindu-Arabic numerals (0, 1, 2, 3, 4, 5, 6, 7, 8, 9) to represent numbers. Our numeration system follows a **base-10 place-value** scheme. As we move to the left in any number, each place value is 10 times the place value to the right. Similarly, as we move to the right, each place value is one-tenth the place value to the left. For example, in the number 543, the value of the place that the 5 is in (100s) is 10 times the value of the place that the 4 occupies (10s). The place value of the 3 is one-tenth the place value of the 4.

Expanded notation can show the value of each number in its place. Using the same number 543, the values are $(5 \times [10 \times 10]) + (4 \times [10 \times 1]) + (3 \times 1)$. **Exponential notation** can show the value of each number. Using the same number 543, the exponential values are $(5 \times 10^2) + (4 \times 10^1) + (3 \times 10^0)$.

The Four Basic Operations

Operations indicate what one does with any given group of numbers. There are four main operations: addition, subtraction, multiplication, and division. Multiplication is repeated addition. Division is repeated subtraction.

Addition is an operation that, when performed on numbers of disjoint sets (sets with different members), results in a **sum**. One can show addition on a number line by counting forward. Addition is also a **binary operation**, meaning it combines only two numbers at a time to produce a third, unique number. Adding two whole numbers always results in a whole number. The **algorithm** of addition is the form in which we write and solve an addition example. Familiar short forms are

2 (addend) + 3 (addend) = 5 (sum) and

$$\begin{array}{r} 2 \text{ (addend)} \\ + 3 \text{ (addend)} \\ \hline 5 \text{ (sum)} \end{array}$$

The operation of **subtraction** is the **inverse** of addition: what addition does, subtraction undoes. Like addition, subtraction is a binary operation; that is, we work on only two numbers at a time. The result is a third, unique number called the **difference**. Given two whole numbers, subtracting the smaller number from the larger one results in a whole number. However, subtraction of whole numbers does not result in a whole number if the larger whole number is subtracted from the smaller one. The algorithm of subtraction is the form in which we write and solve a subtraction example. Familiar short forms are

5 − 3 = 2 and

$$\begin{array}{r} 5 \text{ (addend)} \quad \text{minuend} \\ - 3 \text{ (addend)} \leftarrow \text{subtrahend} \\ \hline 2 \text{ (sum)} \quad \text{difference} \end{array}$$

Addition problems with a missing addend are solved with the operation of subtraction. For example, the subtraction equation given above solves the following addition problem: (addend) + 3 (addend) = 5 (sum).

Multiplication, like addition and subtraction, is a binary operation. The result of the operation of multiplication is the **product**. The product of multiplying two whole numbers is always a whole number.

The operation of **division** has the same inverse relation to multiplication as subtraction has to addition: what multiplication does, division undoes. For example, multiplying 4 by 9 results in a product of 36; dividing 36 by 9 "gives back" a **quotient** of 4. Teaching division should parallel teaching multiplication.

Modeling the Operations

There are four ways to model the operations:

Concrete method: With the concrete method, the teacher allows the students to use real objects. The students can represent a set and take away objects from it (subtraction), or they can combine two sets with no common objects (addition).

Semiconcrete method: With the semiconcrete method, the students work with visual representations (pictures) instead of actual objects.

Semiabstract method: With the semiabstract method, the students work with one symbol (tally marks, x's, y's, etc.) to represent objects; instead of actual objects, pictures, or abstract (numerical) representations, the students use one symbol. The semiabstract method can be used to represent, for instance, a multiplication problem. If there are three rabbits and if each rabbit eats four carrots each day, how many carrots will the rabbits eat in one day?

Rabbit 1	////
Rabbit 2	////
Rabbit 3	////

Abstract method: With the abstract level, the student matches the elements of a given group with abstract numbers. To represent three rabbits eating four carrots daily using the abstract method, the student would set up the problem as 3 × 4.

Regrouping in Addition and Subtraction

Regrouping in addition, a process that teachers and students once called *carrying*, is evident in addition problems, such 16 + 7 and 26 + 6. To begin working with students on this process, the teacher would ideally drop back to the concrete level. For example, to work on the problem 16 + 7, the teacher would have the students make one bundle of 10 straws and lay 6 straws to the side; when the students see 7 straws added to the 6 straws, they realize that they need to make another bundle of 10 straws. When they make that second bundle, they have the answer: two groups of 10 and 3 extra straws, or 23.

Regrouping in subtraction, a process that teachers and students once called *borrowing*, is evident in problems such as 23 − 7. The students can readily see that they cannot subtract the big number 7 from the small number 3; to begin this process, the students again can use concrete objects. With two bundles of 10 straws and one group of 3 straws on the table, the students should count out 7 straws; when the students see that they cannot subtract 7 from 3, they can unbundle one packet of 10 straws and place the 10 straws with the 3 straws. The students can pull 7 straws from the 13; 6 straws will be left along with one bundle of 10—the answer: 16.

Modeling Multiplication

As noted earlier, pairs of operations that "undo" each other are **inverse**. Multiplication and division are inverse of, or "undo," one another.

An **array** can model a multiplication problem. The first number in a multiplication problem is the vertical number in an array; the second number is the horizontal number. The following is the array for 2 × 3 = 6:

x	*x*	*x*
x	*x*	*x*

Multiplication Properties and Algorithms

The **multiples** of any whole number are the results of multiplying that whole number by the counting numbers. For example, the multiples of 7 are 7, 14, 21, 28, and so on. Every whole number has an infinite number of multiples.

Terms related to multiplication and key properties of the multiplication operation include the following:

Multiplicative identity property of 1: Any number multiplied by 1 remains the same. For instance, $34 \times 1 = 34$. The number 1 is called the **multiplicative identity**.

Property of reciprocals: The product of any number (except 0) multiplied by its reciprocal is 1. The **reciprocal** of a number is 1 divided by that number. Remember that dividing by 0 has no meaning; avoid dividing by 0 when computing or solving equations and inequalities.

Commutative property for addition and multiplication: The order of adding addends or multiplying factors does not determine the sum or product. For example, 6×9 gives the same product as 9×6. Division and subtraction are not commutative.

Associative property for addition and multiplication: Associating, or grouping, three or more addends or factors in a different way does not change the sum or product. For example, $(3 + 7) + 5$ results in the same sum as $3 + (7 + 5)$. Division and subtraction are not associative.

Distributive property of multiplication over addition: A number multiplied by the sum of two other numbers can be handed out, or distributed, to both numbers, multiplied by each of them separately, and the products added together. For example, multiplying 6 by 47 gives the same result as multiplying 6 by 40, multiplying 6 by 7, and then adding the products. That is, $6 \times 47 = (6 \times 40) + (6 \times 7)$. The definition of the distributive property of multiplication over addition can be stated simply: the product of a number and a sum can be expressed as a sum of two products. The simple notation form of the distributive property is

$$a(b + c) = (a \times b) + (a \times c)$$

Another major concept in multiplication is **regrouping**, or carrying. The term *regrouping* indicates the renaming of a number from one place value to another. The short algorithm we are most familiar with does not show the steps that illustrate the regrouping. Students must be able to use the multiplication facts, multiply by 0, and apply regrouping to solve problems such as 268×26.

Special Properties of 0 and 1

The **natural numbers** include the set of counting numbers (1, 2, 3, 4, 5, . . .) and the set of whole numbers (0, 1, 2, 3, 4, 5, . . .). The natural number 0 has special mathematical significance with respect to the operation of addition. The number 0 added to any natural number yields a sum that is the same as the other natural number; 0 is, therefore, the **additive identity**, or the **identity element of addition**.

Because multiplication is repeated addition, 0 holds a special property with both multiplication and addition. The **multiplication property of 0** states that when a factor is multiplied by 0, then the product is 0. The **identity element of multiplication** is 1; the identity element of multiplication means that any factor multiplied by 1 gives that factor. Zero is not an identity element for subtraction or for division. Subtraction does not have an identity element. Even though $4 - 0 = 4$, it is not true that $0 - 4 = 4$. Division by 0 is not possible, so 0 is not an identity element for division.

Factors, Primes, Composites, and Multiples

Factors are any of the numbers or symbols in mathematics that, when multiplied together, form a product. For example, the whole-number factors of 12 are 1, 2, 3, 4, 6, and 12. A number with only two whole-number factors—1 and the number itself—is a **prime number**. The first few primes are 2, 3, 5, 7, 11, 13, and 17. Most other whole numbers are **composite numbers** because they are *composed* of several whole-number factors. The number 1 is neither prime nor composite; it has only one whole-number factor: 1.

As noted earlier, the **multiples** of any whole number are the results of multiplying that whole number by the counting numbers. For example, the multiples of 7 are 7, 14, 21, 28, and so on. Every whole number has an infinite number of multiples.

Modeling Division

Division, the inverse of multiplication, can be represented in two ways: measurement and partition. With **measurement division**, the students know how many are in each group

$400 \div 5 = ?$

(set) but do not know how many sets. Here is an example: A homeowner has a group of 400 pennies. He plans to give each trick-or-treater 5 pennies. How many trick-or-treaters can receive a treat before the homeowner has to turn out the porch light? In this case, the students know the number of pennies (measurement) each child will receive; they need to find the number of children.

$8 \div 4 = ?$

In **partitive division**, students know the number of groups (sets), but they do not know the number of objects in each set. Here is an example: There is a plate of eight cookies on the table. There are four children at the table. How many cookies does each child get if they divide the cookies evenly? The question asks the students to determine how many are in each group.

No properties of division—commutative, associative, and so on—hold true at all times. Division is the most difficult of the algorithms for students to use. Division begins at the left, rather than at the right. Also, to solve a division problem, students must not only divide but subtract and multiply as well. Students must use estimation with the trial quotients; sometimes it takes several trials before the trial is successful.

Rational Numbers, Fractions, Decimals, and Percents

Rational numbers are all the numbers that can be expressed as the quotient of two integers; **integers** are counting numbers, the opposite of counting numbers, and zero. Rational numbers can be expressed as fractions, percents, or decimals.

Common **fractions** are in the form a/b, where a and b are whole numbers. Integers can be expressed as fractions, but not all fractions can be expressed as integers. For example, the number 4 can be expressed as 4/1. However, the fraction 1/4

PRAXIS Pointer

Take the practice tests under the same conditions you will take the actual test.

cannot be expressed as an integer or as a whole number. There are more fractions than whole numbers; between every integer is a fraction. Between the fraction and the whole number is another fraction; between the fraction and the other fraction is another fraction, and so on. Negative and positive fractions are not integers unless they are equivalent to whole numbers or their negative counterparts.

Decimal numbers are fractions written in special notation. For instance, 0.25 can be thought of as the fraction 1/4. All decimal numbers are actually fractions. When expressed as decimals, some fractions terminate and some do not. For instance, 0.315 is a terminating decimal; 0.0575757 . . . is a repeating (nonterminating) decimal. All fractions, however, can be written as decimals. There are more decimals than integers. Fractions, decimal numbers, and percents are different ways of representing values. It is useful to be able to convert from one to the other. The following paragraphs provide some conversion tips.

The practical method for changing a fraction into a decimal is by **dividing the numerator by the denominator**. For example, 1/4 becomes 0.25 when 1 is divided by 4, as follows:

$$4\overline{)1.00}^{\,.25}$$

Naturally, this can be done longhand or with a calculator. (If the fraction includes a whole number, as in $2^3/_5$, the whole number is not included in the division.) The decimal number may terminate or repeat. Converting a simple fraction to a decimal number never results in an irrational number. **Irrational numbers** are all the real numbers that are not rational; irrational numbers include the square roots of 2 and 3, pi, and so on. **Rational numbers** are all numbers that can be expressed as the quotient of two integers. (A number cannot be expressed with 0 in the denominator.) **Real numbers** are all the numbers that can be represented by points on the number lines. The set of real numbers includes all the rational numbers (positive numbers, negative numbers, and 0) and all the irrational numbers ($\sqrt{2}$, $\sqrt{3}$, pi, etc.). To convert a nonrepeating (terminating) decimal number to a fraction in lowest terms, write the decimal as a fraction with the denominator a power of 10, and then reduce to lowest terms. For example, 0.125 can be written as 125/1,000, which reduces to 1/8. Any decimal number can be converted to a **percent** by shifting the decimal point two places to the right and adding the percent symbol (%). For instance, 0.135 becomes 13.5%. (If the number before the percent symbol is a whole number, there is no need to show the decimal point.)

A percent can be converted to a decimal number by shifting the decimal point two places to the left and dropping the percent symbol. For example, 98% becomes 0.98 as a decimal.

A percent can be converted to a fraction by putting the percent (without the percent symbol) over 100 and then reducing. In this way, 20% can be shown as 20/100, which reduces to 1/5.

Ratio, Percent, and Proportion

Ratio notation is an alternative method for showing fractions. For example, 2/5 can be expressed as "the ratio of 2 to 5." The use of ratio notation emphasizes the relationship of one number to another. To show ratios, one may use numbers with a colon between them; 2:5 is the same ratio as 2 to 5 and 2/5.

To illustrate the equivalencies and conversions just described, consider the fraction 19/20. As a decimal, it is 0.95. As a percent, it is 95%. As a ratio, it is 19 to 20, or 19:20. **Proportion** is an equation of two equivalent ratios. For example, 2/5 = N/10 asks the problem solver to supply the missing numerator to make the two fractions equivalent.

INFORMAL GEOMETRY AND MEASUREMENT

Types of Angles or Pairs of Angles

An **angle** consists of all the points in two noncollinear rays that have the same vertex. More simply, an angle is commonly thought of as two "arrows" joined at their bases; the point at which they join is called the **vertex**. Two angles are **adjacent** if they share a common vertex, they share only one side, and one angle does not lie in the interior of the other.

Angles are usually measured in **degrees** (°). A circle has a measure of 360°, a half circle 180°, a quarter circle 90°, and so forth. If the sum of the measures of two angles is 90°, the two angles are **complementary**. If the sum of the measures of the two angles is 180°, the two angles are **supplementary**. If two lines intersect, they form two pairs of **vertical angles**. If a third line intersects two intersecting lines at the same point of intersection, the third intersecting line is called a **transversal**. In the following drawing, t is the transversal:

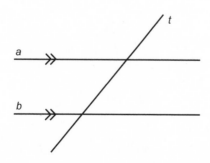

Two lines crossed by a transversal form eight angles. The four angles that lie between the two lines are called **interior angles**. The interior angles that lie on the same side of the transversal are called **consecutive interior angles**. The interior angles that lie on opposite sides of the transversal are called **alternate interior angles**. In the previous figure, angles *A* and *D* are alternate interior angles, as are angles *B* and *C*.

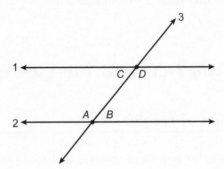

Consider the following drawing. The four angles that lie outside the two lines are the **exterior angles**. Exterior angles that lie on the same side of the transversal are the **consecutive exterior angles**, and those that lie on opposite sides of the transversal are the **alternate exterior angles**. Angles *A* and *D* are alternate exterior angles; they have the same degree measurement. Angles *B* and *C* are also alternate exterior angles. An interior angle and an exterior angle that have different vertices and have sides on the same side of the transversal are the **corresponding angles**.

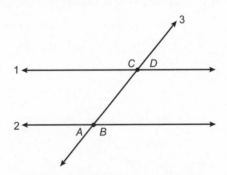

If the measures of two angles are the same, the angles are **congruent**. An angle with a measure of 90° is a **right angle**. An angle measuring less than 90° is an **acute angle**. An angle measuring more than 90° is an **obtuse angle**.

Identifying Lines and Planes as Intersecting, Perpendicular, or Parallel

If lines have a point or points in common, they are said to **intersect**. Lines are **perpendicular** if they contain the sides of a right angle. Lines are **parallel** if they do not intersect.

Through any two points, there is exactly one **straight line**; straight lines are one-dimensional. A **plane** is two-dimensional (think of a surface without elevations or depressions). These concepts form the foundation of other important geometric terms and ideas.

The Pythagorean Theorem in Solving Geometric Problems

Triangles have various properties. One is that the sum of the measures of the three angles of any triangle is 180°. If students know the measures of two angles, they can deduce the third using first addition and then subtraction. The **Pythagorean theorem** states that in any right triangle with legs (shorter sides) a and b and a hypotenuse (longest side) c, the sum of the squares of the sides equals the square of the hypotenuse. In algebraic notation, the Pythagorean theorem is given as $a^2 + b^2 = c^2$.

Basic Characteristics of Geometric Shapes

Point

Students in the elementary grades typically solve problems involving two- and three-dimensional geometric figures (for example, perimeter and area problems, volume and surface-area problems). A fundamental concept of geometry is the notion of a point. A **point** is a specific location, taking up no space, having no area, and frequently represented by a dot. A point is considered one dimensional. Through any two points, there is exactly one straight line; straight lines are one dimensional.

Plane

A **plane** is two dimensional (think of a surface without elevations or depressions). That definition forms the foundation for other important geometric terms and ideas. The **perimeter** of a two dimensional (flat) shape or object is the distance around the object. **Volume** refers to how much space is inside a three dimensional, closed container. **Area** is a measure that expresses the size of a plane region; it is expressed in square units. It is useful to think of volume as how many cubic units fit into a solid. If the container is a rectangular solid, the volume is the product of width times length times height. If all six faces (sides) of a rectangular solid are squares, the object is a cube.

Polygons

A **polygon** is a simple closed curve formed by the union of three or more straight sides; a **regular polygon** is one whose angles are equal in measure. Every polygon that is not regular is irregular.

In an n-sided regular polygon, the sides are all the same length (**congruent)** and are symmetrically placed about a common center (that is, the polygon is both equiangular and equilateral). Only certain regular polygons are "constructable" using the classical Greek tools of the compass and straightedge.

The terms *equilateral triangle* and *square* refer to regular polygons with three and four sides, respectively. The words for polygons with more than five sides (for example, *pentagon*, *hexagon*, *heptagon*, etc.) can refer to either regular or nonregular polygons, although the terms generally refer to regular polygons unless otherwise specified.

Regular Rectangle

A **regular rectangle** is a quadrilateral (four-sided figure) in which sides opposite each other are both of equal length and parallel. A square is the special case of a regular rectangle whose angles are equal (90°) and all sides are of equal length and parallel. If each side of a regular rectangle is of length l, the area (A) and perimeter (P) would be given as follows:

$$A = s^2$$

$$P = 4s \text{ (square)}$$

If the length (l) and width (w) of a regular rectangle differ, that is, the rectangle is not a square, area (A) and perimeter (P) would be given as follows:

$$A = l \times w$$

$$P = l + l + w + w \text{ (or } 2l + 2w) \text{ (quadrilateral)}$$

Regular Triangle

The area of a triangle is the product of half its base multiplied by its height. Using either the Pythagorean theorem or trigonometric functions, one can assign each side a length of b and can describe the height of a **regular triangle** (an equilateral triangle) in terms of the length of its sides. The length is equal to b multiplied by the square root of ¾, so that the area and perimeter are as follows:

$$A = \frac{b^2}{4}\sqrt{3}$$

$$P = 3b$$

Polygons in a Plane

In a plane, three-sided polygons are *triangles*, four-sided polygons are *quadrilaterals*, five sides make *pentagons*, six sides are *hexagons*, and eight-sided polygons are *octagons*. (Note that not all quadrilaterals are squares.) If two polygons (or any figures) have exactly the same size and shape, they are *congruent*. If they are the same shape, but different sizes, they are *similar*.

Applying Geometric Concepts

Symmetry can be thought of as an imaginary fold line producing two congruent, mirror-image figures. Some geometric figures do not have symmetry. Polygons may have lines of symmetry. For example, squares have four lines of symmetry, and nonsquare rectangles have two, as shown later. Circles have an infinite number of lines of symmetry; a few are shown on the circle:

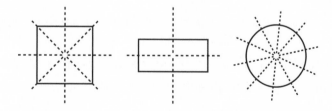

Geometric figures are **similar** if they have exactly the same shape, even if they are not the same size. In the following figure, triangles A and B are similar:

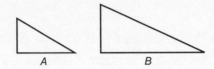

Corresponding angles of similar figures have the same measure, and the lengths of corresponding sides are proportional. In the following figure of similar triangles, $\angle A \cong \angle D$ (meaning "angle A is congruent to angle D"), $\angle B \cong \angle E$, and $\angle C \cong \angle F$. The corresponding sides of the triangles are proportional, meaning that

$$\frac{AB}{DE} = \frac{BC}{EF} = \frac{CA}{FD}$$

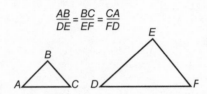

A **tessellation** is a collection of plane figures that fill the plane with no overlaps and no gaps. The following chart provides some examples:

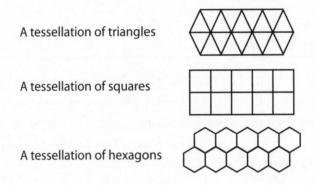

A tessellation of triangles

A tessellation of squares

A tessellation of hexagons

Scaling that is uniform is a linear transformation that enlarges or reduces an object; the scale factor is the same in all directions. The result of uniform scaling is an object that is similar (in the geometric sense) to the original. Scaling may be directional or may have a separate scale factor for each axis direction. This type of scaling may result in a change in shape.

Transformations include a variety of different operations from geometry, including rotations, reflections, and translations. Students will have experiences in such transformations as flips, turns, slides, and scaling. For example, the teacher might ask students to select a shape that is a parallelogram. Then the teacher might ask the students to do the following:

- Describe the original position and size of the parallelogram. Students can use labeled sketches if necessary.

- Translate (or slide) the parallelogram several times. (A **translation** of a figure occurs if it is possible to give an object a straight shove for a certain distance and in a certain direction.) Rotate the parallelogram two times. Students should list the steps they followed.

- Challenge a friend to return the parallelogram to its original position.

- Determine if the friend used a reversal of the original steps or a different set of steps.

Determining and Locating Ordered Pairs

The **coordinate plane** is useful for graphing individual ordered pairs and relationships. The coordinate plane is divided into four quadrants by an x-axis (horizontal) and a y-axis (vertical). The upper-right quadrant is quadrant I, and the others (moving counterclockwise from quadrant I) are quadrants II, III, and IV.

Ordered pairs indicate the locations of points on the plane. For instance, the ordered pair (–3, 4) describes a point that is three units *left* from the center of the plane (the **origin**) and four units *up*, as shown in the following diagram:

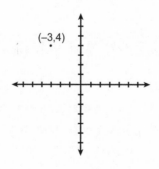

Ordered pairs are sets of data that one can display in a chart and graph on the coordinate plane. For example, the following set of data demonstrates four ordered pairs:

X	Y
3	5
4	6
5	7
6	8

Using Networks to Construct Three-Dimensional Geometric Shapes

A **network** (or net) is a union of points (its vertices or nodes) and the segments (its arcs) connecting them. The nets are, in effect, patterns for building three-dimensional triangles, cubes, and other geometric figures. The teacher may distribute the nets, and the students may construct the figures by cutting, folding, and taping. Using the concrete level is an excellent way to develop geometric understanding in students; following the levels of learning mentioned earlier (concrete, semiconcrete, semiabstract, and abstract), the concrete level should come before using drawings alone to solve problems. Nets can help make this understanding possible. The following is a net for a tetrahedron—a tetranet:

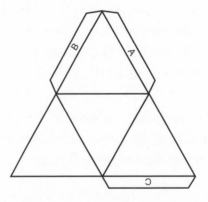

STANDARD UNITS OF MEASUREMENT

Customary units of measurement are generally the same as **U.S. units**. Customary units of length include inches, feet, yards, and miles. Customary units of weight include ounces, pounds, and tons. Customary units of capacity (or volume) include teaspoons, tablespoons, cups, pints, quarts, and gallons.

The **metric system of measurement** relates to the base-10 place-value scheme. The following chart lists the common metric prefixes:

Prefix	Meaning
Kilo-	Thousand (1,000)
Deci-	Tenth (0.1)
Centi-	Hundredth (0.01)
Milli-	Thousandth (0.001)

The basic unit of linear measure in the metric system is the **meter**, abbreviated as **m**. The relationships among the commonly used linear units of measurement in the metric system are

1 kilometer (km) = 1,000 m

1 meter (m) = 1.0 m

1 decimeter (dm) = 0.1 m

1 centimeter (cm) = 0.01 m

1 millimeter (mm) = 0.001 m

The centimeter is the metric unit of length used for short distances; about 2.5 centimeters equals 1 inch. The kilometer is a metric unit of length used for longer distances; slightly more than 1.5 kilometers equals a mile. A very fast adult runner could run a kilometer in about three minutes.

The basic unit of measurement for mass (or weight) in the metric system is the **gram**, abbreviated as **g**. The relationships among the commonly used units of measurement for mass in the metric system include

1 kilogram (kg) = 1,000 g

1 gram (g) = 1.0 g

1 milligram (mg) = 0.001 g

A large paper clip weighs about 1 gram; it takes about 28 grams to make 1 ounce.

The basic unit of measurement for capacity (or volume) in the metric system is the **liter**, represented by **L** or **l**. The relationships among the most common metric units of capacity include

1 liter (l) = 1,000 milliliters (ml)

1 deciliter (dl) = 100 ml; 10 centileter (cl)

1 cl = 10 ml

A liter is slightly smaller than a quart; it takes more than four liters to make a gallon.

Here are some frequently used customary-to-metric ratios (values are approximate):

1 inch = 2.54 centimeters

1 yard = 0.91 meter

1 mile = 1.61 kilometers

1 ounce = 28.35 grams

1 pound = 2.2 kilograms

1 quart = 0.94 liter

One can determine the metric-to-customary conversions by taking the reciprocals of each of the factors just listed. For instance, 1 kilometer = 0.62 mile (computed by dividing 1 by 1.61).

An important step in solving problems involving measurement is to decide what is being measured. Generally, such problems will fall under one of these categories: length, area, angles, volume, mass, time, money, and temperature. Solving measurement problems will likely require knowledge in several other areas of mathematics, especially algebra. The following is one example of a measurement problem that requires knowledge of several math topics (geometry, multiplication, conversions, estimation, measurement, etc.):

Sophie's Carpet Store charges $19.40 per square yard for the type of carpeting Tony would like in his bedroom (padding and labor included). How much would Tony pay to carpet his 9 × 12 foot room?

One way to find the solution is to convert the room dimensions to yards (3 × 4 yards) and multiply to get 12 square yards. The final step is to multiply 12 by the price of $19.40 per square yard, for a total price of $232.80.

PROBABILITY AND STATISTICS

Concepts of Central Tendency and Range

Measures of central tendency of a set of values include the mean, median, and mode. The **mean** is found by adding all the values and then dividing the sum by the number of values. The **median** of a set is the middle number when the values are in numerical order. (If the set comprises an even number of values, and therefore no middle value, the mean of the middle two values gives the median.) The **mode** of a set is the value occurring most often. (Not all sets of values have a single mode; some sets have more than one.) Consider the following set:

$$6, 8, 14, 5, 6, 5, 5.$$

The mean, median, and mode of the set are 7, 6, and 5, respectively. (Note that the mean is often referred to as the average, but all three measures are averages of sorts.)

The **range** of a set of numbers is a measure of the spread of, or variation in, the numbers.

Mean, Median, Mode, and Range

To determine the mean of a set of numbers, add the set of numbers and divide by the total number of elements in the set. For example, to find the mean of 15, 10, 25, 5, and 40, you would use the equation $(15 + 10 + 25 + 5 + 40) \div 5 = 19$.

To find the median, order a given set of numbers from smallest to largest; the median is the "middle" number. That is, half the numbers in the set of numbers are below the median and half the numbers in the set are above the median. For example, to find the median of the set of whole numbers 15, 10, 25, 5, and 40, the first step is to order the set of numbers: 5, 10, 15, 25, 40. Because 15 is the middle number (half of the numbers are below 15, half are above 15), 15 is the median of this set of whole numbers. If a set has an even number of numbers, the median is the mean of the middle two numbers. For instance, in the set of numbers 2, 4, 6, and 8, the median is the mean of 4 and 6, or 5.

The mode of the set of numbers 15, 10, 25, 10, 5, 40, 10, and 15 is the number 10 because it appears most frequently (three times).

The **range** of a set of numbers is obtained by subtracting the smallest number in the set from the largest number in the set. For example, to determine the range of the set 15, 10, 25, 5, and 40, you would use the equation $40 - 5 = 35$.

Determining Probabilities

Probability theory provides models for chance variations. The likelihood or chance that an event will take place is called the **probability** of the event. The probability of any event occurring is equal to the number of desired outcomes divided by the number of all possible events. Thus, the probability of blindly pulling a green ball out of a hat (in this case the desired outcome) if the hat contains two green and five yellow balls is 2/7 (about 29%).

The probability of 2/7 can also be expressed as the ratio of 2:7. We can also write the mathematical sentence with words:

$$\text{Probability of a particular event occurring} = \frac{\text{Number of ways the event can occur}}{\text{Total number of possible events}}$$

PROBLEM SOLVING

Selecting the Appropriate Operation(s) to Solve Problems

The key to converting word problems into mathematical problems is attention to **reasonableness**, with the choice of operations being crucial to success. Often, individual words and phrases translate into numbers and operation symbols; making sure that the translations are reasonable is important. Each word problem requires an individual approach, but keeping in mind the reasonableness of the computational setup should be helpful. Another way to solve a problem is to set up a chart. In solving problems involving percents, students must always consider reasonableness in their thinking and estimating. Mathematical reasoning includes analyzing problem situations, making conjectures, organizing information, and selecting strategies to solve problems. Students must rely on both formal and informal **reasoning processes**. A key informal process relies on reasonableness. Look for **key words** in solving problems. The words may provide a clue as to which operation to use. The following chart gives some examples:

Operation	Key Words
Addition	*Added to, combined, increased by, more than, sum, together, total of*
Subtraction	*Decreased by, difference between, difference of, fewer than, less, less than, minus*
Multiplication	*Decreased by a factor of, increased by a factor of, multiplied by, product of, times*
Division	*Divide, equal groups, how many groups, how many to each, quotient, separate, share*

Using Estimation and Other Problem-Solving Strategies

Estimation is a useful tool in predicting and in checking the answer to a problem. Estimation is at the second level in Bloom's Taxonomy—the comprehension level. Thinking at the comprehension level requires students not only to recall or remember information but also to understand the meaning of information and to restate it in their own words.

The ability to render some real-life quandaries into mathematical or logical problems—workable using established procedures—is an important part of finding solutions. Because each quandary will be unique, so too will be students' problem-solving plans of attack. Still, many real-world problems that lend themselves to mathematical solutions are likely to require one of the following strategies:

Guess and check: This is not the same as "wild guessing." With this problem-solving strategy, students make their best guess and then check the answer to see whether it is right. Even if the guess does not immediately provide the solution, it may help students get closer to it so that they can continue to work on it.

Make a sketch or a picture: Being able to visualize a problem can help to clarify it.

Make a table or a chart: Sometimes organizing the information from a problem into a table or chart makes it easier to find the solution.

Make a list: Like a table or chart, a list can help organize information and perhaps provide, or at least hint, at a solution.

Act it out: Sometimes literally "doing" a problem—with physical objects or even their bodies—can help students produce a solution.

Look for patterns: This technique encourages students to ask, "What's happening here?"

Work a simpler problem: By finding the solution to a different but simpler problem, students might spot a way to solve the harder one. Estimating can be thought of as working a simpler problem. To find the product of 23×184 when no calculator or pencil and paper are handy, students could estimate the product by getting the exact answer to the simpler problem, 20×200.

Write an open math sentence (an equation with one or more variables, or "unknowns") and then solve it: This is sometimes called "translating" a problem into mathematics.

Work backward: Consider this problem:

> If you add 12 to some number and then multiply the sum by 4, you will get 60. What is the number?

Students could find a solution by *starting at the end*, with 60. The problem states that the 60 came from multiplying a sum by 4. When 15 is multiplied by 4, the result is 60. The sum must be 15; if 15 is the sum of 12 and something else, the "something else" can only be 3.

CALCULATORS, COMPUTERS, AND OTHER TECHNOLOGY IN INSTRUCTION

Calculators, computers, and technology are important instructional and problem-solving tools. Their effectiveness, however, depends on the accuracy of the input and the ability of the user to operate the devices correctly.

The effective teacher includes resources of all types in the curriculum-planning process. The educator should be very familiar with the school library, the local library, education service center resources, and the libraries of any colleges or universities in the area. Another important set of resources is the audiovisual aids that the teacher can borrow: kits, films, filmstrips, videos, laser disks, and computer software, among others. Audiovisual aids can relate to curricular objectives. Many librarians have keyed their resources to objectives in related subject areas, and these keys enable the teacher to incorporate library holdings with ease into the lessons. However, teachers should never use resources with a class unless they have previewed and approved them. The teacher should include the list of resources for a lesson or unit in the curriculum guide or the lesson plan to make use more efficient.

The effective teacher determines the appropriate place in the lesson for audiovisual aids. If the material is especially interesting and thought provoking, the teacher can use it to introduce a unit. For example, a travel video on coral reefs or snorkeling might be an excellent introduction to the study of ocean depths and how to graph them. Textbooks do not stay up-to-date on batting averages and stock reports. The Internet; radio and television news reports; and local, state, and national newspapers and magazines all are important resources for teaching mathematics. Figuring batting averages and watching the stock reports are practical lessons in mathematics. Some newspapers and magazines provide special programs to help teachers use their products in the classroom. Local newspapers may even be willing to send specialists to work with students or act as special resource people.

> **PRAXIS Pointer**
>
> When you feel anxious, close your eyes and take a couple of long, deep breaths—hold it—exhale slowly. Imagine a peaceful place to visit.

Technology experts argue that tools such as the Internet make available such a substantial amount of wide-ranging content that today's teachers have a greater role than ever in helping students acquire process skills (such as critical and creative thinking) rather than merely in teaching content skills. Content changes and expands, but thinking processes remain salient and necessary, regardless of the content. Spreadsheets are especially useful to the math classroom. The reader can see rows and columns of numbers linked to produce totals and averages. Formulas can connect information in one cell (the intersection of a row and column) to another cell. Teachers often keep grade books on spreadsheets because of the ease in updating information. Once formulas are in place, teachers can enter grades and have completely up-to-date averages for all students. Some spreadsheet programs also include charting functions that enable teachers to display class averages on a bar chart to provide visual comparisons of performance among various classes.

Students can use spreadsheets to collect and analyze numerical data and then sort the data in various orders. For example, students could enter population figures from various countries and then draw various types of graphs—lines, bars, pies, and scatter plots, and so on—to convey information. This type of graphic information can also become a part of multimedia presentations. Various stand-alone graphing and charting software packages are also available.

Graphics or paint programs allow users to draw freehand to produce any type of chart, graph, or picture. In addition, many word-processing programs have some graphic functions. Students can use these programs to produce boxes, circles, or other shapes to illustrate classroom presentations or individual research projects. For teachers, these relatively simple tools make it easy to create handouts and instructional materials with a very professional and polished appearance.

Today's teachers also need to acquire and demonstrate skill in using presentation software (such as Microsoft PowerPoint) to prepare instructional lessons. In many classrooms, the use of presentation software makes the traditional use of transparencies on an overhead projector obsolete. Presentation software also makes it possible to provide students with instructional handouts and outlines to complement classroom instruction. In some situations and in some schools, Web authoring experience and skills will also prove useful.

Teachers must supplement lectures with an array of visual materials that will appeal to both visual and auditory learners. Putting words or outlines on the board or a transparency is very helpful; however, this is still basically a verbal strategy. Drawings, diagrams, cartoons, pictures, caricatures, and graphs are attention-getting visual aids for lectures. Teacher drawings need not be highly artistic, merely memorable. Often a rough or humorous sketch will be more firmly etched in students' minds than elaborate drawings. Using a very simple sketch is a better means of teaching the most critical information than is a complicated drawing. The major points stand out in a simple sketch; the teacher can add details once students understand the basic concepts.

Social Studies Pedagogy

SCOPE AND SEQUENCE OF SOCIAL STUDIES

There is a typical scope and sequence for teaching the social studies in U.S. schools. Although the schools do not rigorously follow it because the United States does not have a national system of education, the pattern that frequently emerges and that has been in use since the 1920s is the **expanding horizon approach**, or the **widening horizon curriculum**. Based on the original belief that children learn about their environment in gradually expanding concentric circles, this type of curriculum begins with what the children supposedly already know and moves outward. The following lists the typical topics for each grade:

Kindergarten–grade 1: Family, home, school

Grade 2: Community

Grade 3: State history and geography and/or holidays and history of the United States

Grade 4: Regions of the world or state history and geography

Grade 5: American history and American geography

Grade 6: World history and geography

Grade 7: State history and/or U.S. history

Grade 8: Civics, American history

In addition, the national learned societies and state curriculum guidelines also influence the scope and sequence of the curriculum.

INSTRUCTION AND ASSESSMENT IN SOCIAL STUDIES

Identifying Appropriate Resources for Teaching Social Studies Concepts

The ability to understand and apply skills and procedures related to the study of social sciences involves knowledge of the use of **systematic inquiry**. Inquiry is essential for use in examining single social sciences topics or integrated social sciences. Being able to engage in inquiry involves the ability to acquire information from a variety of resources and to organize and interpret that information. The process of inquiry begins with **designing and conducting investigations** that lead to the identification and analysis of social sciences issues.

Systematic social science inquiry uses various resources. Among the most commonly used **primary sources** are diaries, ledgers, oral histories, artifacts, and census reports; **secondary sources** include textbooks and **encyclopedias**.

The effective teacher uses a variety of educational resources (including people and technology) to enhance both individual and group learning. Resources of all types are also key elements of the curriculum planning process. The effective teacher should be very familiar with the school library, the local public library, education service center resources, and the library of any college or university in the area. Another important set of resources is the audiovisual aids the teacher can borrow: kits, films, filmstrips, videos, laser discs, and computer software, among others. All used audiovisual aids should relate to curricular objectives.

Many librarians have keyed their resources to objectives in related subject areas and have thus enabled the teacher to incorporate them with ease into the lessons. However, teachers should never use resources with a class without previewing the resources and approving their use with the class. The curriculum guide or the lesson plan should ideally include the list of resources the teacher might use.

The effective teacher determines the appropriate place in the lesson for audiovisual aids. If the material is especially interesting and thought provoking, the teacher can use it to introduce a unit or to summarize it. Throughout the unit, the teacher and students may use the Internet for research.

Print Resources

The most common print material is the textbook, which teachers usually select from a list of books approved by the state. The use of textbooks has some disadvantages. The cost of textbooks has increased drastically in recent years, and some do not match curriculum guidelines. The adoption process is a long one, and textbooks (particularly for history) can become out-of-date quickly; therefore, the teacher must use additional, more recently published resources.

Another limitation of textbooks is their tendency to provide sketchy or minimal information, partly because publishers must include such a broad range of topics. An ineffective teacher may use the "chapter a week" theory of "covering" a textbook. This method gives no consideration to the importance of information in each chapter or its relevance to the overall district curriculum. Merely covering the material does not promote critical thinking on the part of the teacher or the student. Students tend to believe the textbook is something they must endure and not necessarily employ as a tool for learning. The effective teacher chooses sections from the textbook that are relevant to the learning goals and omits the rest. The teacher may supplement the sketchy textbook treatments by using an abundance of other resources.

Local, state, and national newspapers and magazines are important sources of up-to-date information not available in textbooks. Some newspapers and magazines have special programs to help teachers use their products in the classroom as sources of information and for reading and writing opportunities. Local newspapers may even be willing to send specialists to work with students or act as special resource people.

Visual Materials

The most available visual tools in classrooms are the chalkboard and the overhead projector. Several principles apply to both. The teacher must write clearly and in large letters. Overhead transparencies should never be typed on a regular typewriter because the print is too small. Computers allow type sizes of at least 18 points, which is the minimum readable size. Also, both boards and transparencies should be free of clutter. Teachers must remove old information from the board or screen before adding new information. These tools work more effectively if the teacher plans their use ahead of time. Using different colors emphasizes relationships or differences.

Posters and charts can complement lessons, but they should not clutter the walls so that students are unable to focus on what's important for the current lesson. Teachers may display posters and charts on a rotating basis.

A multimedia production can include images, text, and sound from a videodisc, compact disc (CD), graphics software, word-processing software, and a sound-effects program. Teachers can develop classroom presentations, but students can also develop learning units as part of a research or inquiry project. The cost of a multimedia system remains relatively high, but students can use it to develop high-level thought processes, collaborative work, research skills, content knowledge, and understanding.

The Internet is essential to the students and the teachers in gathering information. Computer programs, filmstrips, films, and videos are appealing to students because visual images on television, computers, and video games already surround them. Films, computer displays, and filmstrips have the advantage of large-screen projection so all students can see clearly, but many projection devices are expensive.

Teachers may stop videos, films, and filmstrips for discussion. Students comprehend better and remember longer if the teacher introduces a video or film appropriately and stops it frequently to discuss it with the students. This method also helps keep students' attention focused and assists them in learning note-taking skills. Some of the best graphic aids are those that individual students or groups of students develop. While learning about subject-area concepts, students become familiar with the design and presentation of information. Students can take pictures of their products to put in a portfolio or scrapbook.

CDs and Interactive Video

CDs provide a sturdy, condensed system of storage for pictures and sound. These discs can store many separate frames of still images, up to two hours of music, or two hours of motion pictures with sound. An advantage of a CD rather than videotape is that one can assess each frame separately and quickly by inputting its number. The simplest level of use involves commands to play, pause, forward, or reverse.

A CD or video program can become interactive with a computer link. The teacher can then access individual images, sequence images, and pace the information from the interactive system. A social studies teacher with a collection of pictures of the

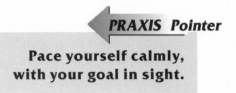

PRAXIS Pointer

Pace yourself calmly, with your goal in sight.

world's art treasures can choose which pictures to use, order the images, and design custom-made lessons for repeated use or for easy revision. The teacher can develop numerous lessons from one CD or videotape. More comprehensive interactive programs use the computer to present information, access a disc to illustrate main points, and ask for responses from the student.

Human Resources

Parents and other members of the community can be excellent local experts from whom students can learn about any subject: economics from bankers, history from veterans, music from a specific period from local musicians or recording collectors, community history from local historians or librarians, business from owners of companies—the list of possibilities is endless. Effective teachers make sure that any invited guest understands the purpose of the visit and the goals or objectives of the presentation. Preparation can make the class period more focused and meaningful.

Field trips are excellent sources of information, especially about careers and current issues like pollution control. One field trip can yield assignments in mathematics, history, science, English, art, architecture, music, or health. Teachers can collaborate with each other to produce thematic assignments for the field trip or simply to coordinate the students' assignments. Often a history report can serve as an English paper as well. Data can be analyzed in math classes and presented with the aid of computers.

Evaluating Examples of Primary Source Documents for Historical Perspective

Evaluating primary source documents to gain a historical perspective involves the ability to analyze and interpret the past. Analysis and interpretation result from an understanding that history is logically constructed; this conclusion results from careful analysis of documents, eyewitness accounts, letters, diaries, artifacts, photos, historical sites, and other primary sources. It is through these primary source documents that history can come alive.

The Library of Congress has on-line a wide range of primary source documents, from the Declaration of Independence and the Constitution to recordings and photographs made during the Great Depression. Students can even conduct interviews with veterans and examine the diaries, letters, and discharge papers that veterans or members of their families or communities may possess. Visits to local museums, libraries, and courthouses can also uncover primary source documents.

CONCEPTS IN SOCIAL STUDIES

Geography in the Social Studies Curriculum

Identifying the Five Themes of Geography, Including the Specific Terms for Each Theme

The five themes of geography are place; location; human–environmental interaction; movement and connections; and regions, patterns, and processes. An understanding of these themes would include the ability to use them to analyze regions, states, countries, and the world to gain a perspective about interrelationships among those areas. When a teacher uses the five themes, students should gain the ability to compare regions:

1. In this world of fast-breaking news from throughout the globe, students must be able to recognize the **place** names of continents, countries, and even cities. In addition to geography, the theme of place encompasses the fields of political science.

2. An understanding of the theme of **location** requires knowledge of both absolute and relative location. **Absolute location** is determined by longitude and latitude. **Relative location** deals with the interactions that occur between and among places. Relative location involves the interconnectedness among people because of land, water, and technology. For example, the Silver River brought commerce and steamboats to the Silver Springs area of Florida; the 99.8 percent pure artesian spring waters in one of the largest artesian spring formations in the world offered respite and beauty to settlers and tourists alike. Hullam Jones invented the glass-bottom boat

there in 1878 and enabled visitors to view the underwater world of fish, turtles, crustaceans, and fossils more than 10,000 years old. The location of Silver Springs has contributed to the area's economic development and vitality. In addition to geography, the theme of location encompasses the fields of technology, history, and economics.

3. An understanding of the theme of **human–environmental interaction** involves consideration of how people rely on the environment, how people alter it, and how the environment may limit what people are able to do. For example, Silver Springs is at the headwaters of the Silver River. In the 1850s, barges carried cotton, lumber, and nonperishables up the Silver River to the area's growing population. The development of a stagecoach line and the bringing of conventional steamboats to Silver Springs in 1860 aided in the development of Silver Springs and the nearby areas. In addition to geography, the theme of human-environmental interaction encompasses the field of ecology.

4. An understanding of the theme of **movement and connections** requires identifying how people are connected through different forms of transportation and communication networks and how those networks have changed over time. This would include identifying channels of the movement of people, goods, and information. For example, the automobile industry had a profound impact on the number of visitors to Silver Springs, Florida, and on the movement patterns of ideas, fashion, and people. In addition to geography, the theme of movement and connections encompasses the fields of communications, history, anthropology, economics, and sociology.

5. An understanding of the theme of **regions, patterns, and processes** involves identifying climatic, economic, political, and cultural patterns within regions. To comprehend why these patterns were created, students need to understand how climatic systems, communication networks, international trade, political systems, and population changes contributed to a region's development. With an understanding of a particular region, students can study its uniqueness and relationship to other regions. In addition to geography, the theme of regions, patterns, and processes encompasses the fields of economics, sociology, and politics.

The study of global issues and events includes comprehending the interconnectedness of peoples throughout the world (sociology and political science). For example, knowing the relationship between world oil consumption and oil production helps students understand the impact that increased demand for oil in China would have on the price of a barrel of oil, which in turn could affect the decisions of consumers of new vehicles in the United States.

Interpreting Maps and Other Graphic Representations and Identifying Tools and Technologies to Acquire, Process, and Report Information from a Spatial Perspective

Any study of maps should begin with a study of the globe—a model of the earth with a map on its surface. The globe is more accurate than a flat map. Constantly using the globe helps bring understanding of the earth's shape and structure.

Some of the points on the globe that students should be able to locate include the equator, Antarctic Circle, Arctic Circle, prime meridian, international date line, the North Pole, the South Pole, meridians, parallels, the Great Circle Route, and time zones. The use of maps requires students to identify four main types of map projections: conic, cylindrical, interrupted, and plane. Additional graphics that students use in geography include charts, graphs, and picture maps.

Interpreting Geologic Maps, Including Topographic and Weather Maps That Contain Symbols, Scales, Legends, Directions, Latitudes, and Longitudes

Geologic maps provide much information about the earth and present a perfect opportunity to integrate social studies and science. By reading a **topographical map**, a student can find out about **altitudes** (heights above and below sea level) and landforms. **Symbols** on the map may represent rivers, lakes, rapids, and forests. **Map scales** allow the student to determine distances. The **legends** of a map furnish additional information, including the locations of mineral deposits and quarries, dams and boat ramps, fire and ranger stations, and more. Often a map displays a **compass rose**, which gives the cardinal directions: north, south, east, and west.

Parallels and meridians grid the earth. **Meridians** run from pole to pole, and 360 of them surround the earth in 1° increments. Every hour, a given location on the earth's surface rotates through 15° of longitude. Meridians help measure longitude, the distance east and west of the prime meridian, which has a measurement of 0° east-west. **Parallels** are the lines that run in an east-west direction; parallels help measure **latitude**, the distance north and south of the equator. Geologic maps often contain all this information. A geologic map usually differs from a political map, which shows political boundaries, counties, cities, towns, churches, schools, and other representations of government and people.

Identifying the Factors That Influence the Selection of a Location for a Specific Activity

Factors that influence the selection of a location for a specific activity include the area's population density, government, latitude (distance from the equator), altitude (height above sea level), distance from bodies of water, culture, economics, landforms, sociology, vegetation, and climate (temperature, rainfall, etc.).

The human development of the area also affects selection. For instance, methods of transportation, highways, airports, communication, waterways, water travel, buildings, industries, and facilities are only a few of the factors that influence location for a specific activity. For some industries, nearness to sources of raw materials for production and ways of transporting the goods after production may be important in selecting an area in which to locate.

Two types of location—absolute and relative—describe the positions of people and places on the earth's surface. Determining **absolute location** requires the use of longitude and latitude on a grid system. The longitude and latitude coordinates identify exact (absolute) location. **Relative location**, on the other hand, recognizes the interdependence of people and places. Places do not exist in isolation. Geographers attempt to identify relationships between or among places and to determine the factors that might encourage those relationships.

Identifying the Relationship between Natural Physical Processes and the Environment

One can approach geography—the study of places on the earth's surface—from various perspectives. One study approach is **physical geography**—locating and describing places according to physical features (climate, soils, landforms, vegetation, etc.). Physical geography must take into account how the earth's movements around the sun, the tilt of the earth, the sea, weather patterns, the distance from the equator, the altitude, and the air affect the earth's surface. The physical approach alone, however, is a narrow methodology from the social science point of view because it ignores the human factor.

Interpreting Statistics That Show How Places Differ in Their Human and Physical Characteristics

For geography (the study of the earth) to be a true social science, it must take into account the human factor. Some notice of the interaction of the humans and animals that live on the earth—whether the interaction is deliberate or incidental—is an important part of the social sciences. The relationship between a place and the humans and animals that inhabit it is **cultural geography**.

Location affects both plant and animal life. The physical environment—climate, resources, terrain, and so on—impinges on the life of people by affecting diet, shelter, clothing, accessibility, inventions, religion, resources, and prosperity. In fact, in prehistoric times—even before history, government, or economics—the earth (geography) was the most important element in human life. Geography is still important in society today. Studying a map of the rivers and the fall line (a physical feature that indicates the navigability of rivers) in North Carolina, for example, reveals why many people decided to settle there. In the late 1800s, textile mills were often built near the fall line so they could use water as a power source. Many people who needed employment and were not highly skilled sought work in the textile mills. This example shows how the physical characteristics of a place can affect the people who move there.

Identifying How Conditions of the Past, Such As Wealth and Poverty, Land Tenure, Exploitation, Colonialism, and Independence, Affect Present Human Characteristics of Places

Three generalizations of geography relate the past to human characteristics of places:

1. Physical factors and cultural factors are related. For instance, the types of houses that families build reflect the available materials and climates. Therefore, physical differences can arise among houses in various places. The richness of the physical environment can affect the wealth of the people.

2. Change is a constant. The effects of change on people are both physical and cultural. For example, the people themselves bring about some

changes; they may modify the environment by cutting trees and affecting the landscape now and in days to come.

3. People modify the environment to suit their changing needs and wants. For example, when tenant farmers lived on another person's land, they had little say over the use of the land; planting gardens for their own families' uses may have been out of the question. Once they were able to purchase land, their use of the land changed; many began planting gardens and fruit trees for their families. Today, people living in an area damaged by a storm may be able to repair the damages caused by the storm and even change the place to suit their current needs and wants.

Identifying Ways in Which People Adapt to an Environment through the Production and Use of Clothing, Food, and Shelter

Although the environment can affect the way people live, people can change the environment to meet their wants and needs. For example, the jobs that people hold enable them to get money for food, clothing, and shelter. Some jobs—farming, logging, and mining, for example—have a profound effect on the environment. In parts of the world without adequate rainfall, farmers have to use irrigation to grow their crops. Through their adaptation of the environment, the farmers acquire the things they need to survive but, in the process, may damage their environment and ultimately threaten the survival of future generations.

Ideally, people will explore a damaged environment to determine the causes of water and air pollution. They will also determine whether there is any harm to local plants and animals and will ascertain the cause if there is damage. The people will ideally work to change damages to the environment and prevent further harm.

Identifying How Tools and Technology Affect the Environment

The period from the emergence of the first-known hominids, or humans, around 2.5 million years ago until approximately 10,000 B.C.E. has been designated as the Paleolithic period, or the Old Stone Age. During that period, human beings lived in very small groups of perhaps 10 to 20 nomadic people who were constantly moving from place to place. Human beings had the ability to make tools and weapons from stone and the bones of animals they killed. Hunting large game such as mammoths, which the hunters sometimes drove off cliffs in large numbers, was crucial to the survival of early humans. The meat, fur, and bones of the hunted animals were essential to the survival of prehistoric people, who supplemented their diets by foraging for food.

Early human beings found shelter in caves and other natural formations and took the time to paint and draw on the walls of their shelters. Created during the prehistoric period, cave paintings in France and northern Spain depict scenes of animals, such as lions, owls, and oxen. Around 500,000 years ago, humans developed the means of creating fire and used it to provide light and warmth in shelters and to cook meat and other foods. They also developed improved techniques of producing tools and weapons. Tools and technology can improve the lives of people; needless to say, tools and technology can also harm the lives of people. Likewise, people can use tools and technology both to improve their environment and to harm or even destroy their immediate areas or even the world. For example, as Alfred Nobel learned after he developed dynamite, escalating the power of weapons has never successfully prevented war. As weapons become more powerful, the danger from the technology increases.

PRAXIS Pointer

To relax, tense up your shoulder muscles by bringing your shoulders up toward your ears. Hold it for 10 seconds—release and relax. Do this technique 2 –3 times. Then try it with other muscles.

Identifying Physical, Cultural, Economic, and Political Reasons for the Movement of People in the World, Nation, or State

The people living in a particular area determine the characteristics of that area. The physical, cultural, economic, and political characteristics are important to most area residents and may affect their original decision to settle there.

If the characteristics of an area become unacceptable to residents, the inhabitants may consider moving to a different location. With the ease of transportation today, most people can move more easily than they could have a generation ago. The move may be to another region of their state, the nation, or the world.

Economic reasons for moving include the finances of an individual considering relocating and the economic level required to live comfortably in the area. Some residents may move to a more expensive area, but others may decide to go to a less expensive area. Many change their places of residence, therefore, to get ahead economically or to raise their standard of living.

Some people decide to relocate for **cultural reasons**. These people might consider their neighbors too similar to them and decide to move to an area with more diversity. On the other hand, some people would rather live with others who are similar to them.

Physical reasons can also affect a person's decision to relocate. An understanding of the theme of human–environmental interaction involves considering how people rely on the environment, how they alter it, and how the environment can limit what people are able to do. Sometimes people move to a place where they can satisfy their physical wants or needs. In some cases, people can modify their environment or bring the needed goods to their area without having to relocate. For example, an adaptation of the environment that aided the Illinois shipping industry was the development of the lock and dam system on the Mississippi River.

An understanding of the theme of location, movement, and connections involves identifying how people are connected through different forms of transportation and communication networks and how those networks have changed over time. This would include identifying the channels of movement of people, goods, and information. For example, the textile industry in North Carolina in the 1930s had a profound impact on the movement patterns of ideas and people; many of those without work came to the textile regions seeking jobs. When the textile mills began closing in the 1990s, many people began to leave the area in search of other employment.

Political reasons also compel the movement of people. Many people equate the political system with government. There is a distinction, however. Government carries out the decisions of the political system. The organizations and processes that contribute to the decision-making process make up the political system. Individuals may move to another region or area if they are unhappy with the government and/or political systems in their area and are unable to bring about change. On the other hand, an attractive system of government may bring people to an area.

Comparing and Contrasting Major Regions of the World

There are many ways of dividing the world into regions. Perhaps the simplest is to consider the equator as a dividing line between the Northern Hemisphere and the Southern Hemisphere. Another way of dividing the world in regions is to draw a line from pole to pole. Such a line may separate the globe into the Eastern Hemisphere and Western Hemisphere. Another way geographers might divide the world into regions is by landmasses, or continents, specifically Africa, Asia, Australia, Europe, North America, and South America; some geographers also include Antarctica as a separate continent. Other geographers prefer to group the regions according to political characteristics. Still others prefer to designate regions by latitudes: low, middle, and high.

Two important higher-order thinking skills that teachers should encourage among their students are comparing and contrasting. The use of regions is an ideal place to work with these skills of comparing and contrasting two (or more) things (or concepts). The process of finding similarities between or among the things or concepts that appear dissimilar on the surface requires deeper thought. W. J. J. Gordon describes a process of synectics, which forces students to make an analogy between two concepts, one familiar and the other new. At first, the concepts might seem completely different, but through a series of steps the students discover underlying similarities. By comparing something new with something familiar, students have a "hook" that will help them remember and understand the new information (Huitt 1998; Gordon 1961).

For example, a biology teacher might ask students to draw an analogy between a cell (new concept) and a city government (familiar concept). Although they seem impossibly different, both concepts involve systems for transportation, systems for disposing of unwanted materials, and parts that govern those systems. After discussion of this analogy, students trying to remember the functions of a cell would find help by relating the functions of the cell to the systems of city government.

Anthropology, Sociology, and Psychology

Anthropology is the study of human culture. Anthropologists study both modern-day and prehistoric culture. There are several types of anthropologists:

1. Archaeologists excavate and scientifically analyze the remains of extinct people to attempt reconstruction of their way of life. Richard Leakey is an archaeologist.

2. Primatologists study the group behavior of primates (nonhuman) such as gorillas, baboons, and chimpanzees. Jane Goodall is a primatologist.

3. Ethnographers gather information about culture through fieldwork done on site. Margaret Mead was an ethnographer.

4. Linguistic anthropologists study languages, particularly language in a social context.

5. Physical (or biological) anthropologists study living and fossil human beings and primates, such as chimpanzees and monkeys.

Sociology is the study of the social behavior of humans within a group. The groups studied can include families, mobs, workers in large organizations, criminals, medical groups, men, women, and so on; of particular concern is how the groups and the institutions interact. The sociologist and Nobel Prize winner Gunnar Myrdal was a prominent sociologist; his *An American Dilemma* (1944) dealt with the "Negro in America [which] represents nothing more and nothing less than a century-long lag of public morals" (24). He saw the problem as being "an integral part of, or a special phase of, the whole complex of problems in the larger civilization. It cannot be treated in isolation" (xlix).

Psychology is the study of human behavior—individuals and small groups of people. Educators are perhaps most familiar with psychologists Jean Piaget (a developmental psychologist who studied individuals over a lifespan) and B. F. Skinner (a behavioral or experimental psychologist). Social psychologists study the behavior of people in groups. Cognitive psychologists are interested in how people think and learn. Clinical psychologists study abnormal behavior. It is interesting, however, that some people do not classify psychology as a social studies subject.

Assessment in Teaching Social Science Concepts

The basic goals of assessment are to enhance teachers' knowledge of learners and their needs, to monitor students' progress toward goals and outcomes, and to modify instruction when progress is not sufficient.

Purposes of Assessment

The effective teacher understands the importance of ongoing assessment as an instructional tool for the classroom and uses both informal and formal assessment measures. Informal measures can include observation, journals, written drafts, and conversations. Formal measures can include teacher-made tests, district exams, and standardized tests.

REFERENCES

Alvarez, Lizette. "Census Director Marvels at the New Portrait of America." New York Times, January 1, 2001.

Cayne, Bernard S., ed. *Merit Students Encyclopedia*. Chicago: Crowell-Collier, 1969.

Chitwood, Oliver Perry, Frank Lawrence Owsley, and H. C. Nixon. *The United States: From Colony to World Power*. New York: D. Van Nostrand, 1949.

Congress for Kids. "Constitution: Amendments." *www.congressforkids.net/Constitution_amendments.htm*.

Davis, Anita Price. *North Carolina during the Great Depression: A Documentary Portrait of a Decade*. Jefferson, NC: McFarland, 2003.

Florida Smart. "Florida Population and Demographics." *www.floridasmart.com/facts/demographics.htm*.

Gordon, W. J. J. *Synectics*. New York: Harper and Row, 1961.

Halsey, William D., and Bernard Johnston, eds. *Merit Students Encyclopedia*. New York: Macmillan, 1991.

Harrington, Michael. *The Other America: Poverty in the United States*. New York: Macmillan, 1962.

Huitt, W. "Critical Thinking: An Overview." *Educational Psychology Interactive*. Valdosta, GA, 1998. *http://chiron.valdosta.edu/whuitt/col/cogsys/critthnk.html*. Last accessed July 11, 2008.

Martin, Philip L. "Immigration in the United States." Institute of European Studies, University of California, Berkeley. *http://ies.berkeley.edu/pubs/workingpapers/ay0102.html*.

Myrdal, Gunnar with the assistance of Richard Sterner and Arnold Rose. *An American Dilemma: The Negro Problem and Modern Democracy*. New York: Harper and Brothers Publishers, 1944.

Noyce, Ruth M., and James F. Christie. *Integrating Reading and Writing Instruction in Grades K–8*. Boston: Allyn and Bacon, 1989.

NATO Official Homepage. *www.nato.int*.

Schieffer, Bob. "Government Failed the People." *CBS News* (September 4, 2005).

Schug, Mark C., and R. Beery. *Teaching Social Studies in the Elementary School.* Prospect Heights, IL: Waveland Press, 1987.

Schuncke, George M. *Elementary Social Studies: Knowing, Doing, Caring.* New York: Macmillan, 1988.

"United Nations Educational, Scientific, and Cultural Organization," *http://portal. unesco.org.*

U.S. Census Bureau, *Current Population Survey*, March 2000. *www.census.gov/ population/socdemo/foreign/p20-534/tab0314.txt.*

U.S. Census Bureau. "Countries of Birth of the Foreign-Born Population, 1850– 2000." *Profile of the Foreign-Born Population in the United States: 2000. www. Infoplease.com/ipa/A0900547.html.* Last accessed July 17, 2008.

U.S. Census Bureau. "State and County Quickfacts: Florida." *http://quickfacts. census.gov/qfd/states/12000.html.*

Woolever, Roberta, and Kathryn P. Scott. *Active Learning in Social Studies: Promoting Cognitive and Social Growth.* Glenview, IL: Scott Foresman, 1988.

Science Pedagogy

HISTORY AND NATURE OF SCIENCE AND INQUIRY

Basic Science Processes

The **scientific method** is *not* a specific set of steps that is rigorously followed whenever a question arises that can be answered using the knowledge and techniques of science. Rather, it is a process of observation and analysis used to develop a reliable, consistent, and objective representation and understanding of our world. The scientific method is useful for answering many but not all questions. The processes that make up the scientific method are identifying a problem or question, observing and describing, formulating hypotheses, making predictions based on the hypotheses and testing those predictions (experimenting), interpreting results, and deriving conclusions.

Scientists—and students—must carefully observe their surroundings and consider the data available. The scientific method is best applied to situations in which the experimenter can control the variables, eliminating or accounting for all extraneous factors, and can perform repeated independent tests that change only one variable at a time. Scientists and students must be able to find similarities and differences and to classify the information, objects, plants, and animals accordingly.

Scientists and students must be able to communicate to share their observations and their questions. This communication can be either written or oral. To communicate data clearly enough to foster sound interpretation, the scientists or students can present the information in various formats: graphs, diagrams, maps, concrete models, role playing, and charts, among others.

Quantifying the results of observing and classifying is part of effective communication. Effective quantifying requires the selection of appropriate tools for observing, describing, measuring, comparing, and computing. The **microscope** and **telescope** extend the range of human observation beyond human physiology. The **spectroscope** separates visible light into its component colors, and the **spectrophotometer** measures the selective absorption of those colors as a function of some property of a solution, solid, or gas. **Mathematics** is a tool to evaluate the results of our observations, to organize large quantities of data into averages, ranges, and statistical probabilities. The fundamental uncertainty of the measuring device limits quantifying and measurements. The concept of **significant figures** derives from the simple assumption that calculations on measurements cannot generate results that are more precise than the measurements themselves. For example, if you divide one pie into three pieces, a calculator might report that each piece represents 0.33333333 (depending on the number of digits on the calculator display). You know from experience that there will be crumbs left in the pan and that no amount of care in dividing the pieces will result in the level of accuracy the calculation suggests. Most of us assume every measuring device to be accurate to the smallest of the subdivisions marked, and every measurement with such a device should include one additional estimated digit. For example, when you use a ruler with one centimeter as its smallest division, you should record your measurements to the tenth of a centimeter, the smallest measured digit plus one estimated digit. The following terms form an indispensable part of the vocabulary used in scientific experimentation:

Observation: The act of sensing some measurable phenomenon.

Organization: Relating parts to a coherent whole.

Experimental: Testing the effect of an independent variable on a dependent variable in a controlled environment.

Inference: Reducing a conclusion from a measurement or observation that is not explicit to either. For example, you can infer that a classroom of

30 students has 16 girls if you know that there are 14 boys. Here the inference is done by subtracting 14 from 30.

Prediction: Stating the outcome of an experiment in advance of doing it. An example would be predicting that a plot of velocity versus time for a freely falling object will be a straight line.

Integrated Science Processes

As noted in the previous section, the processes that make up the scientific method are observing and describing, formulating hypotheses, making predictions based on the hypotheses and testing those predictions (experimenting), and deriving conclusions.

In planning experiments, the scientist or student is generally attempting to test a hypothesis. A **hypothesis** is an educated guess about the relationship between two variables that is subject to testing and verification. The outcome of the test in a well-designed experiment answers questions suggested by the hypothesis in a clear and unambiguous way. In planning and conducting an experiment, the scientist or student must (1) identify relevant variables, (2) identify equipment and apparatus to be used to measure and record the variables, (3) eliminate or suppress any other factors that could influence measured variables, and (4) decide on a means of analyzing the data obtained. In conducting experiments, it is imperative that questions raised by the hypotheses be testable and that the data recorded be sufficiently accurate and repeatable.

Testable Questions

An example of a testable question might be, "Does mass have an influence on acceleration for bodies subjected to unbalanced forces?" This question is testable because it identifies specific variables (force, mass, and acceleration) one can measure and control in any experiment that seeks to establish a connection. Thus, testable questions must specify variables that are subject to both measurement and control.

Data Representation

Data is often represented in graphical form, where raw data is plotted. The independent (controlled) variable is usually displayed on the *x*-axis of a graph (horizontal), and the dependent variable is usually displayed on the *y*-axis (vertical). Graphs can either be linear (a straight line) or nonlinear. Often equations can be fitted to graphs obtained for purposes of finder analyses. Use of a graphing calculator and specialized software can facilitate both the data collection and data representation in graphical form. Note that x–y plots are not the only means of data representation. Charts, diagrams, and tables are also often used to display results.

Interpreting Experimental Results

Sometimes experimental work involves measurements that do not directly yield the desired variable value but can be interpreted or reduced to provide the desired value. The experimental approach in that case is indirect.

An example is the measurement of acceleration of gravity, or g, a fundamental gravitational constant. One common method is to measure displacement over time for a falling body. The resulting graph is then reduced (interpreted) to yield a plot of velocity versus time. This plot in turn is then reduced (interpreted) to yield a plot of acceleration versus time, from which the acceleration of gravity, g, can be read. Inherent to each of the reductions was finding the slope (the rise divided by the run) at various points, which is a mathematical technique that enables interpretation of the results.

Variables

The science fair project is a common tool for instruction in the scientific method. Many formal and informal sources, often Web based, provide lists of suggested science fair topics, but not all are experiments. For the youngest students, it is appropriate and useful for the focus to be on models and demonstrations—for example, a model of the solar system or a volcano, or a clay cross section of an egg. Older students should move to true experiments that focus on identifying a testable hypothesis and controlling all experimental variables but the one of interest.

Many projects that begin as models or demonstrations can be elevated to experiments. A proposal to demonstrate how windmills work can be made an experiment when the student adds quantitative measurements of one variable against variations in one other variable; the student must hold all other variables constant. For example, using an electric fan, the student could measure the number of rotations per minute as a function of the fan setting (low, medium, or high). Then, while keeping the fan setting constant, the student could conduct several experiments that vary the number of fans, the sizes of fans, or the shapes of fans, measuring the rotational speed at each variation.

Collecting and Presenting Data

Scientifically literate individuals have detailed and accurate content knowledge that is the basis of their scientific knowledge. They do not try to recall every detail of that knowledge but build conceptual frameworks on which they can add both prior knowledge and new learning. From this framework of facts, concepts, and theories, scientifically literate individuals can reconstruct forgotten facts and use them to answer new questions not previously considered. Scientifically literate individuals are lifelong learners who ask questions that can be answered using scientific knowledge and techniques.

Scientific information is communicated to nonscientific audiences to inform, guide policy, and influence the practices that affect all of society. This information is presented through text, tables, charts, figures, pictures, models, and other representations that require interpretation and analysis. Scientifically literate individuals can (1) read and interpret these representations and (2) select appropriate tools to present the information they gather.

Science is based on experimentation, but not all knowledge is derived daily from first principles. Scientifically literate individuals are informed by existing knowledge and are aware of the sources, accuracy, and value of each source. Not every source is equally reliable, accurate, or valid. Classroom teachers are advised to use trusted educational sites.

Scientifically literate individuals can evaluate critically the information and evidence they collect and the conclusions or theories to which that information and evidence leads. Such analysis incorporates an understanding of the limitations of knowledge in general and, more specifically, the limitations of all measurements and information based on the quality of the experimental design. Scientifically literate individuals can evaluate claims for scientific merit, identify conflicting evidence, and weigh the value and credibility of conflicting information. They can also recognize that not every question can be answered using scientific knowledge. They should value the contributions of other cultures and other ways of knowing, including art, philosophy, and theology.

Measurement

Measurement includes (1) estimating and converting measurements within the customary and metric systems; (2) applying procedures for using measurement to describe and compare phenomena; (3) identifying appropriate measurement instruments, units, and procedures for problems involving length, area, angles, volume, mass, time, money, and temperature; and (4) using a variety of materials, models, and methods to explore concepts and solve problems involving measurement.

Inquiry Approach to Learning Science Concepts

Effective teachers use not one but many methods and strategies to enhance student learning. Teachers choose various strategies to meet both content- and student-driven purposes. If the purpose is to investigate current problems without specific answers, the teacher might choose an inquiry lesson.

To engage in **inquiry**, a student must be able to acquire information from a variety of resources and organize and interpret that information. Inquiry may involve designing and conducting investigations that lead to the identification of issues to analyze. Inquiry is essential for examining single topics or integrated sciences.

Scientists and students should understand the principles and processes of scientific investigation and how to promote the development of scientific knowledge and skills, including the use of scientific thinking, inquiry, reasoning, and investigation. Effective science-teaching methods include the following:

- Determining the type of scientific investigation (for example, experimentation, systematic observation) that best addresses a given question or hypothesis

- Demonstrating a knowledge of considerations and procedures, including safety practices, related to designing and conducting experiments (for example, formulation of hypotheses; use of control and experimental groups; and recognition of variables being held constant, those being manipulated, and those responding in an experiment)

- Recognizing how to use methods, tools, technologies, and measurement units to gather and organize data, compare and evaluate data, and describe and communicate the results of investigations in various formats

- Understanding concepts, skills, and processes of inquiry in the social sciences (for example, locating, gathering, organizing, formulating hypotheses) and how to promote students' development of knowledge and skills in this area

Teaching methods can be divided into two categories: inductive and deductive. Using **inductive** methods, teachers encourage students to study, conduct research, collect and analyze data, and then develop generalizations and rules based on their findings. During inductive lessons, first a hypothesis or concept is introduced, and then generalizations are developed based on inferences from data.

Inquiry or discovery lessons are inductive in nature. An inquiry lesson starts with a thought-provoking question for which students are interested in finding an explanation. After posing the question, the teacher guides students in brainstorming a list of what they already know about the topic and then categorizing the information. Students use these categories as topics for group or individual research. The lesson typically ends with students presenting their research to the class.

A teacher who uses inquiry strategies takes the role of a facilitator who plans outcomes and provides resources for students as they work. In their role as inquirers, students must take responsibility for their own learning by planning, carrying out, and presenting research and projects.

CONCEPTS IN SCIENCE

Earth Science

Revolution of the Earth

Earth revolves around the sun. The axis of Earth is tilted at a 23.5° angle, and the axis always points toward the North Star (Polaris). The tilt and the revolution about the sun cause the seasons. **Earth's distance from the sun does not cause the seasons**. In fact, the Northern Hemisphere is closer to the sun in the winter—not in the summer. This closeness of the Earth to the sun in the winter is because of the elliptical pattern that the Earth follows as it revolves about the sun.

The Northern Hemisphere experiences **summer** when it is tilted toward the sun. Summer begins in the Northern Hemisphere on June 21, when the rays of the sun shine directly on the area. The hours of daylight are longer in the summer in the Northern Hemisphere, and the rays of the sun cover a smaller part of the surface of Earth in the summer. At that time of year, therefore, the Northern Hemisphere has hot surface temperatures and, because of the tilt of Earth, more hours of sunlight than darkness. This means that the longer direct rays of the sun hit the Earth for a longer period of time in the summer. When the Northern Hemisphere is tilted away from the sun, it experiences **winter**. Winter begins in the Northern Hemisphere on December 22. During this season, the days are shorter, fewer direct rays from the sun reach the Northern Hemisphere, and the hours of night are longer than

PRAXIS Pointer

Wear a (noiseless) watch.

in the summer. When it is summer in the Northern Hemisphere, it is winter in the Southern Hemisphere. When it is winter in the Northern Hemisphere, it is summer in the Southern Hemisphere. In the **fall** and

spring, Earth is not tilted toward or away from the sun; it is somewhere between. The days and nights have an almost equal number of hours in the spring and fall. The Northern Hemisphere has days and nights of equal duration at the **vernal equinox** (March 21) and at the **autumnal equinox** (September 23).

Earth History

Processes That Shape the Earth

Geology is the study of the structure and composition of the Earth. The three layers that compose the earth are the core, mantle, and crust. Solid iron and nickel make up the **core**, which is about 7,000 kilometers in diameter. The **mantle** is the semi-molten layer between the crust and the core. It is about 3,000 kilometers thick. The **crust** is the solid outermost layer, composed of bedrock overlaid with mineral and/or organic sediment (soil) and ranging from 5 to 40 kilometers thick.

At times, large sections of the earth's crust move and create faults, earthquakes, volcanoes, and mountains. These moving sections of the earth are **plates**, and the study of their movements is **plate tectonics**.

Faults are cracks in the crust and are the results of the movements of plates. **Earthquakes** occur when plates slide past one another quickly. Volcanoes may also cause earthquakes. A seismograph measures earthquakes and uses the Richter scale. **Volcanoes** are mountains that form when two plates move away from one another to let magma reach the crust. **Magma** is molten rock beneath the earth's crust. **Lava** is molten rock on the Earth's surface. A volcano shoots out magma, which eventually hardens into lava, and releases ash. Sometimes the erupting volcano forms rivers of lava.

Volcanoes exist all over the world—for example, the Pacific Ocean, the Hawaiian Islands, and the southeastern border of Asia. The composition of volcanoes is fiery igneous rock, ash, and many layers of dirt and mud that have hardened from previous eruptions. Volcanic activity causes the crust of the Earth to buckle upward and form mountains.

Plate tectonics is a relatively new theory that has revolutionized the way geologists think about the Earth. According to the theory, large lithospheric plates form the surface of the Earth. The size and position of these plates change over time. The edges of the plates, where they move against each other, are sites of intense geologic activity such as earthquakes, volcanoes, and mountain building. Plate tectonics is a combination of two earlier ideas: continental drift and seafloor spreading. **Continental drift** is the movement of continents over the Earth's surface and their change in position relative to each other. **Seafloor spreading** is the creation of new oceanic crust at mid-ocean ridges and movement of the crust away from the mid-ocean ridges.

The following are some of the evidence of continental drift and the underlying plate tectonics:

- The shapes of many continents are such that they look as though they are separate pieces of a jigsaw puzzle. For example, the east coasts of North America and South America and the west coasts of Africa and Europe appear to fit together.

- Many fossil comparisons along the edges of continents that look as if they fit together suggest species similarities that would make sense only if the two continents were joined at some point in the past.

- Much seismic, volcanic, and geothermal activity occurs more frequently along plate boundaries than in sites far from boundaries.

- Ridges, such as the Mid-Atlantic Ridge, occur where plates are separating because of lava welling up from between them as they pull apart.

Likewise, mountain ranges are forming where plates are pushing against each other (for example, the Himalayas, which are still growing).

﹀ Physical Science

Identifying the Physical and Chemical Properties of Matter

Matter is everything that has mass and volume. **Mass** is the amount of matter in an object; one way to measure mass is by using a lever-arm balance. **Volume** is the amount of space an object occupies. Water is matter because it takes up space (that is, it has volume); light is not matter because it does not take up space.

Weight, although sometimes incorrectly interchanged with mass, is a measure of the force of gravity on an object; a spring scale can determine weight. An electronic scale may display an object's mass in grams, but the scale is dependent on gravity for its operation. An electronic scale, such as some butchers use, is accurate only when an expert (usually with the state trade agency) has adjusted the electronics for the local gravitational force. Although an object appears "weightless" as it floats inside the space shuttle, it is not; gravitational forces from both the earth and the sun keep it in orbit and affect the object. The force of gravity is proportional to the product of the masses of the two objects under consideration divided by the square of the distance between them. Earth, being larger and more massive than Mars, has proportionally higher gravitational forces. This is the basis of the observation in H. G. Wells' *The War of the Worlds*, in which he describes the Martian invaders as "the most sluggish things I ever saw crawl." (Wells 1898).

Density is the ratio of mass to volume. An intrinsic property, density depends on the type of matter but not the amount of matter. Thus, the density of a five-ton cube of pure copper is the same as that of a small copper penny. However, the modern penny is a thin shell of copper over a zinc plug, and the density of the coin may be significantly lower than that of the older pure copper coin.

Density is related to **buoyancy**. Objects sink in liquids or gases alike if they are denser than the material that surrounds them. Archimedes' principle, also related to density, states that an object is buoyed up by a force equal to the mass of the material the object displaces. Thus, a 160-pound concrete canoe will easily float in water if the volume of the submerged portion of the canoe is equal to the volume of 20 gallons of water. (The weight of water is approximately 8 pounds per gallon; therefore, 8 lbs/gal × 20 gal = 160 lbs.)

Matter can undergo chemical and physical changes. A **physical change** affects the size, form, or appearance of a material. These changes can include melting, bending, or cracking. Physical changes do not alter the molecular structure of a material. **Chemical changes** do alter the molecular structure of matter. Examples of chemical changes are burning, rusting, and digestion. Under the right conditions, compounds can break apart, combine, or recombine to form new compounds; this process is called a **chemical reaction**.

Characteristics of Elements, Compounds, and Mixtures

Classifications of matter also include elements, compounds, mixtures, or solutions. An **element** consists of only one type of atom. An example is iron. A symbol of one or two letters, such as Fe (iron) or C (carbon), represents an element. A **compound** is matter that comprises atoms chemically combined in definite weight proportions. An example of a compound is water, which is oxygen and hydrogen combined in the ratio of two hydrogen molecules to one oxygen molecule.

A **mixture** is made up of one or more types of molecules, not chemically combined and without any definite weight proportions. For example, milk is a mixture of water and butterfat particles. Mixtures can be separated by either physical or chemical means. An example of a physical means would be straining the butterfat from milk to make skim milk. **Solutions** are **homogeneous** mixtures—that is, mixtures with evenly distributed substances. An example of a solution is seawater. Separating the salt from seawater requires the process of evaporation. The three main **states of matter** are solids, liquids, and gases. A **solid** has a definite volume and a definite shape; an example is ice. A **liquid** has a definite volume but has no definite shape; an example is water. A **gas** has no definite volume or shape; an example is water vapor or steam.

Knowledge of the Processes of Life

Comparing and Contrasting Living and Nonliving Things

Biology is the study of living things. Living things are differentiated from nonliving things by the ability to perform a specific set of life activities at some point in a normal life span. Table 6-1 describes the activities that define life.

Table 6-1. Required Activities of Living Things

Activity	Description
Food getting	Procuring the food needed to sustain life by eating, absorption, or photosynthesis
Respiration	Exchanging of gases
Excretion	Eliminating wastes
Growth	Increasing in size over part or all of a life span
Repair	Repairing damaged tissue
Movement	Willfully moving a portion of a living thing's body, or channeling growth in a particular direction
Response	Reacting to events or things in the environment
Secretion	Producing and distributing chemicals that aid digestion, growth, metabolism, etc.
Reproduction	Making new living things similar to the parent

It is important to note that living things *must*, during a typical life span, be able to perform *all* these activities. It is quite common for nonliving things to perform one or more of these activities. For example, robots can move, respond, and repair, and crystals can grow; neither robots nor crystals, of course, are living things.

A **cell** is the basic structural unit of living things. In a living thing, a cell is the smallest component that can, by itself, be considered living. Plant cells and animal cells, though generally similar, are distinctly different; for example, plant cells have unique plant structures, cell walls, and vacuoles that animal cells do not have.

Differentiating Structures and Functions of Plant and Animal Cells

As discussed earlier, a cell is the basic structural unit of living things and the smallest unit that can, by itself, be considered living. Plant cells and animal cells, though generally similar, are distinctly different. Figure 6-1 illustrates the structures of animal and plant cells. Cells are made of several smaller structures called **organelles**, which are surrounded by cell fluid, or cytoplasm. The functions of several cell structures are listed in Table 6-2.

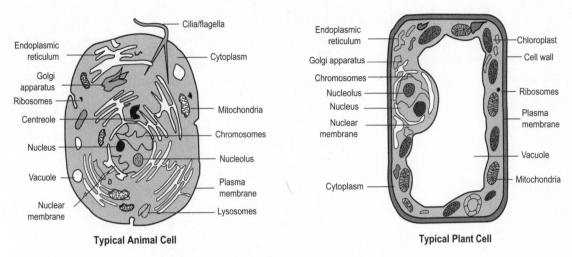

Figure 6-1. Typical Animal and Plant Cells

Table 6-2. Cell Structures and Their Functions

Organelle	Function
Cell membrane	Controls movement of materials into and out of cells
Cell wall	Gives rigid structure to plant cells
Chloroplast	Contains chlorophyll, which enables green plants to make their own food
Cytoplasm	Jellylike substance inside a cell; comprises the cytosol and organelles but not the nucleus
Mitochondrion	Liberates energy from glucose in cells for use in cellular activities
Nucleus	Directs cell activities; holds DNA (genetic material)
Ribosome	Makes proteins from amino acids
Vacuole	Stores materials in a cell

The Plant Physiological Process

Cells perform several chemical processes to maintain essential life activities. The sum of these necessary chemical processes is called **metabolism**. Table 6-3 lists the processes related to metabolism and the organelles involved.

Table 6-3. Processes of Cell Metabolism

Process	Organelle	Life Activity
Diffusion	Cell membrane	Food getting, respiration, excretion
Osmosis	Cell membrane	Food getting, excretion
Phagocytosis	Cell membrane	Food getting
Photosynthesis	Chloroplasts	Food getting
Respiration (aerobic)	Mitochondrion	Provides energy
Fermentation	Mitochondrion	Provides energy

Cells need to move materials into their structures to get energy and to grow. The **cell membrane** allows certain small molecules to flow freely across it. This flow of chemicals from areas of high concentration to areas of low concentration is called **diffusion**. **Osmosis** is diffusion of water across a semipermeable membrane. Particles too large to pass through the cell membrane may be engulfed by the cell membrane and stored in vacuoles until they can be digested. This engulfing process is called **phagocytosis**.

All cells need energy to survive. Sunlight energy is made biologically available when plant cells convert it to chemical energy during **photosynthesis**. Photosynthesis is carried out in the **chloroplasts** of green cells. **Chlorophyll**, the pigment found in chloroplasts, catalyzes (causes or accelerates) the photosynthetic reaction that turns carbon dioxide and water into glucose (sugar) and oxygen. Sunlight and chlorophyll are needed for the reaction to occur. Chlorophyll, because it is a catalyst, is not consumed in the reaction and may be used repeatedly.

The term *respiration* has two distinct meanings in the field of biology. As a life activity, respiration is the exchange of gases in living things. As a metabolic process, respiration is the release of energy from sugars for use in life activities. All living things get their energy from the digestion (respiration) of glucose (sugar). Respiration may occur with oxygen (aerobic respiration) or without oxygen (anaerobic respiration, or fermentation). Most often the term *respiration* is used to refer to aerobic respiration. Aerobic respiration occurs in most plant and animal cells. **Fermentation** occurs in yeast cells and other cells in the absence of oxygen. Fermentation by yeast produces the alcohol in alcoholic beverages and the gases that make yeast breads rise and have a light texture.

Reproduction is a process whereby living plant or animal cells or organisms produce offspring. Individual plants have growth limitations imposed by inherited characteristics and environmental conditions. If the plant grows excessively, any number of reproductive processes may be simulated. However, in plants, reproduction may be either sexual or asexual. **Asexual plant propagation**, also known as vegetative reproduction, is the method by which plants reproduce without the union of cells or nuclei of cells. The product of asexual plant propagation is genetically identical to the parent. Asexual propagation takes place either by **fragmentation** or by special asexual structures. An example of fragmentation is growing new plants from cuttings. **Sexual plant propagation** almost always involves seeds produced by two individuals, male and female. Most plant propagation is, in fact, from seed, including all annual and biennial plants. Seed **germination** begins when a sufficient amount of water is absorbed by the seed, precipitating biochemical changes that initiate cell division.

Water is essential for plant life. The plant needs the water to make food, among other uses. A plant usually takes in more water than it needs. To get rid of excess water, the stomata of the leaves allow the water to pass out as water vapor. This evaporation of water from the plant is **transpiration**.

Identifying the Structures and Functions of Organs and Systems of Animals, Including Humans

Not all cells are alike. Cells that perform different functions differ in size and shape. A group of the same kind of cells is called a **tissue**. A group of the same kind of tissues working together is an **organ**. Examples of animal organs are the brain, stomach, heart, liver, and kidneys. A group of organs that work together to accomplish a special activity is a **system**. The complex organism known as the human body is made up of several organ systems.

The **skeletal system** is composed of bones, cartilage, and ligaments. The area where two or more bones come together is called a **joint**. Bone surfaces in a joint are often covered with **cartilage**, which reduces friction in the joint. **Ligaments** are connective tissues that hold bones together. The human skeleton consists of more than 200 bones connected at joints by ligaments. Movements are effected by contractions of the skeletal muscles, to which tendons attach the bones. Muscular contractions are controlled by the nervous system. The **muscular system** controls movement of the skeleton and movement within organs. Three types of muscle exist: striated (voluntary), smooth (involuntary), and cardiac. Skeletal muscles work in pairs. The alternating contractions of muscles within a pair cause movement in joints.

The **nervous system** has two divisions: the somatic, allowing voluntary control over skeletal muscle, and the autonomic, or involuntary, controlling cardiac and glandular functions. Voluntary movement is caused by nerve impulses arising in the brain, carried by cranial or spinal chord nerves connecting to skeletal muscles. Involuntary movement occurs in direct response to outside stimulus. Involuntary responses are called reflexes. Various nerve terminals called receptors constantly send impulses to the central nervous system. There are three types of receptors:

Exteroceptors: Pain, temperature, touch, and pressure receptors

Interoceptors: Internal environment receptors

Proprioceptors: Movement, position, and tension receptors

Each receptor routes nerve impulses to specialized areas of the brain for processing.

The energy required for sustenance of the human body is supplied by food. The **digestive system** receives and processes food. The digestive system includes the mouth, esophagus, stomach, large intestine, and small intestine. The **excretory system** eliminates wastes from the body. Excretory organs include the lungs, kidneys, bladder, large intestine, rectum, and skin. The lungs excrete gaseous waste. The kidneys filter blood and excrete wastes, mostly in the form of urea. The bladder holds liquid wastes until they can be eliminated through the urethra. The large intestine absorbs water from solid food waste, and the rectum stores solid waste until it can be eliminated. The skin excretes waste through perspiration.

The **circulatory system** is responsible for internal transport in the body. It is composed of the heart, blood vessels, lymph vessels, blood, and lymph. The **immune system** is important for health and indeed life. The body defends itself against foreign proteins and infectious microorganisms by means of a complex dual system that depends on recognizing a portion of the surface pattern of the invader. Lymphocytes and antibody molecules are generated to destroy the invader molecules. The **respiratory system** performs the essential process of respiration. In humans, respiration involves the expansion and contraction of the lungs. Some animals, however, make use of gills and other means of respiration. The **reproductive system** is essential for the continuance of life in animals and in humans.

Identifying Parts and Sequences of Biogeochemical Cycles of Common Elements in the Environment

The amount of oxygen and carbon dioxide in the air remains the same as a result of the **carbon dioxide–oxygen cycle**. To make food, green plants take in carbon dioxide from the air. The waste product that plants give off in the process is oxygen. When animals breathe in oxygen to digest their food, they give off carbon dioxide as a waste product.

The amount of nitrogen in the air remains constant as a result of the **nitrogen cycle**. Nitrogen-fixing bacteria live in the soil and in the roots of legumes (for example, beans, peas, and clover). Bacteria change the nitrogen in the air (that plants cannot use) into nitrogen materials that plants can use. After animals eat plants, they give off waste materials that contain nitrogen. Bacteria in the soil act on the animals' waste materials and on dead plants and animals, breaking them down and making the remaining nitrogen available. **Nitrifying bacteria** return the nitrogen to the soil for plants to use. **Denitrifying bacteria** change some of the nitrogen in the materials and the dead plants and animals to free nitrogen, which returns to the air and continues the nitrogen cycle.

The air today is different in composition from what it was when the earth was formed. Large amounts of hydrogen and helium characterized the composition of air millions of years ago. As the earth cooled, water vapor, carbon dioxide, and nitrogen became components of the air. When the water vapor condensed, carbon dioxide and nitrogen remained. The plants reduced the amount of carbon dioxide in the air and increased the amount of oxygen in the air. Today pollution is changing the composition of the air.

SCIENCE SAFETY AND EQUIPMENT

Identifying the Appropriate Laboratory Equipment for Specific Activities

A variety of tools or instruments are used in scientific experimentation. These include microscopes, scales, graduated cylinders, meter sticks, micrometers, voltmeters, and ammeters. In general, these devices measure mass, volume, length, and voltage.

Inherent to the proper use of measuring devices is a recognition of their limitations in accuracy and precision. Precision concerns the number of places that one can reliably read from any measurement device. For example, a meter stick is generally good to three-place precision, the first two places being determined by scale markings and the third place determined by the estimated position between scale markings.

Scientific process skills, including the proper and accurate use of laboratory equipment, are an important component of science education. Instruction is necessary to guide the effective use of each measurement or observation tool: rulers, microscopes, balances, laboratory glassware, and so forth. As students develop their measuring skills, they move from simple observations and conformist activities to using these tools to find answers to questions that they develop themselves.

Safety Procedures for Teaching Science

Rules and regulations on safety procedures for teaching science may change. It is important to review the current rules and regulations. Some general rules are listed here:

Handling Living Organisms Safely

- Live vertebrates are not appropriate for elementary students, except for observation.

- Students should not touch or handle reptiles; the animals may carry *Salmonella* bacteria.

- Some plants may be toxic and should not be used in the classroom.

- Wash hands after handling plants and animals.

- Use gloves when handling animals that might bite or scratch.

- Generally, children should not bring pets to class. If they are brought, only the owner should handle the animals.

- Treat animals with care and respect.

- Remember that animal hair, scales, and waste can cause allergic reactions.

- Plant and animal specimens from ponds, ditches, canals, and other bodies of water may contain microorganisms that can cause disease. Suppliers can provide cultures that are safer.

- Set aquariums on stable furniture out of traffic ways. Be sure electrical accessories are plugged into a ground fault circuit interrupter (GFCI) outlet. Ensure that thermostats and heating elements are working correctly.

Safety Equipment and Fire-Prevention Measures for Classrooms

- Teachers and students must wear eye-protective devices when using hazardous materials in activities such as heating of materials, tempering a metal, working with caustic or explosive materials, and working with hot liquids or solids.

- School boards should give out or sell plano (safety) glasses to students, teachers, and visitors.

- Fire extinguishers must be available to classrooms.

- Fire blankets must be available in each classroom where a fire hazard exists.

- Fire alarms, detector systems, lighting, and electrical outlets should be in operating condition, even in storage rooms.

- Outlets should be grounded.

- Outlets within two feet (six feet for new construction) of water supplies must have a GFCI protection device.

- All buildings must have GFCI-protected outlets.

- Extension cords must be in only continuous lengths, and must not be stapled; run through or over doors, windows, or walls; or spliced or taped.

- Adapters must be approved by the Underwriters Laboratories (UL) and must have overcurrent protection with a total rating of no more than 15 amperes.

- Every classroom with electrical receptacles at student workstations should have an emergency shut-off switch that is unobstructed within 15 feet of the teacher's workstation.

Preparation, Use, Storage, and Disposal of Chemicals and Other Materials

An elementary classroom usually does not contain hazardous chemicals or equipment, but the following rules are necessary for classrooms where they are present:

- Rooms where students handle materials or chemicals that are harmful to human tissue must have a dousing shower, a floor drain, and an eye-washing facility.

- Rooms where students handle materials or chemicals that are harmful should have emergency exhaust systems, fume hoods, and fume hood supply fans that shut down when emergency exhaust fans are operating.

- Lockable cabinets are required for hazardous materials or hazardous chemicals.

Monitoring Guide for Chemical Storage

- Chemical storage areas must be secured with lock and key and have limited student access.

- Signs prohibiting access to students must be posted clearly.

- Chemical storage areas must be well lighted to avoid mix-ups.

- The floor space must not be cluttered.

- The area must be inventoried at least once a year. The chemical labels and the inventory list must have the name, supplier, date of purchase of mix, the concentration, and the amount available.

- Chemicals must be purged at least once a year.

- Chemical storage must use recognized storage patterns; chemicals should be stored in compatible groups—not in alphabetical order.

- Chemical storage areas must include materials to dilute and absorb a large-volume (one-gallon) chemical spill.

- Certain chemicals that present a potential for explosion are not allowed in science classrooms or chemical storage areas. These include benzoyl peroxide, phosphorus, carbon disulfide, ethyl ether, disopropyl ether, picric acid, perchloric acid, potassium chlorate, and potassium metal.

- Some chemicals present a danger as a human carcinogen and are not allowed in science classrooms or chemical storage areas. These include arsenic compounds, benzene, chloroform, nickel powder, asbestos, acrylonitrile, benzidine, chromium compound, ortho-toluidine, cadmium compounds, and ethylene oxide.

Table 6-4 and Table 6-5 are checklists for teachers to use to ensure that their classrooms are safe places for students to learn science.

Through active, hands-on activities, science instruction is made a richer and more meaningful experience. From simple observations and activities at early grades to detailed controlled experiments at higher grades, students who do science to learn science understand science better. While students are engaged in the process of discovery and exploration, the teacher must be engaged in protecting students' health and safety. The hazards vary with the discipline; thoughtful planning and management of the activities will significantly reduce the risks to students. In all cases, students must use appropriate personal hygiene (hand washing) and wear personal protective equipment (goggles, gloves) while engaged in laboratory or field activities.

Table 6-4. Checklist for Chemical Storage in Schools

Ventilation
Temperature
Heat detector
Secured
Well illuminated
Uncluttered floor
Chemical inventory
Chemicals purged annually
Chemicals grouped correctly
Labels on chemical containers
Flammables cabinet
Spill protection
No explosives
No carcinogens

Substitution of less hazardous materials whenever possible is a high priority. For example, in the physical sciences, teachers can (1) replace mercury thermometers with alcohol or electronic ones, (2) replace glass beakers and graduated cylinders with ones made of durable polyethylene, and (3) eliminate or reduce the use of hazardous chemicals. In the earth sciences, (1) rocks and minerals used in class should not contain inherently hazardous materials, (2) students should not be allowed to taste the minerals, and (3) reagents like hydrochloric acid used for identification of carbonate minerals should be dispensed from spill-proof plastic containers. In the life sciences, special care should be given to (1) safe practices with sharp objects, (2) the safe handling of living organisms, and (3) the care and use of microscopes. Experiments or activities involving the collection or culture of human cells or fluids should be discouraged and proper sterilization procedures followed to prevent the growth or spread of disease agents. When possible, field activities like visiting nature centers or other outdoor facilities or museums can bring valuable enrichment to the science curriculum in all disciplines. However, the teacher must assume responsibility for planning and implementing activities that not only increase students' learning but also maintain their health and safety.

Table 6-5. Checklist for Science Classroom

Fire extinguisher
Fire blanket
Gas cut-off (present and labeled)
Water cut-off (present and labeled)
Electrical cut-off (present and labeled)
Dousing shower
Floor drain
Eye-washing facility
Room ventilation adequate
Fume hood
Grounded receptacles
Ground fault circuit interrupters where students are likely to be in contact with water or conductive liquids
No flammable storage
Face protection meet standards
Face protection in sufficient numbers
Face protection sanitized

SCIENCE AND TECHNOLOGY

Identifying the Interrelationship of Science and Technology

Technology can be loosely defined as the application of science for the benefit of people. For political, geographic, and economic reasons, not all people have the same ready access to clean, safe water supplies or to adequate food supplies, despite the technological capabilities that basic science has provided. Science certainly can be beneficial, but arguably it can also harm humankind and the environment.

Science gives us the knowledge and tools to understand nature's principles; that knowledge can often be applied for some useful purpose. Few would debate the benefits of the wheel and axle, the electric light, the polio vaccine, and plastic. The benefits of science and technology become more complicated to evaluate when discussing the applications of gene splicing for genetically modified foods, of cloning, of nuclear energy to replace fossil fuels, or of atomic energy to prepare weapons of mass destruction. Science can tell us how to do something, not whether we should.

PRAXIS Pointer

> **Study the directions and format of the practice tests. Become familiar with the structure of the test so that you can save time. This way, you can also cut your chances of experiencing any unwanted surprises.**

Scientific literacy helps us participate in the decision-making process of our society as well-informed and contributing members. Real-world decisions have social, political, and economic dimensions; scientific information can often support or refute those decisions. Understanding that the inherent nature of scientific information is unbiased and based on experimental evidence that can be reproduced by any laboratory under the same conditions can help us all make better decisions, recognize false arguments, and participate fully as active and responsible citizens.

The science teacher should incorporate the effective use of technology to plan, organize, deliver, and evaluate instruction for all students. Moreover, the effective teacher includes resources of all types in the curriculum-planning process. As mentioned in previous chapters, among the resources educators should be very familiar with are the school library, the city or county library, education service center resources, and the library of any college or university in the area.

Teachers should have lists of all audiovisual aids that they can borrow, such as kits, films, filmstrips, videos, laser discs, and computer software. All audiovisual aids should be related to curricular objectives. Many librarians have keyed their resources to objectives in related subject areas, making it easy for teachers to incorporate them into their lessons. However, the teacher should be sure to preview and approve all resources before using them with a class. The list of resources to accompany a lesson or unit should ideally be a part of the curriculum guide or the lesson plan.

Presentations

Although it is very likely that prospective teachers have had some background in instructional design, some basic guidelines for creating and presenting effective slide presentations are worth repeating (Truehaft 1995). First, it is important that teachers consider the purpose of the presentation: what is the message? Teachers should avoid the temptation to include "bells and whistles" or any advanced technology so dazzling that it detracts from the message.

Second, it is important for the presentation to be consistent; that is, the transitions from slide to slide should, in general, be the same. The backgrounds (or templates) should remain the same. Typefaces and font sizes should be consistent. The use of color to high-light or separate text should also be consistent.

Third, students must be able to see clearly and read easily. The type size must be large enough. Projecting a presentation onto a television screen causes the images to appear smaller than when an LCD projector is used. To ensure that the presentation is easy to read, the teacher should limit the amount of text on each slide. Students may find it dif-ficult to read a slide with more than six or eight lines of type on it. Lots of "white space" gives a presentation a clean, easy-to-read appearance. The teacher should use just one or two kinds of fonts. For small pieces of text (titles or labels, for example), a sans serif typeface may be best (such as **Arial** or **Helvetica**); however, if you have long passages of text, a serif typeface (such as **Times New Roman** or **Bookman**) is easier to read.

Just as it is desirable to limit the amount of text on a slide and to limit the fonts used, it is also important to limit the number of graphic elements used. Each slide should include only one or two graphics and one message or main point. Visibility is a primary consider-ation. Whether the text is readable depends on the contrast between the text color and the background. It is best to use dark text on a light background or vice versa (such as black on white or white on black). An accent color (such as red) can emphasize important points.

Before making a presentation, the teacher must ensure that all equipment is function-ing and that he or she knows how to use the computer and the projection-device controls. If using sound, the teacher should check the volume. To maintain students' attention, the teacher must be fully in charge of the presentation.

Computers

When computers first appeared in classrooms, they were primarily used to give stu-dents drill and practice in simple skills like arithmetic operations. As the technology advanced, elaborate systems of practice and testing with management capabilities enabled teachers to track student achievement.

Drill-and-practice software is useful for students who need considerable practice in certain skills because it gives students immediate feedback; they need not wait for the teacher to correct their papers to know if they chose the correct answers. Many of these programs have game formats to make the practice more interesting. One disadvantage of drill-and-practice software is that they generally employ lower-level learning.

Tools and Technology Used for Data Collection and Problem Solving

Reliability of data obtained in any experiment is always a concern. At issue is reproducibility and accuracy. In general, data must be **reproducible** by the experimenter and others using the same apparatus. Results that cannot be reproduced are suspect. **Accuracy** is often limited by the measurement instruments used in the experiment. Any reported numerical result must always be qualified by the uncertainty in its value. A typical example might be a voltage meter readout of 3.0 volts. If the meter has a full-scale reading of 10 volts and accuracy of 3 percent, the actual value could be anywhere between 2.7 volts and 3.3 volts.

Computer programs and on-line resources make data collection and problem solving easier and more accurate. Compared to the goose quill, the modern ballpoint pen is a dramatic advancement in the technology of written communication. However, neither replaces the critical, analytical, and creative act of authorship. Likewise, although many tools are available to assist in observation, data collection, analysis, and the presentation of scientific information, no technology can replace the role of the investigator who must formulate meaningful questions, perform critical analyses, reach meaningful conclusions, and recognize how to use scientific tools effectively. Technology provides the tools on which all of modern science is based. By making some of these tools available in their classrooms, teachers give students the opportunity to participate firsthand in the process of inquiry and discovery.

Technology used in the classroom must facilitate student learning, remove barriers to understanding, and prevent the creation of new barriers that might delay or obscure the scientific concepts being taught. Scientific process skills, including the proper and accurate use of laboratory equipment, are an important component of science education. Instruction is necessary to guide the effective use of each measurement or observational tool: rulers, microscopes, balances, laboratory glassware, and so forth. As students develop these skills, they move from simple observations to using these tools to find answers to questions that they develop themselves.

TECHNOLOGY IN THE CLASSROOM

Identifying the Purposes and Functions of Common Computer Software

Many software tools are extremely useful for teachers and students. **Word-processing programs** allow students to write, edit, and polish written assignments, such as term papers and research reports. Most programs include spelling and grammar checkers that enable students to enhance the quality of their written assignments. With most word processors, students can put the text into columns topped by headlines of varying sizes to produce periodic newsletters. For example, a class could write a series of reviews of scientific articles and add information about class activities in science. **Desktop-publishing programs** allow students to integrate text and graphics to produce more complex publications like a school newspaper or yearbook.

Databases are like electronic file cards; they allow students to input data and then retrieve it in various formats and arrangements. For example, science students can input data about an experiment on temperature, volume, or time, for instance, and then manipulate the data to call out information in a variety of ways. The most important step in learning about databases is dealing with huge quantities of information. Students need to learn how to analyze and interpret the data to discover connections among isolated facts and figures and how to eliminate unnecessary information.

On-line databases are essential tools for research. Students can access databases related to science as well as many other subject areas. Through electronic mail (e-mail), students can communicate over the computer with scientific associations and scientists from around the world. Massive bibliographic databases are also available to help students and teachers find the resources they need. One can usually obtain many of the print materials through interlibrary loan. The use of electronic systems can geometrically increase the materials available to students.

Spreadsheets are similar to teacher grade books. One can link rows and columns of numbers to produce totals and averages. Formulas can connect information in one cell (the intersection of a row and column) to another cell. Teachers often keep grade books on a spreadsheet because of the ease in updating information. Once formulas are in place, teachers can enter grades and have completely up-to-date averages for all students. Some spreadsheet programs also include charting functions that enable teachers to display class averages on a bar chart and thus provide a visual comparison of performance among various classes. Several stand-alone graphing and charting software packages are also available.

Students can use spreadsheets to collect and analyze numerical data, sort the data in various orders, and create various types of graphs, bars, columns, scatter plots, histograms, and pies to convey information. Students can use the graphics they produce to enhance written reports or in multimedia presentations.

Computer-Assisted Instruction

In the past, teachers used computers strictly for **drill-and-practice** lessons, giving students an alternative to printed worksheets to practice simple skills like arithmetic operations. Publishers developed many elaborate systems of practice and testing with management systems that enabled teachers to keep track of students' progress. As mentioned earlier, drill-and-practice software is useful for students who need to hone basic skills. One advantage of these programs is the immediate feedback they provide to students; they know if they chose the correct answer without having to wait for the teacher to correct their papers. Many drill-and-practice programs have game formats to make students' practice sessions more interesting. One disadvantage of the programs is they generally require low-level thinking skills.

Tutorials are a step above drill-and-practice programs because they also include explanations and information. A student makes a response, and then the program branches to the most appropriate section based on the student's answer. Tutorials often help with remedial work but are also useful for instruction in any topic—for instance, the metric system. Improved graphics and sound allow non-English-speaking students to listen to correct pronunciation while viewing pictures of words. Tutorials can supplement, not supplant, teacher instruction.

Selection and Evaluation Criteria

The effective teacher uses criteria to evaluate audiovisual, multimedia, and computer resources. The first thing to look for is congruence with lesson goals. If the software does not reinforce student outcomes, the teacher should not use it, no matter how flashy or well crafted it is. A checklist for instructional computer software could include appropriate sequence of instruction, meaningful student interaction with the software, learner control of screens and pacing, and motivation. Other factors to consider are the ability to control sound and progress, effective use of color, clarity of text and graphics, and potential as an individual or group assignment.

In addition to congruence with curriculum goals, the teacher needs to consider students' strengths and needs, their learning styles or preferred modalities, and their interests. Students' needs can be determined through formal or informal assessment. Most standardized tests include an indication of which objectives the student did not master. Students can receive help in mastering these objectives from computer or multimedia aids.

Identifying Ways Technology Can Be Used by Students to Represent Understanding of Science Concepts

Graphics or paint programs allow students to produce freehand drawings of cells viewed under a microscope, plants or animals observed outdoors, or other images. Students can use these programs to illustrate classroom presentations, individual research projects, or multimedia presentations. Many word-processing programs have some graphic functions.

Simulations or **problem-solving programs** provide opportunities for students to have experiences that otherwise could not take place in the classroom because of time or cost constraints or simply because the classroom setting does not allow for such experiences. For example, several simulation programs available give students the opportunity to "dissect" animals. Using the program rather than attempting to perform real dissections saves time and materials, is less messy, and allows students who might be reluctant to dissect real animals to learn about them. Other software might explore the effects of weightlessness on plant growth, a situation that would be impossible to set up in the classroom lab.

Students may even teach each other through multimedia presentations. Students in an inquirer role often take responsibility for their own learning by planning, carrying out, and presenting research and projects.

Demonstrating Knowledge of Legal and Ethical Practices as They Relate to Information and Technological Systems

Computer technology is becoming a larger focus of the classroom. In addition to being part of the curriculum, educators frequently use computers as aids in storing information and developing lesson materials. Computer software programs and databases fall under the domain of copyright law. As defined by federal law, computer programs, such as a word-processing software or graphic design programs, are "a set of statements or instructions to be used directly in a computer in order to bring about a certain result" (Public Law 96-517, Section 117).

Often a teacher will make a backup, or copy, of a computer program, in case the original disk containing the program becomes damaged. A backup copy is not considered an infringement of the copyright law as long as the teacher follows these rules when creating the backup:

1. The teacher must make the new copy or adaptation only to facilitate use of the program in conjunction with the machine.

2. The new copy or adaptation must be for archival purposes only, and all archival copies must be destroyed in the event that continued possession of the computer program should cease to be rightful.

3. Any copies prepared or adapted may not be leased, sold, or otherwise transferred without the authorization of the software copyright owner. Copies of a computer program cannot be shared or borrowed. The original disk should not be used to install a program on more than one machine unless the owner has a license to do so from the computer software company. If unsure about the licensing status of a computer program, the teacher can check with the media specialist or school administrator.

Teachers are role models for their communities; therefore, all educators must be aware of the software copyright law and be in complete compliance.

The Internet

The Internet and the World Wide Web have a profound effect on students and teachers alike. This very powerful learning tool is best viewed as a source of information. By linking computers around the world, the Internet serves as a network of networks. From 500 hosts in 1983, the Internet has rapidly grown to about 541 million hosts in 2008, and the number continues to mount at a dramatic rate. At the start of the twenty-first century, an estimated 360 million people had access to the Internet; today there are over 1.4 billion Internet users (Internet World Stats 2008).

Oscar Wilde once argued that there is no such thing as a good or bad book and that a work of literature exists apart from issues of morality. The same logic could be applied to the Internet. Like any source of information, the Internet can be used well or badly. The amount of information available is so enormous that people often have difficulty finding the exact information they are seeking. Moreover, because no form of quality control exists to filter the massive amounts of information posted on the Internet, much of what is available is inaccurate, misleading, or false. Consequently, teachers must instruct students in using critical-thinking skills to judge the accuracy of information, look for evidence and substantiation of claims, and separate facts from opinions. Educators and parents alike must also be concerned about the appropriateness of the information accessed by students; a wide range of material is available and some of it is unsuitable for children.

To safeguard children and provide some kind of quality control, federal law requires public schools to use Internet filters. These tools are designed to limit access to unsuitable material; however, some of the filters do not discriminate adequately, so that questionable material may still be accessed while some acceptable material may be blocked. Thus, teachers must carefully supervise students' use of this powerful resource.

The Internet offers many tools that classroom teachers will find valuable. Basically, teachers should be familiar with common Internet browsers (such as Microsoft Internet Explorer and Netscape) and popular search engines (such as Yahoo!, Excite, Lycos, and Google) that make it possible to research any topic. Many Web sites offer teaching tips and tools, so teachers will want to investigate these and bookmark the ones that are most pertinent and reliable. Communicating with colleagues, parents, and even students is made convenient through e-mail. The Internet, then, is a common tool of the twenty-first century, used by both teachers and students. Internet sites are constantly being developed and renovated, so sites that are popular today may be gone tomorrow. However, the following sites have been popular with teachers for many years:

- U.S. Department of Education: *www.ed.gov/*

- Texas Education Agency: *www.tea.state.tx.us/*

- Education World: *www.education-world.com/*

- National Education Association: *www.nea.org/*

- DiscoveryChannel/Education: *http//school.discovery.com/teachingtools/teachingtools.html*

- TeachersFirst: *www.teachersfirst.com/*

Protecting Children Accessing the Internet

As teachers discover more ways to use the Internet as an instructing tool, they must also be mindful of the Children's Internet Protection Act (CIPA) and the Neighborhood Children's Internet Protection Act (N-CIPA), which passed Congress in December 2000. Both were part of a large federal appropriations measure (Public Law 106-554). The legislation established three basic requirements that schools and libraries using the Internet must meet, or be "undertaking actions" to meet:

1. The school or library must use blocking or filtering technology on all computers with Internet access. The blocking or filtering must protect against access to certain visual depictions, including obscenity, child pornography, and materials harmful to minors. The law does not require the filtering of text.

2. The school or library must adopt and implement an Internet safety policy that addresses the key criteria, including

   a. access by minors to inappropriate matter on the Internet and the Web

   b. the safety and security of minors when using electronic mail, chat rooms, and other forms of direct electronic communications

   c. unauthorized access, including so-called hacking, and other unlawful activities by minors on-line

   d. unauthorized disclosure, use, and dissemination of personal identification information regarding minors

   e. measures designed to restrict minors' access to materials harmful to minors

3. The school or library must hold a public meeting to discuss the Internet safety policy; specifically, the law requires that the school or library "provide reasonable public notice and hold at least one public hearing or meeting to address the proposed Internet safety policy."

REFERENCES

Blough, Glenn O., and Julius Schwartz. *Elementary School Science and How to Teach It.* New York: Rhinehart and Winston, 1969.

Children's Internet Protection Act (CIPA), Public Law No. 106-554 (2000) (codified at 20 U.S.C. § § 6801, 6777, 9134 [2003]; 47 U. S. C. § 254 [2003]).

Computer Software Copyright Act, Public Law Number 96-517, § 10(b), 94 Stat.3028 (1980) (codified at 17 U. S. C. § 117 [1988]).

Copyright. U.S. Code, Title 17. Enacted July 30, 1947, Ch. 391, 61 Stat. 652. Revised in its entirety by Public Law 94-553, Title I, Section 101, October 19, 1976, 90 Stat. 2541.

Digital Performance Right in Sound Recordings Act of 1995 amended section 106 by adding paragraph (6). Public Law No. 104-39, 109 Stat. 336. In 1999, a technical amendment substituted "121" for "120." Public Law No. 106-44, 113 Stat. 221, 222. The Intellectual Property and High Technology Technical Amendments Act of 2002 amended section 106 by substituting sections "107 through 122" for "107 through 121" Public Law No. 107-273, 116 Stat. 1758, 1909.

Internet World Stats. *www.internetworldstats.com* (Accessed June 19, 2008).

Truehaft, J. "Multimedia Design Considerations." Using Technology in Education. Algonquin College, 1995. *www.algonquincollege.com/edtech/mmdesign.html.*

U.S. Congress. Children's Internet Protection Act. 106th Congress. *www.cybertelecom. org/cda/cipatext.htm.*

U.S. Copyright Law. U.S. Copyright Office, Library of Congress. *www.copyright. gov/title17/.*

Victor, Edward. *Science for the Elementary School.* New York: Macmillan, 1975.

Walker, John, ed. *The War of the Worlds by H. G. Wells. www.fourmilab.ch/etexts/ www/warworlds/b1c1.html,* 1995 (Accessed June 9, 2008).

Wells, H. G. *The War of the Worlds by H. G. Wells.* New York: Harper & Brothers, 1898.

CHAPTER 7

Basic Concepts in Art, Music, and Physical Education

ART

Elements of Art and Principles of Design

Ideas, meanings, and human emotions are varied and numerous. To respond to these many stimulations, students must have knowledge of and be able to use many of the elements of art (the things that make up a painting, drawing, or design) and the basic principles of design (what one does with the elements of design). These are the basic principles:

Line: Linear mark from a pen or brush; the edge created where two shapes meet.

Color: Hue. There are three primary colors (red, yellow, blue) and three secondary colors (green, orange, violet); tertiary colors are colors that fall between primary and secondary colors, and compound colors are those containing a mixture of the three primary colors. In addition, complimentary colors are those that lie opposite each other on the color wheel, and saturated colors are those that lie around the outside of the color wheel.

Shape: Self-contained, defined area of a form (geometric or organic). A positive shape in a painting automatically results in a negative shape. Whenever you put any kind of mark or image on the page, you create two shapes: the named shape is the positive shape and the leftover shape is the negative shape. If you make the letter *A* on a page, the letter is the positive shape and the rest of the page is the negative shape. We become so accustomed to seeing the positive image that it is difficult to focus on the negative image.

Form: Total structure; a synthesis of all the visible aspects of a structure or design; all the elements of a work of art independent of their meaning.

Texture: The surface quality of a shape. These qualities include rough, smooth, soft, hard, and glossy. Texture can be physical (felt with the hand; e.g., a buildup of paint, layering, etc.) or visual (giving the illusion of texture; e.g., the paint gives the impression of texture, but the surface remains smooth and flat).

Balance: Similar to balance in physics. For example, a large shape close to the center can be balanced by a smaller shape that is close to the edge; a large light-toned shape can be balanced on the surface by a small dark-toned shape.

Movement: A way of combining elements of art to produce the appearance of action; a representation of or suggestion of motion; implied motion.

Strategies to Develop Creative Responses

To respond creatively through art to text images, music and visual suggestions, and speech and movement ideas, students need a variety of techniques and media. This means that they must work with many art forms. Ideally, even the child in the earliest grades engages in drawing, painting, designing, constructing crafts, sculpting, weaving, finger painting, and—to a limited extent—Styrofoam carving. In grades 3 through 5, students should work further with drawing, painting, designing, constructing crafts, and sculpting and should start new techniques like printmaking, sponge painting, graphics, film animation, and environmental design. In the upper-elementary grades, students should continue with the earlier activities, media, and techniques and add jewelry making and intaglio. ?

Materials and Tools for Developing Basic Skills

Both large and small motor skills are involved in art activities. For example, students might use larger motor skills in painting a mural on a cement-block fence than in painting a small clay figure.

Art materials for the elementary art program include scissors, wet and dry brushes, fabrics, wrapping paper, film, computers, clay, glue, Styrofoam, construction paper, crayons, beads, and much more (South Carolina Visual and Performing Arts Curriculum Framework Writing Team 1993).

Strategies and Materials to Assess Artistic Skills

The overall goals of art education include

- developing aesthetic perception

- providing opportunities to examine many art forms of both natural and human in form

- providing opportunities to reflect on and discuss observations and reactions

- providing opportunities to develop and extend their own art abilities

- providing opportunities to identify symbols and characteristics of art, objects of arts, and natural art forms

- increasing awareness of tactile art

- fostering the ability to select and enjoy arts (natural and human made)

- promoting the ability to analyze and enjoy forms based on informed judgments

Critiquing a Work of Art Using Vocabulary Appropriate for Description, Analysis, Interpretation, and Evaluation

Students should be able to describe a work of art using terms like *line*, *color*, *value*, *shape*, *balance*, *texture*, *repetition*, and *rhythm*. Students should be able to discuss some of the major periods in the history of the visual arts. It is important that students be able to confront a work and judge its aesthetic merits, regardless of their ability to recognize it from memory. Analytical questions a teacher might ask include the following:

- What is the purpose of the work? Religious? Entertainment? Philosophical? Emotional? Didactic? Pure form? Social or political commentary?

- To what culture does it belong, and to what geographical region and period? How does it reflect that context?

- Is its origin and/or function popular or commercial?

- Does it derive organically from the needs or celebratory functions of a community, or is it a self-conscious artistic creation of one individual?

- What style is it in? For example, is the music baroque, classical, or romantic? Is it influenced by ethnic or popular music?

Often after answering such questions, some students might be able to determine the specific artist by putting all the clues together, as in a detective story.

Identifying Characteristics of Style in Works of Art

A **style** is an artist's manner of expression. When a group of artists during a specific period (usually a few months, years, or decades) have a common style, it is called an **art movement**. Art movements seem to occur only in the West and may occur in both visual art and architecture.

Identifying Strategies for Developing Students' Analytical Skills to Evaluate Works of Art

To judge the quality of a work of visual art—whether it is or is not good art—students need to consider the following questions:

- Does the work achieve its purpose?

- Has the artist spoken with a unique voice, regardless of style, or could this artwork just as easily be the work of someone else?

- Is the style appropriate to the expressed purpose of the work?

- Is the work memorable and distinctive?

- Has the artist used all the technical elements available to the particular discipline with accomplished skill?

Any activity that encourages children to use their thinking skills can help students develop the analytical skills needed to evaluate visual arts. The thinking skills, according to Benjamin Bloom's Taxonomy (Krathwohl, Bloom, and Masia 1964), proceed from knowledge, comprehension, application, analysis, and synthesis to evaluation. The skill of **analysis** requires looking at the parts that make up the whole. Viewing many types of art, examining the works of many artists, and experimenting with various media themselves help students to analyze art forms. Using the vocabulary associated with art helps them form and express their opinions.

MUSIC

Music is the arrangement of sounds for voice and musical instruments and, like dance and visual art, requires training and repetitive practice. For most of history, music has been an outgrowth of a community's or an ethnic group's need to celebrate; it is often linked to storytelling or poetry. In Europe, a system of musical notation developed during the Middle Ages, and the use of notation (written symbolic indications of pitch and duration of tones) is a convenient way to distinguish "art" (or classical, or complexly composed) music from folk and ethnic music.

Traditional instruments have been indigenous variations on drums, horns, pipes (such as flutes), and hollow boxes fitted with vibrating strings (such as lyres or lutes). Since the seventeenth century, orchestral instruments of the West have multiplied to include pianos, saxophones, clarinets, cellos, and, in our own era, electronic synthesizers.

Table 7-1. Art Strategies, Materials, Skills, Techniques, Creativity, and Communication

Grades	Strategies	Materials	Skills	Techniques	Creativity	Communication
Kindergarten–2	Provide a wide variety of art: natural and human-made forms	Use art materials in the art room and classroom	Use terms such as *line, color, value, shape, balance, texture, repetition,* and *rhythm*	Try various art media and produce art forms	Experiment with various art supplies	Create feelings, ideas, and impressions through art products
	Experiment with art materials	Use art forms from nature and humans, slides, art shows, visiting guests, trips, the computer, etc.	Respond to art	Behave as a responsible member of an audience	Create simple art projects	Use art terms and concepts to express thoughts about art
	Provide opportunities to view art in the classroom, the art room, and elsewhere		Describe feelings and ideas while viewing art	Use an art program to locate exhibits at an art show	Respond to art in an individual way	
			Use various art materials to produce art in the art room and classroom			
			Use a program from an art exhibit			
			Practice acceptable behavior at an art exhibit or as a member of an audience			
3–5	Provide occasions to experience art of many periods and many cultures through art exhibits, computer, slides, speakers, etc.	Use actual art materials in the classroom and art room	Continue to use terms such as *line, color, value, shape, balance, texture, repetition,* and *rhythm*	Try various art media and produce art forms	Encourage to express self through art	Create art using various materials to express self
		Use actual art forms from speakers and teacher	Continue to respond to art	Behave as a responsible member of an audience	Encourage to create art	Create original art
					Encourage to improvise	Hear, read, and learn about careers in art

Grade				
	Experiment with ways to produce art using many media	View slides; use computer programs, etc. Attend programs and study written programs	Become more adept at describing feelings and ideas while producing and viewing art Continue to use various art materials to produce art in the art room and classroom Use a program from an art exhibit Practice acceptable behavior at an art exhibit or as a member of an audience Distinguish between classical and popular art	Use an art program to locate exhibits at an art show Describe feelings about own art and the art of others Encouraged to respond to art	Practice basic etiquette for showing own art and as a member of an audience Read art programs Express ideas about origin, culture, etc., of art
6–8	Provide occasions to view art of many cultures and many periods through exhibits, slides, books, computer searches, speakers, etc. Encourage to respond to art and create own art Communicate orally and in written form about art Use a range of types of art	Use many art media, including those for weaving, film, crafts, etc. Reseach and access art through compact discs (CDs), Internet searches, slides, books, etc. Study programs for art shows Attend exhibits and guest speaker lectures	Use art to express self Use many different art media to produce many art forms Identify major artists, media, and periods	Produce simple art products Demonstrate understanding of terms when others use them Use correct terminology Read about art	Realize that art can be a career Produce an original art piece for display Express a feeling for an event by producing art Analyze art Talk about ways that art can be used as a career

Identifying the Elements of Music

There are several elements of music:

Rhythm: The contrast among the various lengths of musical tones. For instance, in "The Star-Spangled Banner," the rhythm is short, short, medium, medium, medium, long.

Harmony: The vertical aspect of the groups of notes. The sheet music uses simultaneous combinations of musical tones to indicate harmony.

Melody: The succession of the notes. Melody is the horizontal aspect of the notes. Sometimes the teacher may refer to the melody as the *tune*.

Form: The structure of the song, or the way that it is put together. Sometimes there is a refrain that is repeated; sometimes there is a chorus that is used after each verse.

Texture: The context in which simultaneous sounds occur. The sounds can be chords (harmony) or even counterpoint (concurrent melodies of equal importance).

Timbre or tone: The quality of the musical sound.

Dynamics: The volume or the loudness of the sound or the note. The two basic dynamic indications are *p* (for *piano*, meaning softly or quietly) and *f* (for *forte*, meaning loudly or strong).

These elements work together to express a text, ideas, certain emotions, settings, time, and place through music.

Identifying Appropriate Vocal Literature for Children

Children's **vocal ranges** vary from one child to the next. However, in a 1979 study, Sylvesta ("Sally") Wassum found that first-grade children had a vocal range of one octave, 64 percent were able to sing as high as C_5 (C_4 is middle C), and 90 percent could sing as low as C$_4$. Of the singers in sixth grade, 98 percent had a vocal range of an octave or more; 52 percent could vocalize two octaves or more.

The voice ranges of girls and boys remain about the same until the boys' voices begin to change—usually, sometime during junior high. When selecting vocal literature (music for singing), the teacher must consider the age-appropriate range of the students and their vocal abilities.

The materials used for a quality music program in any grade should reflect various musical periods and styles, cultural and ethnic diversity, and a gender balance. The goal of a quality music program is to make students aware that music is both a part of and a reflection of many cultures and many ethnic groups. The teacher should provide and encourage students to sing, play, and listen to music of many cultural and ethnic groups. The teacher should include diverse **styles** (basic musical languages) and **genres** (categories); the main musical styles are discussed later in the chapter.

Developmentally Appropriate Singing Techniques

The voices of singing children should sound as if they are "floating out" rather than forced. To help students achieve the preferred sound, the teacher might ask students to imagine trying to support a feather fluttering a few inches from their mouths.

Posture is an important part of good singing. Children should not slouch when they are singing; they should stand or sit erectly as they sing. An excellent way to attain the desired straight spine is to have the students stand. Standing helps to allow for sufficient breath.

Inhaling the **breath** should mimic directing it to the area just below the rib cage; as the child takes in a breath, the wall of the child's abdomen should move out. The expansion that is necessary for the inhalation should not come from raising the shoulders or from puffing up the chest; instead, the inhalation should result from the diaphragm moving toward the waistline. Because the flow of air should be steady, the child's mouth should remain open. The child should not try to manipulate the voice box; the idea is not to sing *with* the larynx but to sing *through* the larynx (Hoffer 1982). Whether standing or sitting, children should make sure that both feet are flat on the floor. When standing, children should be certain that their hands are down at their sides or clasped loosely in front; children should not clasp their hands tightly in the back or place their hands in their pockets.

The **tone** is the musical sound of the voice; it may describe the quality of the musical sound. For instance, one might say that someone sings with a "nasal tone," a "thin tone," or a "full tone." A synonym for *tone* is *timbre*.

The voice of the average child is similar to the voice of the adult in terms of range but not quality. The teacher should not encourage children to imitate the heavier and fuller quality of the mature adult voice. Children can sing high, but as in an adult, tension results when the pitch is too high. The average voice range is from around middle C to F (fifth line); D and E-flat (fourth line and space) are, however, far more comfortable. For the beginner, a very comfortable range is from E-flat (first line) to B-flat or C.

Identifying Correct Performance Techniques for Rhythmic and Melodic Classroom Instruments

As defined earlier, *music* is the arrangement of sounds for voice and musical instruments and, like dance, requires training and repetitive practice. Making music is a basic experience. Mothers sing to their babies. Children beat sticks together, make drums, and sing during their play. Adults whistle or sing along with tunes on the radio. Sound and music naturally draw people; music is an important part of culture, religious practice, and personal experience for all people. Some people become professional musicians, whereas others whistle, sing, or play for their own enjoyment and nothing more.

It is important that students have the opportunity to experience as many ways to make music as possible. It is through the acquisition of basic skills in singing and playing instruments that people grow in their ability to express themselves through music. As students develop skills, they are also exposed to basic musical concepts such as melody, harmony, rhythm, pitch, and timbre (tone). With experience, students come to make decisions about what is acceptable or not acceptable within a given cultural or historical context and thereby develop their own aesthetic awareness. Only a very small segment of society does not make music. These people would likely choose to make music if they could but are unable as a result of a physical impairment or personal choice (e.g., a vow of silence). Music making is a natural part of human experience.

PRAXIS Pointer

Be prepared. Don't waste time on "beat-the-test" strategies. Organize a study schedule and keep to it—you will avoid test anxiety.

There is a distinction between the study of simple instruments and the study of orchestral instruments. The child does not usually begin the study of orchestral instruments until the fourth or fifth grade; a music teacher—not the classroom teacher—gives instruction in orchestral instruments. The instruments that the classroom teacher normally teaches include the **rhythmic instruments** (e.g., triangle, tambourine, blocks, and sticks), **melodic instruments** (e.g., melody bells and simple flutes), and **harmonic instruments** (e.g., chording instruments, such as the autoharp).

Rhythmic Instruments

After the students have a chance to move with the music in the manner that the music suggests and after singing games and action songs, they may be ready to try rhythmic instruments. The students will need opportunities to experiment with triangles, tambourines, sticks, and blocks, among others, to experience the sounds they make; students might try striking the tambourine with the hand to get one sound and with the knee to get another, for instance. After this experimentation, the teacher and class will be ready to try something new.

If the teacher decides on which instruments the class will use, who will use them, and when, music instruction becomes a teacher-directed activity that can stifle the children's creativity. Allowing the students to make decisions about what and when to play is a more engaging technique than the teacher-directed approach. For example, the teacher might write out a piece of music on a large sheet of paper and allow the students to draw pictures where they should play their instruments. Another student-directed approach to music instruction is first having students listen to a piece of music and then allowing them to decide on the instruments they want to play and when it seems right to play them. This more creative approach is appropriate for young children who cannot read music or even for music readers who want to produce their own performance techniques. Upper-grade students can even try making their own instruments.

Melodic Instruments

Melodic bells are melodic instruments that the child strikes with a mallet. The child may use the bells before the flutes. The simple flutes include the trade names of Flutophone, Song Flute, and Tonette. Teachers usually include these melodic instruments with the music instruction at about the fifth grade. For most of these instruments, the child supports the flute using the right thumb; to play the notes, the child covers the various holes with the fingers. The use of the fingers to help attain the sounds varies from one instrument to the other. The melodic instruments are helpful to use as the children are learning to read music.

Harmonic Instruments

The wooden base of an autoharp (which is approximately rectangular in shape) has wire strings stretched across it. The child can press the wooden bars attached at right angles; when the child presses the bars and strums the wires, the instrument produces chords. Students can experiment with harmony using the autoharp. They will find that sometimes a variety of choices of chords "sound right" but that at other times only one choice works.

Reading and Interpreting Simple, Traditional, and Nontraditional Music Notation

Music notation is a way of writing music. Teaching students to use, read, and interpret music notation will heighten their enjoyment of music. Students can begin with **simple music notation**. For example, students might try listening to a simple melody and making dashes on the board or on their papers to indicate the length the notes are held. As they sing "Three Blind Mice," for instance, they would mark dashes of similar length for the words/notes *three* and *blind*.

With **traditional music notation**, the students use the lines and spaces on the staff. They observe that there are four spaces and five lines, for instance. They also notice that the appearance of the notes indicates the length, and the placement of the notes on the staff indicates the various tones. **Nontraditional music notation** is something that many students in the upper grades may have noticed in their books. In the South, for example, many of the hymnals use a nontraditional type of music notation called shape notes. Instead of the elliptical note head in the traditional notation, the heads of the notes are in various shapes to show the position of the notes on the major scale. Another nontraditional music notation is Braille notation.

Identifying Characteristics of Style in Musical Selections

Often, after listening to a piece of music, a person might be able to determine the specific artist by putting several clues together, as in a detective story. To help students reach this level of discernment, the teacher should expose them to diverse styles (basic musical languages) and genres (categories). Dividing music into categories is difficult. Styles are constantly emerging. Many songs include multiple genres. Nevertheless, the main groupings are as follows:

- Classical
- Gospel
- Jazz
- Latin American
- Blues
- Rhythm and blues
- Rock
- Country
- Electronic

- Electronic dance
- Electronica
- Melodic
- Hip hop
- Rap
- Contemporary African
- Punk
- Reggae
- Dub

Because music often reflects the events of the time, the technology, the composer and performer(s), the beliefs, and the cultures, music changes over time. The ancient Greeks accompanied the recitation of poetry with the stringed lyre, and choral songs were heard between recited passages. In the early Christian era, plainsong, or unaccompanied religious chant, was codified and arranged with early forms of music notation by Pope Gregory the Great (late sixth century). This is the origin of Gregorian chant. By the twelfth and thirteenth centuries, the important form of polyphony, upon which the distinctive art music of the West is based, enabled supportive melodies to be added to the main chant. Throughout the later Middle Ages, both religious and secular polyphonic music was composed and melodies and rhythms became more diversified.

During the Renaissance, the spirit of humanism and rationalism pervaded polyphonic music, and music began to be seen as a mark of culture. Emphasis was placed upon secular music and dance and instrumental music ensembles.

Composers

Baroque music of the seventeenth and early eighteenth centuries employed a greater complexity of contrapuntal, or multimelodic, form, and the beginnings of harmony, the use of colorful instrumental ensembles, and great drama and emotion. Other innovative forms included the oratorio, the cantata, the sonata, the suite, the concerto, and the fugue. The great works of baroque music were composed by Antonio Vivaldi and Johann Sebastian Bach.

The greatest composers of the classical period of the latter half of the eighteenth century, marked by clarity of form, logical thematic development, and strict adherence to sonata form, were Franz Joseph Haydn and Wolfgang Amadeus Mozart. Mozart's structurally exquisite works approach perfection of form while adding to music inventive melodic diversity. The German composer Ludwig van Beethoven ushered in the romantic school of symphonic music. His symphonies and piano sonatas, concertos, and string quartets explode with dramatic passion, expressive melodies and harmonies, and complex thematic development.

Romantic composers included Frédéric Chopin, Hector Berlioz, Franz Liszt, Richard Strauss, and Felix Mendelssohn. Other important symphonic composers of the nineteenth century were Robert Schumann, Johannes Brahms, Peter Ilyich Tchaikovsky, and Gustav Mahler. Nineteenth-century music includes the use of ethnic influences or folk melodies and music of a nationalistic vein, as well as of popular song (often linked to composers who were outstanding melodists and harmonic innovators).

The concert music of the twentieth century increasingly endeavored to enlarge the boundaries of rhythm, form, and harmony, seemingly parallel to the direction in the visual arts away from traditional structure and melodic-harmonic connections with listeners and toward more personal or intellectual experiments in abstraction. Ethnic and popular influences continued to exert an important pull in the creation of twentieth-century music. Ragtime, blues, jazz, and other popular folk, dance, and commercial music provided material for some of the most innovative and exciting work in twentieth-century music. Composers after World War II experimented with tape-recorded sound (Edgard Varèse) and conceptual music based on indeterminacy or chance (John Cage).

Identifying Strategies for Developing Students' Analytical Skills to Evaluate Musical Performance

As with analyzing visual arts, any work that encourages children to use their thinking skills can help develop the analytical skills needed to evaluate musical performance. For example, a teacher might ask young children, after they played "Here We Go 'Round the Mulberry Bush," some questions requiring them to perform some very basic analysis of the music. A simple question might be, "Do you think this song would be good to march to on the playground?" Upper-elementary students might listen to *Peter and the Wolf*, by Sergei Prokofiev, and try to identify the instruments in the recording. The students might talk about why the composer used certain instruments for a character, suggest other instrument sounds for the characters, and give their justifications for the new instrument. Because these activities involve analysis, they help develop the upper-level thinking skills needed to evaluate musical performance.

Strategies and Materials to Assess Skills, Techniques, Creativity, and Communication in Music

The overall goals of music education include

- encouraging responsiveness to music

- increasing involvement in music

- aiding in music discrimination

- promoting understanding of music and music structure

- increasing listening awareness

- developing sensitivity to the expressive qualities of music

Critiquing Musical Performance Using Vocabulary Appropriate for Description, Analysis, Interpretation, and Evaluation

Although students can experience music and find it satisfying, challenging, or beautiful without prior knowledge of a piece or an understanding of its form, cultural significance, and so forth, some knowledge can enrich the experience. People respond to music naturally. They do not need prompting or help to respond. However, to share their thoughts and feelings about music, students must learn how to put their responses into musical terminology. Some people call music a language, but it does not function as a spoken language. It does not provide specific information, instructions, or reactions. Rather, music sparks thoughts, feelings, and emotions. To put their experiences into words, musicians and artists have developed vocabularies and approaches to discussing music and art. This does not mean there is only one way to respond to or talk about music or art. However, students will more easily understand music and musicians, art and artists, if they first understand and can use the kind of vocabulary and approaches that musicians or artists use to discuss their work. This includes terms as basic as *melody* and *harmony* and as profound as the *aesthetic experience*.

People cannot express themselves or effectively communicate if they do not understand the structures and rules that underlie the "language" that they are trying to use. Although music does not provide the kind of specific communication that spoken language does, it has structures. When students are able to think about and discuss music, they gain a deeper understanding of the music and can better express their responses to the music.

The aesthetic experience is what draws people to music. The experience is one that most people have had but one that some people cannot describe. In fact, words seem clumsy when it comes to something that can be so profound and wonderful. The type of music, the period, or the performer does not necessarily limit the aesthetic experience. It is equally as possible to have an aesthetic experience when listening to a child sing a simple melody as it is when listening to a professional orchestra performing a symphony by Beethoven. The important thing is to share that aesthetic experience. It is part of what makes music and art special.

There are many ways to encourage exploration of and growth through aesthetic responsiveness. A common experience is a crucial starting point. After students listen attentively to several pieces of music, the teacher might ask them to describe how each piece made them feel. It is often best for students to write their responses down before starting a discussion. Then, the teacher might ask them to explain why each piece of music made them feel the way they indicated. To the music, young students will likely provide simple, straightforward emotional responses (e.g., "It made me feel happy!"). Older students should explore why the music affected the feelings that it did and use both musical concepts (e.g., "It made me feel happy because it was in a major key") and non-musical associations (e.g., "It made me feel happy because it sounded like a circus, and I like to go to the circus"). Through this kind of sharing, along with teacher insights and readings about how other people have responded to music, students can explore and come to a deeper understanding of their personal responses to music, other art forms, and possibly the world. In addition, it should provide them with practical ways to express their responses or reactions to what they experience in life.

In addition to having aesthetic experiences, recognizing their value, and being able to grapple with discussing or sharing those experiences, teachers and students must attempt to foster an appreciation for the arts and their ability to create meaning. The arts provide an opportunity to explore and express ideas and emotions through a unique view of life experiences. It is through the experience of music, or any art form, that people begin to transcend the mundane day-to-day experience and reach beyond to a richer life experience.

When preparing for this part of the exam, you must understand that the primary objectives of music education are teaching the contexts of music, the concepts and skills involved in experiencing music, and the aesthetic and personal dimensions of music. These constitute a broad overview of the field of music and the musical experience.

Music does not exist in a vacuum. The historical or cultural context of a piece of music is very important. Students should know and be able to discuss the context of music by making connections among social studies, reading or language arts, and the fine arts. For example, when students are reading stories about the American Revolution, they should be aware that it occurred during the period known as the classical period in music history. Listening to a piece by Haydn or Mozart, talking about how they reacted to the Old World, and comparing their works to a colonial American tune by William Billings is an effective way to understand the historical, cultural, and societal contexts of music.

> *PRAXIS Pointer*
>
> **Double-check the number of the question on the test and on the answer sheet each time you mark your sheet. Marking one wrong answer can throw off your entire answer sheet and sink your score.**

Similarly, the visual art of Andy Warhol, the music of the Beatles, the assassination of John F. Kennedy, and the war in Vietnam all took place within the same approximate time frame. The teacher can ask students to find contrasts and similarities among these artistic and social events; students can attempt to find ways that the historical context affected music and ways that music affected and reflected history.

These examples from American history are easy for most to grasp quickly. However, the objective seeks to have teachers and students consider the role of music in history and culture beyond the American experience. By having students listen to music from China, Japan, Germany, Australia, or Africa when they are studying these cultures, the teacher enriches the students' learning experience and makes it more memorable for them. It is even more valuable for students to view live or videotaped performances of the music and dance of these cultures because often the music is performed in traditional costume with traditional instruments (sometimes very different from modern instruments). Seeing the costumes and the movement are an important part of understanding the culture.

PHYSICAL EDUCATION

Demonstrating Knowledge of the Interrelatedness of Physical Activity, Fitness, and Health

The axiom "Use it or lose it" certainly holds for the human body. Our bodies thrive on **physical activity**, which is any bodily movement produced by skeletal muscles and resulting in energy expenditure. Unfortunately, Americans tend to be relatively inactive. In a recent survey, 25 percent of adult Americans had not participated in any leisure-time physical activities in the past month; in 2003, 38 percent of students in grades 9 through 12 viewed television three hours or more per day (Centers for Disease Control and Prevention).

Physical fitness enables a person to meet the physical demands of work and leisure comfortably. It is a multicomponent trait related to the ability to perform physical activity. A person with a high level of physical fitness is also at lower risk of developing chronic disease.

Lack of activity can cause many problems, including flabby muscles, a weak heart, poor circulation, shortness of breath, obesity, coronary artery disease, hypertension, type 2 diabetes, osteoporosis, and certain types of cancer. Overall, mortality rates from all causes are lower in physically active people than in sedentary people. In addition, physical activity can help people manage mild-to-moderate depression, control anxiety, and prevent weakening of the skeletal system.

By **increasing physical activity**, a person may improve heart function and circulation, respiratory function, and overall strength and endurance. All of these lead to improved vigor and vitality. Exercise also lowers the risk of heart disease by strengthening the heart muscle, lowering pulse and blood pressure, and lowering the concentration of fat in both the body and the blood. It can also improve appearance, increase range of motion, and lessen the risk of back problems associated with weak bones and osteoporosis.

Table 7-2. Music Strategies, Materials, Skills, Techniques, Creativity, and Communication

Grades	Strategies	Materials	Skills	Techniques	Creativity	Communication
Kindergarten–2	Provide exposure to a wide variety of sounds: recorded music, sheet music, live performances	Play simple instruments	Classify sounds as high and low; use body to show high and low	Play simple rhythm instruments	Walk, run, jump to music	Create symbols to notate sounds of music
	Experiment with ways to change sounds	Use CDs, tapes, records	Play simple rhythm instruments	Sing, especially rote songs	Create simple songs	Use musical terms and concepts to express thoughts about music
	Use simple instruments in the classroom	Attend programs		Move in time with the music		
3–5	Provide experiences with music of many periods and many cultures	Play simple instruments	Sing rounds	Play music	Encourage students to express themselves through music	Sing and play instruments from written notation
	Experiment with ways to change sounds	Use CDs, tapes, records	Sing two-part songs by rote	Dance to music		Create own notation system
	Use simple instruments in the classroom	Attend programs and study written programs	Conduct simple songs	Conduct duple and triple meter	Encourage students to create sounds	Hear, read, and learn about careers in music
	Move to music		Move to music		Encourage students to improvise	Notate a simple phrase
			Distinguish between classical and popular music			Create a simple phrase
						Practice basic etiquette for performing and listening as part of an audience
						Read music notation

(Continued)

Table 7-2. (*Continued from previous page*)

Grades	Strategies	Materials	Skills	Techniques	Creativity	Communication
						Express ideas about origin, culture, etc., of music listened to in class
					Write notation for original song	
					Write own idea of notation for song heard	
					Read notation	
6–8	Provide occasions to listen to music of many cultures and many periods	Play simple instruments	Sing rounds	Play simple accompaniment on autoharp, guitar, etc.	Create some simple songs	
	Encourage students to respond to music and create their own music	Use CDs, tapes, records	Sing three-part songs by rote	Read some music	Create an accompaniment	
	Provide opportunities for students to communicate with notation	Attend programs and study written programs	Conduct simple songs	Use correct terminology	Create a dance	
	Use a range of instruments and types of music	Use the autoharp and/or guitar	Move to music	Perform dance steps		
			Identify major and minor scales			
			Dance			

Each person should engage in regular physical activity and reduce sedentary activities to promote health, psychological well-being, and a healthy body weight. On most days of the week, children should engage in at least 60 minutes of physical activity.

Proper hydration is important during physical activity. Two steps that help prevent dehydration during prolonged physical activity or when it is hot are (1) consuming fluid regularly during the activity and (2) drinking several glasses of water or other fluid after the physical activity is completed (U.S. Department of Agriculture [USDA]).

Nutrition and Its Role in Promoting Health

Along with exercise, a knowledge of and a participation in a healthy lifestyle are vital to good health and longevity. The elements of good nutrition, the role of vitamins, elimination of risk factors, and strategies to control weight are all part of a healthy lifestyle.

In the spring of 2005, the USDA changed the food pyramid to guide Americans in how to eat healthily. As shown in the Figure 7-1, the food pyramid has six rainbow-colored divisions. The climbing figure reminds us all to be active.

Figure 7-1. USDA Food Pyramid

Source: U.S. Department of Agriculture, Steps to a Healthier You, www.mypyramid.gov/.

The food groups indicated on the pyramid are as follows:

1. Grains

2. Vegetables

3. Fruits

4. Fats and oils

5. Milk and dairy products

6. Meat, beans, fish, and nuts

Complex carbohydrates—vegetables, fruits, high-fiber breads, and cereals—should comprise at least one-half of the diet. These foods provide fiber, which helps digestion, reduces constipation, and reduces the risk of colon cancer. Complex carbohydrates also provide water, which is vital to the entire body.

Proteins should make up about one-fifth of the diet. Proteins build and repair the body. Protein sources include fish, beans, peas, lentils, peanuts, and other pod plants; red meat contains protein, but because it is high in saturated fat, one should eat it less often. **Saturated fat** is present also in cocoa butter, palm oil, and coconut oil.

There is a link between high-fat diets and many types of cancer. Diets high in saturated fats cause the body to produce too much **low-density lipoprotein (LDL)**, which is one type of **cholesterol**. The other type of cholesterol is **high-density lipoprotein (HDL)**. Some cholesterol is essential to the brain functions and to the production of certain hormones, but too much LDL cholesterol encourages the buildup of plaque in the arteries. LDL cholesterol can be controlled through proper diet, and HDL cholesterol levels can be raised by exercise. **Triglycerides** are other types of fat in the blood that are important to monitor; triglycerides seem to be inversely proportional to HDLs.

Unsaturated vegetable fats are preferable to saturated fats. Unsaturated fats appear to offset the rise in blood pressure that accompanies too much saturated fat and may lower cholesterol and help with weight loss. Unsaturated fats are present in vegetable products. Although whole milk products contain saturated fat, the calcium they contain is vital to health. For this reason, weight-loss diets still recommend dairy products but in the form of skim milk and low-fat cheese.

Vitamins are essential to good health; however, a person must be careful not to take too much of certain vitamins. The fat-soluble vitamins, A, D, E, and K, are stored in the body, and excessive amounts will cause some dangerous side effects. All other vitamins are water soluble and are generally excreted through the urinary system and the skin when taken in excess. Here is a brief synopsis of the vitamins and minerals needed by the body:

Vitamin A: Needed for normal vision, prevention of night blindness, healthy skin, resistance to disease, and tissue growth and repair. Found in spinach, carrots, broccoli, and other dark green or yellow-orange fruits and vegetables; also found in liver and plums.

Vitamin D: Promotes absorption of calcium and phosphorous and the normal growth of healthy bones, teeth, and nails. Formed by the action of the sun on the skin. Present in halibut liver oil, herring, cod liver oil, mackerel, salmon, and tuna and is an additive to many milk products.

Vitamin E: Protects cell membranes, seems to improve elasticity in blood vessels, and may prevent the formation of blood clots and protect red blood cells from damage by oxidation. Found in wheat-germ oil, sunflower seeds, raw wheat germ, almonds, pecans, peanut oil, and cod liver oil.

Vitamin B_1 (thiamin): Helps with the functioning of nerves, muscle growth, and fertility. Also aids in the production of energy, appetite, and digestion. Found in pork, legumes, nuts, enriched and fortified whole grains, and liver.

Vitamin B_2 (riboflavin): Aids in the production of red blood cells, good vision, healthy skin, mouth tissue, and energy. Found in lean meat, dairy products, liver, eggs, enriched and fortified whole grains, and green leafy vegetables.

Vitamin B_3 (niacin): Promotes the production of energy and appetite, aids the functioning of the digestive and nervous systems, and promotes healthy skin and tongue. Present in beef liver, peanuts, chicken, salmon, and tuna.

Vitamin B$_6$ (pyridoxine): Promotes red blood cell formation and growth. Found in liver, beans, pork, fish, legumes, enriched and fortified whole grains, and green leafy vegetables.

Vitamin B$_{12}$: Promotes healthy nerve tissue, production of energy, and utilization of folic acid. Aids in the formation of healthy red blood cells. Found in dairy products, liver, meat, poultry, fish, and eggs.

Vitamin C: Promotes healing and growth, resists infection, increases iron absorption, and aids in bone and tooth formation and repair. Found in citrus fruits, cantaloupe, potatoes, strawberries, tomatoes, and green vegetables.

Minerals such as the following are also essential to good health:

Sodium: Maintains normal water balance inside and outside cells, regulates blood pressure, and balances electrolytes and chemicals. Found in salt, processed foods, bread, and bakery products.

Potassium: Maintains the volume and balance of body fluids, prevents muscle weakness and cramping, and is important for normal heart rhythm and electrolyte balance in the blood. Found in citrus fruits, leafy green vegetables, potatoes, and tomatoes.

Zinc: Promotes taste, appetite, healthy skin, and wound healing. Found in lean meat, liver, milk, fish, poultry, whole grain cereals, and shellfish.

Iron: Promotes red blood cell formation and oxygen transport to the cells, and prevents nutritional anemia. Found in liver, lean meats, dried beans, peas, eggs, dark green leafy vegetables, and whole grain cereals.

Calcium: Promotes strong bones, teeth, and nails. Helps maintain muscle tone, prevents osteoporosis and muscle cramping, and promotes sound nerve function and heartbeat. Found in milk, yogurt, and other dairy products, and dark leafy vegetables.

Phosphorus: Regulates blood chemistry and internal processes; promotes strong bones and teeth. Found in meat, fish, poultry, and dairy products.

Magnesium: Promotes energy production, helps maintain normal heart rhythm, ensures nerve and muscle function, and prevents muscle cramps. Found in dried beans, nuts, whole grains, bananas, and leafy green vegetables.

Promoting Individual Health and Wellness

One of the primary reasons for the teaching of physical education is to instill in students a willingness to exercise and to encourage students to make good decisions about their health. To that end, it is important that students understand the benefits of participating in a lifelong program of exercise and physical fitness and of avoiding the risks of choosing an unhealthy lifestyle.

Reaping the Benefits, Avoiding the Risks

Fortunately, it is not difficult to find justification for exercising and maintaining a consistently high level of fitness. The benefits of a consistent program of diet and exercise are many. Improvements in cardiac output, maximum oxygen intake, and enhancing the blood's ability to carry oxygen are just a few of these benefits.

Another aspect of physical education concerns awareness and avoidance of the risks that are present in our everyday lives. Some risk factors include being overweight, smoking, using drugs, having unprotected sex, and not eliminating excessive stress. Education is the key to minimizing the presence of these risk factors. Unfortunately, because of the presence of peer pressure and the lack of parental control, the education is sometimes not enough.

Weight-Control Strategies

Statistics show that Americans get fatter every year. Even though countless books and magazine articles are available on the subject of weight control, often the only place a student gets reliable information about diet is in a classroom. The unfortunate reality is that people who are fat do not live as long, on average, as those who are thin. Being overweight has been isolated as a risk factor in various cancers, heart disease, gall bladder problems, and kidney disease. Chronic diseases such as diabetes and high blood pressure are also aggravated by, or caused by, being overweight.

Conversely, being underweight presents a great many problems. Our society often places too much emphasis on losing weight. Women are especially prone to measuring their self-worth by the numbers they read on the bathroom scale. Ideal weight and a good body-fat ratio are the goals when losing weight. A correlation may exist between body fat and high cholesterol. Exercise is the key to a good body-fat ratio. Exercise helps keep the ratio low, improve cholesterol levels, and prevent heart disease.

To lose weight, calories burned must exceed calories consumed. No matter what kind of diet is tried, that principle applies. There is no easy way to maintain a healthy weight. Again, the key is exercise. If calorie intake is restricted too much, the body goes into starvation mode and operates by burning fewer calories. Just a 250-calorie drop a day combined with a 250-calorie burn will result in a loss of one pound a week. Crash diets, which bring about rapid weight loss, are not only unhealthy but also ineffective. Slower weight loss is more lasting. Aerobic exercise is the key to successful weight loss. Exercise speeds up metabolism and causes the body to burn calories. Timing of exercise will improve the benefits. Exercise before meals speeds up metabolism and helps suppress appetite. Losing and maintaining weight is not easy. Through education, people will be better able to realize that maintaining a healthy weight is crucial to a healthy life and should be a constant consideration.

Common Health Problems and Risk Behaviors Associated with Them

The health of students and their families depends not only on individual and family decisions about diet and exercise but also on various social factors. For example, advertising often encourages children to make unhealthy decisions. Students as young as kindergarten and first grade can learn how to recognize advertisements (e.g., for candy or sugar-laden cereal) that might lead them to unhealthy behavior. By third or fourth grade, children should be able to demonstrate that they are able to make health-related decisions regarding advertisements in various media. Teachers can encourage students to (1) avoid alcohol, tobacco, stimulants, and narcotics; (2) get plenty of sleep and exercise; (3) eat a well-balanced diet; (4) receive the proper immunizations; and (5) avoid sharing toothbrushes, combs, hats, beverages, and food with others. In addition, any study of the physical environment—in science, social studies, or other subjects—should relate to health whenever possible. Examples include:

- the effects of pollution on health

- occupational-related disease (e.g., "black lung" disease and the effects of chemicals on soldiers)

- the different health care options available to people in different parts of the world and in different economic circumstances

- differentiation between communicable and noncommunicable diseases

- the importance of even very young children washing their hands frequently

Older children should be able to explain the transmission and prevention of communicable diseases, and all children should learn which diseases cannot be transmitted through casual contact.

Choosing Developmentally Appropriate Instructional Practices

There are three areas or domains of learning:

Psychomotor domain: Pertains especially to physical activities or skills that the individual masters. For example, playing basketball demands many physical skills, including dribbling, making free throws from the free-throw line, and doing a lay-up shot.

Affective domain: Pertains to feelings and attitudes. A basketball player who enjoys playing with the other team members feels more positive about the practices and games than the player who does not enjoy playing with team members. The coach certainly wants the players to feel joy in the game they are playing.

Cognitive domain: Pertains to thinking. Some basketball coaches administer paper-and-pencil tests to be certain that the players understand the rules.

Of course, physical activities or instructional activities in the elementary school must be developmentally appropriate. The characteristics of children in grades 1 through 3 suggest that throwing the ball is easier than catching a ball; therefore, dodge ball is popular. Other characteristics of children age 6 through 8 indicate that they like large-muscle activities, games in which they can shout and chase each other, repetition of favorite games, and free play. Children in the upper-elementary grades are ready for increasing skill development, more games with rules, and activities involving tossing and catching balls.

Factors to Consider When Planning Physical Activities

When planning physical activities—or any classroom activity, for that matter—the teacher should attempt to:

- create and sustain a safe, efficient, supportive learning environment

- evaluate the appropriateness of the physical environment for facilitating student learning and promoting safety

- identify a repertoire of techniques for establishing smooth, efficient, and well-paced routines

- involve students in establishing rules and standards for behavior

- identify emergency procedures for student and campus safety

While certain physical aspects of the classroom are permanent (e.g., size and shape of the room, number of windows, type of lighting, etc.), others are changeable. Windows can have shades or blinds that distribute light correctly and allow for a darkened room for video or computer viewing. If the light switches do not allow some of the lights to remain on, sometimes schools will change the wiring system. If not, teachers can use a lamp to provide minimum lighting for monitoring students during videos or films. Schools often schedule maintenance, such as painting and floor cleaning, during the summer. Often school administrators will comply with teachers' requests for specific colors of paint if they have sufficient time for ordering a different color.

Most classrooms have movable desks, which allow for varied seating arrangements and for opening up areas of the classroom for group games or activities. However, the teacher should ensure that students cannot fall over or bump against furniture and be injured.

The equipment used in physical activities should vary according to the age of the students. For instance, large sports balls are better for young children than are small balls.

Analyzing the Influence of Culture, Media, Technology, and Other Factors When Planning Health and Wellness Instruction

All classrooms should have a bulletin board for the teacher and the students. The effective teacher has plans for changing the board according to units of study. Space for displaying students' work, either on the bulletin board, the wall, or in the hallway, is necessary.

Bare walls can be depressing; however, covering the walls with too many posters can be visually distracting. Posters with sayings that promote cooperation, rules for games, diagrams for warm-up drills, study skills, and content ideas are helpful. Teachers should change the displays several times during the school year because students will ignore them when they become too familiar.

Some physical activities require technological equipment. For instance, a dance class might need a compact disc (CD) player to play music and a video player to watch a film of a finished dance; a softball team might need a computer to check the rules of the game. Technology contributes to effective instruction.

Physical education—on the playground or in the classroom—has definite association with almost every subject in the curriculum. The opportunities for integrating physical education with other subjects in the curriculum are many. For example, students may develop an appreciation for other cultures and for other ways of life if teachers include games and dances from other cultures and other nations in their lesson plans. Teachers can integrate these activities into the curriculum or employ them in isolation during the physical education periods.

Using advertisements, public health brochures, and Web sites can help teachers when planning wellness and health instruction. Students, too, may receive or be able to locate pertinent materials; the teacher can use them as a springboard to instruction.

Chapter 7 PRAXIS II: 0011

Scoring Team, Dual, and Individual Sports

Team, dual, and individual sports all have a prominent place in a successful physical education curriculum. Since one of the attributes of a quality physical education program is its carryover value, it is easy to justify the inclusion of these activities in a curriculum. Learning the rules and keeping score supplies students with a framework for goals and for learning how to deal with both victory and defeat. Here are examples of some sports and games that are useful to achieve the aforementioned goals:

Team Sports

- Volleyball: 6 players, two out of three games. Winner scores 25 points with a margin of 2.

- Basketball: 5 players. Most points at the end of the game wins.

- Softball: 9 or 10 players. Most runs at the end of seven innings wins.

- Field hockey: 11 players. Most goals wins.

- Soccer: 11 players. Most goals wins.

- Flag football: 9 or 11 players. Six points for a touchdown, one or two for a point after, and two for a safety. (The number per team can change to accommodate the ability and size of the class.)

Dual and Individual Sports

- Tennis: Either doubles or singles. Four points: 15, 30, 40, and game. Tie at 40 (*deuce*). Winner must win by a margin of 2. Remember, *love* means 0 points in tennis.

- Badminton: Either doubles or singles. For doubles, 15 points wins; for singles, 21 points wins. Winner must win by a margin of 2.

- Table tennis: Either doubles or singles. In either case, 21 points by a margin of 2 wins.

- Shuffleboard: Either singles or doubles. Participants determine the winning score—50, 75, or 100 points—before the game begins.

ARTS AND PHYSICAL EDUCATION TEACHING STRATEGIES

Motivational Factors

Students often say that they like teachers who motivate them. Although teachers can be highly motivated themselves and demonstrate interest in the subject matter and in their students, in fact, teachers are not responsible for students' motivation. Motivation is a student's responsibility and must come from within the student. However, effective teachers will help students develop self-discipline, self-control, and self-motivation. These skills of self-management can be taught, yet the skills require a great deal of effort and practice for students to gain true proficiency in using them.

When students say that they like or want teachers who motivate them, they are probably referring to some characteristics that teachers possess that are attractive and interesting to learners. So, while it is true that teachers are not responsible for students' motivation, it is also true that teachers can influence motivation and that teachers can promote and/or inhibit motivation in the classroom by their attitudes and their actions.

Three Motivational Principles

Marcia Baxter-Magolda (1992) offers three principles to guide teachers and to lead to greater effectiveness in the classroom. Interestingly, each of these principles leads to empowering students and, thus, is motivational in nature.

Validating Students as Knowers

The first principle is to *validate students as knowers*. The basis of this principle is the idea of the active learner who brings much to the classroom (the dynamic view of human development). How can teachers validate students? Baxter-Magolda suggests that teachers display a caring attitude toward students. This means that it is appropriate for teachers to take an interest in students, to learn about their likes and dislikes, and to find out about their interests and hobbies, both in school and outside school. This also means that it is okay for teachers to show enthusiasm and excitement for their classes, for the subject matter they teach, and for the students they teach. It also means, as Carol Tavris (1994) notes, that it is good for teachers to show empathy for students' emotional needs.

Baxter-Magolda recommends that teachers appropriately question authority by example and that they allow students to ask questions of them. This means that teachers model critical thinking skills in the classroom. Teachers can question authority when they examine and evaluate readings—whether from textbooks or other sources. Teachers can question authorities when they teach propaganda techniques, exposing advertising claims and gimmicks. Teachers can question authority when they discuss the media and how so-called news sources shape and form public opinion. There are numerous opportunities for teachers in dealing with current affairs and public opinion to question authority and inculcate in their students' critical thinking and higher-ordered reasoning skills. Also, when teachers allow students to question them, teachers are acknowledging that everyone is a learner. Everyone should participate in a lifelong process of continuous learning. It is no shame or disgrace for the teacher to admit that sometimes he or she does not know the answer to a question. This gives the teacher the opportunity to show students how adults think, how they have a level of awareness (metacognition) when they do not know something, and how they go about finding answers to their questions. Teachers who admit that they do not have all the answers have the opportunity to show students how answers can be found and/or to reveal to students that there are no easy answers to some of life's most difficult questions.

To validate students as knowers, teachers must also value students' opinions, ideas, and comments. Teachers' affirmations include smiles and nods of approval, positive comments (such as, "That's a good answer"), and encouraging cues (such as, "That may seem like a reasonable answer, but can you think of a better answer?" or "Can you explain what you mean by that answer?"). Validating students as knowers also means supporting students' voices and giving them ample opportunity to express their own ideas, to share their opinions, and to make their own contributions to the classroom. These opportunities can include times of oral discussion as well as written assignments.

Jointly Constructed Meaning

Another principle in Baxter-Magolda's guidelines for teaching effectiveness is for teachers and students to recognize that learning is a *process of jointly constructing meaning*. To explain, Baxter-Magolda says, teachers should create a dialogue with students (also an important concept in Piagetian theory) and emphasize mutual learning. Also in agreement with Piagetian principles, Baxter-Magolda recommends that teachers reveal their own thinking processes as they approach subjects, as they analyze and understand new subjects, and as they solve problems and reach decisions. She further advises that teachers share leadership and promote collegial learning (group work), acknowledging that individual achievement is not the sole purpose or focus for learning. Through the process of collaborating, students will learn significant lessons directly applicable to work situations in which most accomplishments are the result of team efforts, not the sole efforts of individuals.

Situating Learning in the Students' Own Experiences

Baxter-Magolda's final principle for teachers is to *situate learning in the students' own experiences*. To do this, Baxter-Magolda suggests, a teacher must let students know that the he or she wants them in class; using inclusive language (avoiding ethnic and cultural bias and stereotyping and instead using gender-neutral and inclusive language) and focusing on activities will convey the importance of the student.

Activities are important for motivation because they give learners things to do, to become involved in, to arouse their attention and interest, and to provide an outlet for their physical and mental energy. Activities can have an additional positive benefit in that they can serve to connect students to each other, especially when students have opportunities to participate in collaborative learning (the way things happen in the "real world") and to work in groups. Finally, in situating learning in students' own experiences, teachers should consider the use of personal stories in class, as appropriate. (These stories must not violate anyone's right to privacy and confidentiality.) Moreover, teachers can share personal stories that allow them to connect with students in a deeper and more personal way.

In 1993, Robert Coles, the child psychologist, Harvard professor, and author of numerous scholarly and popular books, wrote of his experiences teaching in a Boston inner-city high school. He told of his disillusionment and his struggle to claim students' respect and attention so that he could teach them. Finally, there was a classroom confrontation, followed by a self-revelation (the realization that he had to show his students what he was like as a person). He shared some of his thoughts and feelings about loneliness. He told about his own boyhood experiences of visiting museums with his mother and what she taught him about art. In the end, he, too, had a revelation; he concluded that when teachers share what they have learned about themselves with their students, they often can transcend the barriers of class and race. A teacher can change a "me" and a "them" (the students) into an "us." Building camaraderie this way becomes an optimal starting point for teaching and learning (Coles 1993). Dr. Coles's experience was that telling his story to the class was a step toward helping his students claim some motivation of their own.

When students assume responsibility for their own motivation, they are learning a lesson of personal empowerment. Unfortunately, although personal empowerment is probably one of the most important lessons anyone ever learns, it is a lesson infrequently taught in classrooms across the country. Empowerment has at least four components, one of which is self-esteem. A good definition of *self-esteem* is "my opinion of me, your opinion of you." It is what we think and believe to be true about ourselves, not what we think about others and not what they think about us. Self-esteem appears to be a combination of self-efficacy and self-respect as seen against a background of self-knowledge.

Self-efficacy, simply stated, is one's confidence in one's own ability to cope with life's challenges. Self-efficacy refers to having a sense of control over life or, better, over one's responses to life. Experts say that ideas about self-efficacy get established by the time children reach the age of four. Because of this early establishment of either a feeling of control or no control, classroom teachers may find that even primary grade students believe that they have no control over their life and that it makes no difference what they do or how they act. Therefore, it is all the more important that teachers attempt to help all students achieve coping skills and a sense of self-efficacy.

Control, in this definition of self-efficacy, appears to have both external or internal motivators. For example, external motivators include such things as luck and the roles played by others in influencing outcomes. Internal motivators are variables within the individual. If a student who relies on external motivators does well on a test and is asked, "How did you do so well on that test?" he or she might reply, "Well, I just got lucky," or "The teacher likes me." If that same student failed the test and is asked why, he or she might answer, "Well, it wasn't my lucky day," "The teacher doesn't like me," or "My friends caused me to goof off and not pay attention so I didn't know the answers on the test." A student who relies on internal motivators and who does well on a test may explain, "I am smart and always do well on tests," or "I studied hard and that's why I did well." On the other hand, even the student who relies on internal motivators can do poorly on tests and then may explain, "I'm dumb, and that's why I don't do well," or "I didn't think the test was important, and I didn't try very hard." Even though students have similar experiences regarding issues of control, what is important is how students explain their experiences. If students have external motivators, they are likely to either dismiss their performance (success or failure) as matters of luck, or to credit or blame the influence of others. If students have internal motivators, then they are likely to attribute their performance to either their intelligence and skills (ability) or their effort. Students who have external motivators need help understanding how their behavior contributes to and influences outcomes in school. These students need clarification as to how the teacher will determine their grades and precise information about how the instructor will evaluate their work. Students who have internal motivators but low self-esteem (such as thinking, "I'm dumb") need help identifying their strengths and assets; when students receive information about learning styles and determine their own ways of learning, they may learn more about themselves.

Another factor in empowerment is self-respect. *Self-respect* is believing that one deserves happiness, achievement, and love. Self-respect is treating one's self at least as nicely as one treats other people. Many students are not aware of their internal voices (which are established at an early age). Internal voices are constantly sending messages, either positive or negative. Psychologists say that most of us have either a generally positive outlook on life, and our inner voice sends generally positive messages ("You're okay," "People like you," "Things will be all right," and so forth), or a generally negative outlook on life, and an inner voice sending negative messages ("You're not okay," "You're too fat, skinny, ugly, stupid," and so forth). Many students need to become aware of their inner voice and how it can be setting them up for failure. They need to learn that they can tell their inner voice to stop sending negative messages and that they can reprogram their inner voice to be kinder and gentler and to send positive messages. However, it does require effort, practice, and time to reprogram the inner voice.

Two tools that can help students in the reprogramming process are affirmations and visualizations (Ellis 1991). *Affirmations* are statements describing what students want. Affirmations must be personal, positive, and written in the present tense. What makes affirmations effective are details. For example, instead of saying, "I am stupid," students should say, "I am capable. I do well in school because I am organized, I study daily, I get all my work completed on time, and I take my school work seriously." Students should repeat these affirmations until they can say them with total conviction. *Visualizations* are images students can create whereby they see themselves the way they want to be. For example, if a student wants to improve his or her typing skills, then the student evaluates what it would look like, sound like, and feel like to be a better typist. Once the student identifies the image, then the student has to rehearse that image in her or his mind, including as many details and sensations as possible. Both visualization and affirmation can restructure attitudes and behaviors. They can be tools for students to use to increase their motivation.

Finally, the fourth component of empowerment is self-knowledge. *Self-knowledge* refers to an individual's strengths and weaknesses, assets and liabilities; self-knowledge comes about as a result of a realistic self-appraisal, including a determination and an examination of learning styles. Achieving self-knowledge also requires that students have opportunities to explore their goals and values. Students who have determined their goals and values can more easily see how education will enable them to achieve those goals and values. Conversely, students are not motivated when they do not have goals and values or when they do not know what their goals and values are. In other words, without self-knowledge, motivation is impossible. Therefore, teachers who follow Baxter-Magolda's guidelines for effective instruction and who teach their students about personal empowerment are teachers who realize the importance of motivation and who set the stage for students to claim responsibility for their own successes and failures. Such teachers help students to become motivated to make changes and accomplish more.

REFERENCES

Barry, Leasha M., Betty J. Bennett, Lois Christensen, Alicia Mendoza, Enrique Ortiz, Migdalia Pagan, Sally Robison, and Otilia Salmón. *The Best Teacher's Test Preparation for the Florida Teacher Certification Examination Professional Education Test*. Piscataway, NJ: Research & Education Association, 2005.

Baxter-Magolda, M. B. *Knowing and Reasoning in College: Gender-Based Patterns in Students' Intellectual Development*. San Francisco: Jossey-Bass, 1992.

Califano, Joseph A. Jr. "Teen Tipplers: America's Underage Drinking Epidemic." Statement, National Press Club, Washington, DC, February 26, 2002. *www. casacolumbia.org/absolutenm/templates/articles.asp?articleid=247&zoneid=31*.

Centers for Disease Control and Prevention. "Physical Activity for Everyone: Physical Activity Terms." *www.cdc.gov/nccdphp/dnpa/physical/terms/index.htm*.

Coles, Robert. "Point of View: When Earnest Volunteers Are Sorely Tested." *Chronicle of Higher Education*. Volume XXXIX: 35 (May 5, 1993), A52.

Cummins, James Patrick. "The Role of Primary Language Development in Promoting Educational Success for Language Minority Students." In *Schooling and*

Language Minority Students: A Theoretical Rationale, edited by California State Department of Education. Los Angeles: California State University, 1981, 3-49.

———. "Tests, Achievement, and Bilingual Students." *Focus* Volume IX (February 1, 1982), 1–5.

Elliott, Raymond. *Teaching Music.* Columbus, OH: Charles E. Merrill, 1960.

Ellis, D. *Becoming a Master Student.* Rapid City, SD: College Survival, 1991.

Erikson, E. *Childhood and Society.* New York: Horton, 1963.

Florida State Law, chap. 232.277. *www.fdle.state.fl.us/OGC/Summaries/1997/9701_w95.doc.* (Accessed July 11, 2008)

Goplerud, E. N., ed. *Breaking New Ground for Youth at Risk: Program Summaries.* Rockville, MD: Alcohol, Drug Abuse, and Mental Health Administration, Office for Substance Abuse Prevention, 1990. Rep. No. DHHS-ADM-89-1658 (OSAP Technical Rep. 1).

Hoffer, Charles R. *Teaching Music in the Elementary Classroom.* New York: Harcourt Brace Jovanovich, 1982.

Johnson, Elaine M. *Making Prevention Work.* Rockville, MD: Center for Substance Abuse Prevention, 1998.

Kaufman, P., X. Chen, S. P. Choy, S. A. Ruddy, A. K. Miller, K. A. Chandler, C. D. Chapman, M. R. Rand, and P. Klaus. *Indicators of School Crime and Safety, 1999.* Washington, DC: U.S. Departments of Education and Justice, National Center for Education Statistics and Bureau of Justice Statistics, 1999.

Kohlberg, Lawrence *The Psychology of Moral Development: The Nature and Validity of Moral Stages (Essays on Moral Development).* Vol. 2. New York: Harpercollins, 1984.

Krathwohl, David R., Benjamin S. Bloom, and Bertram B. Masia. *Taxonomy of Educational Objectives.* New York: David McKay, 1964.

National Clearinghouse for Alcohol and Drug Information. *Straight Facts about Drugs and Alcohol.* Rockville, MD: National Clearinghouse for Alcohol and Drug Information, 1998.

National Organization on Fetal Alcohol Syndrome. *www.nofas.org/faqs.aspx?id=9.*

Piaget, J. *The Psychology of Intelligence.* London: Routledge and Kegan Paul, 1950.

Prevention Institute. "What Factors Increase the Risk of Being Involved in Violence?" *www.preventioninstitute.org/schoolviol4.html*.

South Carolina Visual and Performing Arts Curriculum Framework Writing Team. *South Carolina Visual and Performing Arts Framework*. Columbia: South Carolina State Board of Education, 1993.

Tavris, C. "Coping with Student Conflict Inside and Outside the Classroom." Paper presented at Texas Junior College Teachers' Conference, San Antonio, TX, February 25, 1994.

U.S. Department of Agriculture. "Steps to a Healthier You." *www.mypyramid.gov*.

U.S. Department of Education. "Creating Safe and Drug-Free Schools: An Action Guide." September 1996. *www.ncjrs.org/pdffiles/safescho.pdf*.

U.S. Departments of Education and Justice. *Early Warning, Timely Response.* Washington, DC: U.S. Government Printing Office, 1998.

Wassum, Sylvesta "Sally." "Elementary school children's vocal range." *Journal of Research in Music Education,* 27:4 (Winter 1979), 214–26.

Practice Test 1

PRAXIS 0011

This test is also on CD-ROM in our special interactive PRAXIS Elementary Education (0011) TEST*ware*®. It is highly recommended that you first take this exam on computer. You will then have the additional study features and benefits of enforced timed conditions and instantaneous, accurate scoring. See page 4 for instructions on how to get the most out of REA's TEST*ware*®.

ANSWER SHEET FOR PRACTICE TEST 1

1. Ⓐ Ⓑ Ⓒ Ⓓ
2. Ⓐ Ⓑ Ⓒ Ⓓ
3. Ⓐ Ⓑ Ⓒ Ⓓ
4. Ⓐ Ⓑ Ⓒ Ⓓ
5. Ⓐ Ⓑ Ⓒ Ⓓ
6. Ⓐ Ⓑ Ⓒ Ⓓ
7. Ⓐ Ⓑ Ⓒ Ⓓ
8. Ⓐ Ⓑ Ⓒ Ⓓ
9. Ⓐ Ⓑ Ⓒ Ⓓ
10. Ⓐ Ⓑ Ⓒ Ⓓ
11. Ⓐ Ⓑ Ⓒ Ⓓ
12. Ⓐ Ⓑ Ⓒ Ⓓ
13. Ⓐ Ⓑ Ⓒ Ⓓ
14. Ⓐ Ⓑ Ⓒ Ⓓ
15. Ⓐ Ⓑ Ⓒ Ⓓ
16. Ⓐ Ⓑ Ⓒ Ⓓ
17. Ⓐ Ⓑ Ⓒ Ⓓ
18. Ⓐ Ⓑ Ⓒ Ⓓ
19. Ⓐ Ⓑ Ⓒ Ⓓ
20. Ⓐ Ⓑ Ⓒ Ⓓ
21. Ⓐ Ⓑ Ⓒ Ⓓ
22. Ⓐ Ⓑ Ⓒ Ⓓ
23. Ⓐ Ⓑ Ⓒ Ⓓ
24. Ⓐ Ⓑ Ⓒ Ⓓ
25. Ⓐ Ⓑ Ⓒ Ⓓ
26. Ⓐ Ⓑ Ⓒ Ⓓ
27. Ⓐ Ⓑ Ⓒ Ⓓ
28. Ⓐ Ⓑ Ⓒ Ⓓ

29. Ⓐ Ⓑ Ⓒ Ⓓ
30. Ⓐ Ⓑ Ⓒ Ⓓ
31. Ⓐ Ⓑ Ⓒ Ⓓ
32. Ⓐ Ⓑ Ⓒ Ⓓ
33. Ⓐ Ⓑ Ⓒ Ⓓ
34. Ⓐ Ⓑ Ⓒ Ⓓ
35. Ⓐ Ⓑ Ⓒ Ⓓ
36. Ⓐ Ⓑ Ⓒ Ⓓ
37. Ⓐ Ⓑ Ⓒ Ⓓ
38. Ⓐ Ⓑ Ⓒ Ⓓ
39. Ⓐ Ⓑ Ⓒ Ⓓ
40. Ⓐ Ⓑ Ⓒ Ⓓ
41. Ⓐ Ⓑ Ⓒ Ⓓ
42. Ⓐ Ⓑ Ⓒ Ⓓ
43. Ⓐ Ⓑ Ⓒ Ⓓ
44. Ⓐ Ⓑ Ⓒ Ⓓ
45. Ⓐ Ⓑ Ⓒ Ⓓ
46. Ⓐ Ⓑ Ⓒ Ⓓ
47. Ⓐ Ⓑ Ⓒ Ⓓ
48. Ⓐ Ⓑ Ⓒ Ⓓ
49. Ⓐ Ⓑ Ⓒ Ⓓ
50. Ⓐ Ⓑ Ⓒ Ⓓ
51. Ⓐ Ⓑ Ⓒ Ⓓ
52. Ⓐ Ⓑ Ⓒ Ⓓ
53. Ⓐ Ⓑ Ⓒ Ⓓ
54. Ⓐ Ⓑ Ⓒ Ⓓ
55. Ⓐ Ⓑ Ⓒ Ⓓ
56. Ⓐ Ⓑ Ⓒ Ⓓ

57. Ⓐ Ⓑ Ⓒ Ⓓ
58. Ⓐ Ⓑ Ⓒ Ⓓ
59. Ⓐ Ⓑ Ⓒ Ⓓ
60. Ⓐ Ⓑ Ⓒ Ⓓ
61. Ⓐ Ⓑ Ⓒ Ⓓ
62. Ⓐ Ⓑ Ⓒ Ⓓ
63. Ⓐ Ⓑ Ⓒ Ⓓ
64. Ⓐ Ⓑ Ⓒ Ⓓ
65. Ⓐ Ⓑ Ⓒ Ⓓ
66. Ⓐ Ⓑ Ⓒ Ⓓ
67. Ⓐ Ⓑ Ⓒ Ⓓ
68. Ⓐ Ⓑ Ⓒ Ⓓ
69. Ⓐ Ⓑ Ⓒ Ⓓ
70. Ⓐ Ⓑ Ⓒ Ⓓ
71. Ⓐ Ⓑ Ⓒ Ⓓ
72. Ⓐ Ⓑ Ⓒ Ⓓ
73. Ⓐ Ⓑ Ⓒ Ⓓ
74. Ⓐ Ⓑ Ⓒ Ⓓ
75. Ⓐ Ⓑ Ⓒ Ⓓ
76. Ⓐ Ⓑ Ⓒ Ⓓ
77. Ⓐ Ⓑ Ⓒ Ⓓ
78. Ⓐ Ⓑ Ⓒ Ⓓ
79. Ⓐ Ⓑ Ⓒ Ⓓ
80. Ⓐ Ⓑ Ⓒ Ⓓ
81. Ⓐ Ⓑ Ⓒ Ⓓ
82. Ⓐ Ⓑ Ⓒ Ⓓ
83. Ⓐ Ⓑ Ⓒ Ⓓ
84. Ⓐ Ⓑ Ⓒ Ⓓ

85. Ⓐ Ⓑ Ⓒ Ⓓ
86. Ⓐ Ⓑ Ⓒ Ⓓ
87. Ⓐ Ⓑ Ⓒ Ⓓ
88. Ⓐ Ⓑ Ⓒ Ⓓ
89. Ⓐ Ⓑ Ⓒ Ⓓ
90. Ⓐ Ⓑ Ⓒ Ⓓ
91. Ⓐ Ⓑ Ⓒ Ⓓ
92. Ⓐ Ⓑ Ⓒ Ⓓ
93. Ⓐ Ⓑ Ⓒ Ⓓ
94. Ⓐ Ⓑ Ⓒ Ⓓ
95. Ⓐ Ⓑ Ⓒ Ⓓ
96. Ⓐ Ⓑ Ⓒ Ⓓ
97. Ⓐ Ⓑ Ⓒ Ⓓ
98. Ⓐ Ⓑ Ⓒ Ⓓ
99. Ⓐ Ⓑ Ⓒ Ⓓ
100. Ⓐ Ⓑ Ⓒ Ⓓ
101. Ⓐ Ⓑ Ⓒ Ⓓ
102. Ⓐ Ⓑ Ⓒ Ⓓ
103. Ⓐ Ⓑ Ⓒ Ⓓ
104. Ⓐ Ⓑ Ⓒ Ⓓ
105. Ⓐ Ⓑ Ⓒ Ⓓ
106. Ⓐ Ⓑ Ⓒ Ⓓ
107. Ⓐ Ⓑ Ⓒ Ⓓ
108. Ⓐ Ⓑ Ⓒ Ⓓ
109. Ⓐ Ⓑ Ⓒ Ⓓ
110. Ⓐ Ⓑ Ⓒ Ⓓ

TIME: 120 minutes
110 questions

1. Teachers can provide a positive testing environment by

   (A) encouraging students to be anxious about a test.
   (B) providing a comfortable physical setting.
   (C) surprising students with disruptions and distractions.
   (D) emphasizing the consequences of poor performance.

2. The teacher read the students a cinquain, a limerick, and a haiku. The students are most likely studying

   (A) narrative.
   (B) poetry.
   (C) metaphor.
   (D) biography.

3. Second graders are studying weather as their science unit. They read newspapers to gather information on temperature and rainfall in several local cities. Their teacher instructs the students during math time on how to use the data gathered to make simple line graphs to chart the weather. The data is then analyzed during their next science time. This teacher is practicing

   (A) differentiated instruction.
   (B) cooperative learning.
   (C) interdisciplinary instruction.
   (D) performance assessment.

4. The teacher provides groups of students with picture cards of mammals, reptiles and amphibians. Their task is to sort the cards, which uses the scientific process of

   (A) hypothesizing.
   (B) classifying.
   (C) concluding.
   (D) organizing.

5. As the decades change, so do the labels the school systems use to identify students who differ from the mainstream—and may have difficulty with mathematics and other subjects. The school systems of the twenty-first century identify these "differing" students as

   (A) at-risk.
   (B) culturally deprived.
   (C) culturally different.
   (D) slow learners.

6. Goals for individual students

   (A) should be based upon the student's academic record.
   (B) should be the same for all students.
   (C) are created from individual observations only.
   (D) are developed after considering the student's history and motivation.

7. Feedback sessions for a test are most effective

   (A) when they are immediate.
   (B) when they are delayed by a day or so.
   (C) when they are delayed for a few weeks.
   (D) when the feedback is written on paper only.

8. A teacher is instructing third grade students about money. The students have been given mock checkbooks and checks, several catalogues, and a worksheet with instructions. The sheet asks the students to select items from catalogues to purchase for themselves and others. It also directs the students to deposit earned amounts into their checkbooks and write checks to pay bills. The lesson objective is that students will balance a checkbook. The teacher is aware of the importance of

   (A) having students learn how to maintain a budget.
   (B) real-life applications of mathematical concepts.
   (C) practicing basic mathematical computations.
   (D) reviewing concepts taught in previous grades.

9. An important goal of the inclusion of students with disabilities in the least restrictive environment

   (A) is a focus on disability and a decreased focus on ability.
   (B) is a focus on inability.
   (C) is the use of the neighborhood school as the first option for the child with a disability.
   (D) is an educational placement of students with disabilities in the neighborhood school only if there is compelling evidence to do so.

10. Effective praise should be

   (A) authentic and low-key.
   (B) used sparingly.
   (C) composed of simple, positive responses.
   (D) used to encourage high-achieving students.

11. Which of the following sets of problems demonstrates a fact family?

   (A) $5 + 5 = 10$, $3 + 3 = 6$, $7 + 7 = 14$, $2 + 2 = 4$
   (B) $3 \times 4 = 12$, $4 \times 3 = 12$, $12 \div 4 = 3$, $12 \div 3 = 4$
   (C) $4 \times 6 = 24$, $3 \times 8 = 24$, $2 \times 12 = 24$, $8 \times 3 = 24$
   (D) $2 + 5 = 7$, $5 + 2 = 7$, $2 \times 5 = 10$, $5 \times 2 = 10$

12. Teachers/tutors who work with students pulled for a short time from a general-education classroom with inclusion have had most satisfactory results with certain techniques of literacy instruction. The most satisfactory method is

   (A) de-emphasizing skills.
   (B) using only basic texts.
   (C) increased positive reinforcement.
   (D) whole language instruction.

13. Teaching reading through literature is a prevalent method today. Instructors who seek to teach reading through literature should have as a main concern

   (A) the factual aspects of a passage.
   (B) what the words may suggest, for instance an image, a sound, an association, or a feeling.
   (C) neither factual information nor aesthetic purposes.
   (D) the situation, the passages, and the students.

14. During Writer's Workshop time, the teacher has the students write personal narratives. The mini-lessons taught include strategies on using descriptive language, choosing the most important information to include, varying sentence structure, and developing a voice as an author. The method for the teacher to assess the students' personal narratives at the end of the process is

(A) order the students' writing from weakest to strongest and assign letter grades accordingly

(B) rely on students' self-assessments since it is a personal writing piece

(C) use a rubric that takes content, mechanics, and organization into account

(D) use a rubric that takes descriptive language, content, sentence variety, and voice into account

15. A kindergarten teacher creates word cards that are placed throughout the classroom to help build literacy. They serve as labels, such as "blocks," "paint," "sand," "books," "desk," and "table." The closet has a card, as do the windows, whiteboard, wastebaskets, easel, and cubbies. Which of the following is the teacher providing?

(A) Word walls

(B) Phonics instruction

(C) Environmental print

(D) Whole language

16. According to the operant model in behavioral theory, negative reinforcement is

(A) operant behavior.

(B) stimulus for operant behavior.

(C) unknowingly strengthening negative behavior.

(D) removing a stimulus in order to cause a behavior to increase.

17. A teacher of language arts implements a variety of instructional strategies and uses an array of resources. Students read independently, with partners and small groups. Sometimes groups are guided by the teacher while other times they are student led. The teacher provides the students with fiction and nonfiction, as well as learning centers on concepts such as grammar and spelling. This teacher's language arts program is considered a(n)

(A) balanced literacy approach.

(B) skills and drills approach.

(C) interdisciplinary approach.

(D) cooperative approach.

18. When maintaining a running reading record, a teacher is

(A) tape recording while a student reads aloud.

(B) writing what a student reads aloud.

(C) testing for comprehension.

(D) noting what books have been read.

19. During which stage of the writing process would students most likely conference with a peer?

(A) Publishing

(B) Pre-writing

(C) Editing

(D) Drafting

20. The social studies teachers of an inner-city school wanted to change to a more relevant curriculum. The department wanted to have units on economics throughout the world instead of only regions of the United States. Mrs. Dunn was asked to submit a proposal for the new curriculum, related activities, sequencing, themes, and materials. In consultation with the other teachers in the department, a needs assessment was planned. The group would undertake the needs assessment to

(A) help the students make a connection between their current skills and those that will be new to them.

(B) reveal community problems that may affect the students' lives and their performance in school.

(C) foster a view of learning as a purposeful pursuit, promoting a sense of responsibility for one's own learning.

(D) engage students in learning activities and help them to develop the motivation to achieve.

21. When the needs assessment in Question 20 was evaluated, it revealed an ethnically diverse community. Student interests and parental expectations varied, different language backgrounds existed, student exceptionalities were common, and academic motivation was low. The question confronting the teachers was how to bridge the gap from where the students were to where they should be. The available choices were to

    (A) change the text only.
    (B) relate the lessons to the students' personal interests.
    (C) create a positive environment to minimize the effects of the negative external factors.
    (D) help students to learn and to monitor their own performance.

Read the following scenario and answer questions 22 and 23.

During the period of community-involvement field experiences, Ms. Parks continually directs her students' attention to the fact that science is a way of solving problems. Following this field experience period, Ms. Parks asks her students to identify a problem in their school and to devise a scientific way of studying and solving that problem. The students work in groups for two class periods and select the following problem for investigation: It is late spring, and the classroom gets so hot during the afternoon that the majority of the students are uncomfortable. Their research question becomes, "Why is it hotter in our classroom than in the music room, art room, or library? How can we make our classroom cooler?"

22. Of the following choices, what is the most important benefit of allowing the students to select their own problem to investigate, rather than having the teacher assign a problem?

    (A) Students become self-directed problem solvers who can structure their own learning experiences.
    (B) The teacher can best assess each student's academic and affective needs in a naturalistic setting.
    (C) Students will have the opportunity to work with a wide variety of instructional materials.
    (D) Students will learn to appreciate opposing viewpoints.

23. Which of the following is the most important force at work when students are allowed to select their own problem for investigation?

    (A) Increased student motivation
    (B) Increased student diversity
    (C) Increased structure of student groups
    (D) Increased use of self-assessment

24. The following tasks are all asked of third grade students during a unit on multiplication.

    I.   Sort 20 counters into four equal groups
    II. Solve $x \times 5 = 20$
    III. Multiply 4×5
    IV. Draw a picture of 4 plates, each with 5 cookies

    Which of the following shows the tasks correctly ordered from the one involving the most concrete to the most abstract thinking?

    (A) I, II, III, IV
    (B) II, III, IV, I
    (C) IV, I, II, III
    (D) I, IV, III, II

25. $4 \div 2 = 8$ $10 \div 5 = 50$ $3 \div 3 = 9$

    The equations above represent one student's work. If the student continues to make the error shown in these problems, which of the following is likely to be this student's answer to the problem $12 \div 2 =$

(A) 6
(B) 10
(C) 14
(D) 24

26. The teacher wants the students to participate in the planning of their class party. They will decide what refreshments and accompanying supplies are needed during a morning meeting. At math time the students will need to figure out the amount of supplies they need such as cups, plates, napkins, and utensils. This is a good task for the students to practice

(A) estimation.
(B) probability.
(C) exact computation.
(D) measurement.

27. Several students in a fourth grade class do not understand the connection between multiplication and division a few weeks into the unit of study. Which is the best course of action for their teacher to take?

(A) Teach the concept again, paying specific attention to directly addressing the connection between multiplication and division, and incorporating new instructional methods and materials.

(B) Have the students stay in at recess to complete additional worksheets that include problems that involve the connection between multiplication and division.

(C) Repeat several of the lessons that were taught during the initial weeks of the study that focused on the connection between multiplication and division.

(D) Direct the students to the textbook chapters on multiplication and division concepts and practice equations.

28. Fourth grade students are beginning a class-wide author study. The teacher gave a book talk about four books written by the same author. The students were then asked to pick the books they were most interested in reading. Based on this information, the teacher assigned the students one of the books to read with four other classmates. Each of the five students in the group had a job to do that rotated every time the group met. The teacher walked around the room to observe the four groups during reader's workshop time. The groups are most likely considered to be

(A) guided reading groups.
(B) literacy circles.
(C) book clubs.
(D) homogenous groups.

Read the following scenario and answer question 29.

Tom Jones was asked to improve the remedial reading curriculum for upper-elementary-grade students. He found that the students were continually tested and evaluated on reading, that the current objectives were unclear, and that the teaching materials were inappropriate. Following a lengthy observation of Mrs. Ratu's teaching strategies, Mr. Jones concluded that she was teaching basic reading skills in the same manner as did the lower-elementary teachers. The teaching materials used a controlled vocabulary and simple sentences. The students were being taught to rely heavily upon pictures and illustrations for the story. Most of the material was fictional in genre. Rote was Mrs. Ratu's preference for learning. Mr. Jones analyzed the test results and found that many of the students in Mrs. Ratu's class had average scores in the areas of art, math, and music. He concluded that, with the exception of reading, most were normal students and would be successful when their remediation was complete. Mr. Jones made several decisions: (1) the students would be evaluated annually with an achievement test; (2) reading materials of interest to upper-elementary students would be substituted for elementary materials; (3) each student would be encouraged to read about the subject of his or her choice; and (4) roundtable discussions would be developed for each "favorite subject."

29. Mrs. Ratu's method of teaching remedial reading focused upon

   I. the level at which the students should have learned the basic reading skills.
   II. her own minimal competency in instructional design and evaluation.
   III. her lack of understanding of the learners in her class.
   IV. her desire to make remedial reading easy for the students.

   (A) I only
   (B) I and IV only
   (C) II and III only
   (D) II only

30. Language-minority students who speak their native language instead of English in the classroom

   (A) do not have the right to do so.
   (B) have the responsibility to do so.
   (C) have the obligation to do so.
   (D) are a challenge to educators.

31. To help a language-minority student most, recent research (Elley and Mangubhai) suggests that

   (A) listening and speaking proficiency should precede literacy instruction.

   (B) the teacher should help the student develop reading skills coincidentally with speaking skills but independently from writing skills.
   (C) the teacher should help the student develop writing skills before reading skills since motor skills precede reading.
   (D) the teacher should seek to help the students to develop reading and writing concomitantly.

32. While working on determining character motives during their literature study, a third grade class reads a short story. The story involves a group of children who bully a peer. The main character is a bystander who watches but does not try to stop the bullying. The teacher asks the students to write a letter from the perspective of the bystander explaining why they did not step in to help. This task asks students to perform at which level of Bloom's Taxonomy?

   (A) Synthesis
   (B) Evaluation
   (C) Knowledge
   (D) Comprehension

33. Early in the school year a second grade teacher is frustrated with the student's confusion with concepts of time. Most of the students can read basic times on an analog clock, such as hours and half hours. Almost none of the students can calculate elapsed time and none is familiar with the numerical representation of terms such as *a quarter to* or *half past*. The teacher can conclude the students

   (A) are not interested in learning how to tell time.
   (B) are not focused during math time.
   (C) are not developmentally ready to understand these concepts.
   (D) will need to rely on digital clocks to tell time.

34. Which of the following tools would be LEAST appropriate to use during a unit on measurement?

    (A) Scales
    (B) Rulers
    (C) Tangrams
    (D) Calendars

35. During a unit on multiplication, a third grade teacher plans and implements a variety of learning experiences. Students watch a video in which cartoon characters sing about the times tables. They work with counters to create different groupings. The teacher reads several picture books that illustrate principles of multiplication. Students make their own illustrations representing multiplication equations. The class writes a multiplication rap to help them remember the tables. This teacher exemplifies which of the following theories?

    (A) Zone of proximal development
    (B) Learning styles
    (C) Social adjustment
    (D) Cognitive development

36. A teacher consistently returns graded papers to her students within three days of them turning in their work. She writes very complete comments on each paper to help students understand what they have done correctly or incorrectly on their assignments. Doing this is important to the teacher's instructional goals because

    (A) it is easy to fall behind in grading if a teacher doesn't keep up with the workload.
    (B) grading papers is an important part of a teacher's job performance.
    (C) students have a responsibility to keep track of their graded work.
    (D) providing students with information about their performance is one way to help them improve their performance.

37. Inquiry learning is most likely characterized by

    (A) preplanned assignments by which the learner might elicit factual information from a textbook and complete a test for evaluation.
    (B) problem posing by learners or by teachers and problem solving; emphasis is on process—not just content.
    (C) a learner gaining meaning primarily through teacher lecture.
    (D) a teacher conducting short, purposeful, direct-teaching sessions with the class.

38. Writing programs may vary from situation to situation, but the most effective writing program for teaching multicultural students has a main characteristic. The characteristic is that the writing program

    (A) connects students' lives to their classroom writing experience.
    (B) is conducted by a teacher who engages the students in story starters, language games, and worksheets developed for the purpose of creative writing.
    (C) presents the teacher as an authority figure that diverse students can learn from and model.
    (D) has a teacher who is confident, experienced, and willing to present the writing techniques to them systematically.

39. Which of the following authors is NOT known for writing literature for children?

    (A) Pat Conroy
    (B) Beverly Cleary
    (C) Judy Blume
    (D) Shel Silverstein

40. Which of the following is the term given for speech sounds?

    (A) Graphemes
    (B) Semantics

(C) Phonemes

(D) Phonetics

41. Devices used to aid memorization using rhymes, acronyms, songs, or stories are called

(A) choral responses.

(B) repetitions.

(C) codings.

(D) mnemonics.

42. Which stage of literacy does the following statement describe?

Children in this stage are making the leap from just speaking to beginning to write and read with support from others.

(A) Emergent

(B) Transitional

(C) Developing

(D) Mastery

43. A teacher walks around the room stopping at the students' desks during a lesson to review their class work. This would be considered which of the following types of assessment?

(A) Informal

(B) Authentic

(C) Global scan

(D) Alternative

44. Which of the following types of literature is characterized as stories written to explain things that the teller does not understand?

(A) Fairy tale

(B) Myth

(C) Legend

(D) Parable

45. Why should children be encouraged to figure out the structure and the features of the text they are attempting to comprehend and re- member?

I. It helps the students to understand the way the author organized the material to be presented.

II. It helps the students to look at the fea- tures of the text.

III. Talking about the structure of the text provides an opportunity for the teacher to point out the most salient features to the students.

IV. The discussions may help the child make connections between the new material in the chapter and what is already known about the topic.

(A) I and III only

(B) II and IV only

(C) I and IV only

(D) I, II, III, and IV

46. Ms. Smith decided to stage three different ver- sions of *Cinderella* with her students. Knowing that this is one of the world's most famous fairy tales, she located Chinese, Native American, and Russian versions of the story. She found age-appropriate plays of each that could be staged in her classroom. In addition to acting in these plays, her students are creating scen- ery, costumes, and props to use in their perfor- mances. Which of the following best describes what Ms. Smith primarily expects her students to achieve through these activities?

I. Understanding cultural similarities and differences through dramatic literature

II. Understanding theatrical practices

III. Gaining experience with creative drama practices

IV. Gaining experience with adapting stories into plays

(A) I only only

(B) I and II only

(C) III and IV only

(D) I, II, and IV only

47. In order to extend the literacy of others, teachers must engage in some self-reflection to meet the needs of the learners. Teachers will find that

    (A) comparing their own literacy history to that of their students is futile.
    (B) considering how a school setting helped them and making such comparisons with the students they teach is probably inapplicable.
    (C) school experiences have no effect on the self-identity of most of the diverse learners.
    (D) self-evaluation of their own values, attitudes, and dispositions is helpful.

Read the following passage and answer question 48.

Mrs. Gettler teaches 26 third-graders in a large inner city school. About one-third of her students participate in the ESL program at the school. Mrs. Gettler suspects that some of the students' parents are unable to read or write in English. Four of the students receive services from the learning resource teacher. At the beginning of the year, none of the students reads above 2.0 grade level, and some of the students did not know all the letters of the alphabet.

48. Which of the following describes the instructional strategy that is most likely to improve the reading levels of Mrs. Gettler's students?

    (A) An intensive phonics program that includes drill-and-practice work on basic sight words.
    (B) An emergent literacy program emphasizing pattern books and journal writing using invented spelling.
    (C) An instructional program that closely follows the third-grade basal reader.

    (D) Participation by all students in the school's ESL program so they can receive services from the learning resource center.

Read the following scenario and answer questions 49 through 52.

Mrs. Doe began planning a two-week unit of study of Native Americans for her fifth-grade class. To begin the unit, she chose a movie on twenty-first-century Native Americans. As Mrs. Doe reflectively listened, the students asked key questions.

The following day, Mrs. Doe reviewed the use of encyclopedias, indexes, and atlases. She then divided the students into groups and took them to the library. Each group was responsible for locating information on a particular topic. The topics were maps showing the topography of the land; charts illustrating the climate, plants, and animals; a map showing migration routes; and a map showing the general areas where the Native Americans settled.

49. The students' involvement in the unit of study is a result of

    I.   the teacher's reflective listening during the discussion.
    II.   the available resources and materials.
    III. careful planning and its relationship to success in the classroom.
    IV.   the students' personal acquaintance with Native Americans.

    (A) I only
    (B) I and II only
    (C) II and III only
    (D) I and IV only

50. Days 3 and 4 of this unit were spent with each group being involved in library research. They wrote information on index cards. Each group prepared a presentation that included a written explanation of an assigned topic, a shadow box, and a sawdust map or models of Native American clothing. A pictograph was to be used in the telling of a legend or folk story. The presentation concluded with a collage depicting the Native American way of life. Multiple strategies and techniques were used for

    I.   motivation of the group and its effects on individual behavior and learning.
    II. allowing each student regardless of ability to participate in the project.
    III. integrating the project with other subjects.
    IV. developing a foundation for teaching American history.

    (A) I, II, and III only
    (B) I and II only
    (C) III only
    (D) IV only

51. Day 10 of the unit was Field Trip Day, which involved visiting museums. The students were given a choice of museums. Each student was expected to take notes of what was seen, heard, and experienced to share with the remainder of the class on the following day. Field Trip Day and its experiences

    I.   allowed the students to make connections between their current skills and those that were new to them.
    II. allowed external factors to create a learning environment that would take advantage of positive factors.
    III. allowed a sense of community to be nurtured.
    IV. allowed the students to take responsibility for their own learning.

    (A) I and II only
    (B) III only

    (C) IV only
    (D) III and IV only

52. Giving the students a choice of field trip locations was meant

    I.   to enhance the students' self-concept.
    II. to respect differences and enhance the students' understanding of the society in which they live.
    III. to foster the view of learning as a purposeful pursuit.
    IV. as an example of using an array of instructional strategies.

    (A) II only
    (B) II and IV only
    (C) I and II only
    (D) III only

53. To convince the reader that the perspective or course of action suggested by the writer is valid is the purpose of which of the following types of writing?

    (A) Expository
    (B) Persuasive
    (C) Descriptive
    (D) Narrative

54. The strength of requiring a cognitive objective and a performance objective is that

    (A) some students are not test takers and do poorly on paper-and-pencil tests.
    (B) the score for one objective could offset the score for the other objective.
    (C) the developmental level in one domain may affect performance in another domain.
    (D) the teacher is matching the students' learning styles to her teaching style.

55. When developing a unit about the Erie Canal for elementary-age students, how would you handle assessment of the students?

(A) Explain to the students that the unit will cover a variety of projects; therefore, you will be using different assessment tools.

(B) Explain to the students each project in the unit, then describe what they will be asked to do.

(C) Give the students a list of new vocabulary words that they will need to know for the final test.

(D) Explain to the students that they will need to hand in their notebooks at the end of the unit.

56. Rubrics are used by many teachers in elementary schools for the purposes of assessment. What criteria should be used when creating a rubric?

I.   Set clearly defined criteria for each assessment.

II. Include a rating scale.

III. Use only one idea at a time so that students are not confused.

IV. Tell students that they can rate themselves.

(A) IV and III only
(B) III and II only
(C) I and II only
(D) None of the above

57. Mr. O'Brien ends class by telling students that over the next few weeks they will be required to keep a communications journal. Every time they have an eventful exchange—either positive or negative—they are to record the details of the exchange in their journal. This assignment is given as

(A) a way to help students improve their composition and rhetorical skills.

(B) a way of understanding individual students, monitoring instructional effectiveness, and shaping instruction.

(C) a way of helping students become more accountable for the way they manage their time.

(D) the basis for giving daily grades to students.

Read the following scenario and answer questions 58 through 60.

It is the first day of class. Ms. Johnson, the language arts teacher, tells the students a little bit about herself. She tells them that she wants to know about each individual in the class. She asks them to write about themselves and hand their papers to her as they leave the class to go to lunch.

58. By requiring that students write about themselves, Ms. Johnson is

(A) fulfilling her responsibilities as an English teacher.

(B) preparing her class to create autobiographies.

(C) relying on the language experience approach (LEA) for instruction.

(D) preparing her class to read biographies about great Americans from diverse cultural backgrounds.

59. Ms. Johnson collects the students' papers at the end of class. As she reads the papers, she decides that the best way to give her students positive feedback is

(A) not to mark errors on the paper so as not to discourage or inhibit their creativity.

(B) to make at least one positive comment about each paragraph.

(C) begin with one or two positive comments about the paper and then suggest how students could improve their writing.

(D) give everyone a high grade on the paper for participating in the assignment.

60. After Ms. Johnson finishes reading all the students' papers, she observes that some of the students had difficulty identifying and describing their strengths, whether in class or outside class. She believes that all of her students have strengths, and she wants to help them see the assets they possess. She decides that in the next class, students will

(A) take a learning-style assessment to uncover their particular learning strengths and characteristics.

(B) listen to a lecture about how everyone possesses special skills and strengths.

(C) read a chapter from a book about Guilford's Structure of Intellect, as a precursor to a discussion about how intelligence is specialized and diverse.

(D) rewrite their papers, correcting their errors and revising their paragraphs to name at least two additional classroom strengths they possess and at least two additional interpersonal skills they possess.

61. Mr. Swenson teaches mathematics in high school. He is planning a unit for his advanced math students on fractal geometry, using the computer lab for demonstrations and exploration. The students have used various computer programs to solve algebra and calculus problems. As Mr. Swenson plans a unit of study, he determines that a cognitive outcome will be that students will design and produce fractals by using a computer program. An effective outcome is that students will become excited about investigating a new field of mathematics and will show this interest by choosing to develop a math project relating to fractals. The most appropriate strategy to use first would be

(A) explaining the exciting development of fractal geometry over the past 10 to 15 years.

(B) demonstrating on the computer the way to input values into formulas to produce fractal designs.

(C) giving students a few simple fractal designs and asking them to figure out the formulas for producing them.

(D) showing students color pictures of complex fractals and asking them for ideas about how they could be drawn mathematically.

62. Teachers of young children should be aware of the stages of development that students learning to spell and write progress through. Which stage of spelling development does the following statement describe?

The student spells the words the way that they sound.

(A) Pre-phonetic stage
(B) Pre-communication stage
(C) Phonetic stage
(D) Transitional stage

63. What can be determined by behavioral observation?

(A) Concept comprehension
(B) Ability to organize concepts
(C) Amount of time spent on task
(D) Verbal skills

64. Which of the following is the LEAST effective way to increase student motivation and interest at the beginning of a new science unit about mammals?

(A) Provide a fact-based worksheet that can be used for a study guide for the end-of-unit test

(B) Have students explore picture/word cards with photographs of mammals

(C) Read the class a nonfiction picture book about mammals

(D) Show a video or DVD about mammals

65. Students in a third grade science class are learning how to classify types of rocks and minerals. Which of the following assessment

techniques is best suited for identifying student skills for this study?

(A) Have the student take a paper-and-pencil test that involves identifying picture reproductions of a sample of rocks and minerals

(B) Have the student provide a detailed written description of a selection of rocks and minerals

(C) Have the student work at home to create a poster about rocks and minerals

(D) Have the student label actual rock and mineral samples as a demonstration for the teacher

66. The teacher begins her science lab with a poem about chemistry. Towards the end of the chemistry lab activity the teacher requires the students to write about their experience in a science journal. The teacher closes the lesson by having several students share what they have written. For this lesson the teacher clearly demonstrates an awareness of the importance of

(A) hands-on activities.
(B) inquiry-based learning.
(C) literacy in the content areas.
(D) reflective practice.

67. Which of the following shows a number written in expanded notation?

(A) 1,643
(B) 1,000 + 600 + 40 +3
(C) One thousand six hundred forty-three
(D) One thousand, six hundreds, four tens, three ones

68. A fifth-grade math class is composed of twenty-three students who represent a range of abilities in the subject area. There are several students who currently receive in-class support from a math instruction specialist, while several others have been designated as gifted and receive no additional support. The remainder of the stu-

dents are considered at grade level in math. The best way for the teacher to address the needs of all the students is through

(A) whole-class instruction.
(B) differentiated instruction.
(C) small group instruction.
(D) efficient instruction.

69. The teacher of a second-grade class is concerned about how to manage her class at math time. The teacher believes in using manipulatives to introduce new concepts; however every time the students use a new manipulative, they play with them instead of listening to the start of the lesson. The best approach for the teacher to take is to

(A) avoid using manipulatives.
(B) give all students time to explore the manipulatives before the lesson.
(C) only allow the best-behaved students to use manipulatives.
(D) remove the most distracted students from the math class when manipulatives are used.

70. Some students in a fourth-grade class often finish their math problems earlier than the teacher had planned. These students then become a distraction to their classmates who are still working on the original assignment. Which of the following strategies is best?

(A) Have the students who finish early help classmates who are still working
(B) Have the students who finish early read quietly at their desks
(C) Give the students who finish early additional practice problems
(D) Give the students who finish early a challenging extension activity

71. A quiet classroom is

(A) a good classroom.
(B) a negative learning environment.

(C) inappropriate for some learning activities.

(D) the classroom of a teacher who has appropriate control of his/her students.

72. To encourage students to read more books on their own time, a teacher develops a reward system to give students tokens for the books they read depending on the difficulty and the length of the book. At the end of the semester, students will be able to use their tokens to purchase "rewards" from the school store (pens, pencils, erasers, notebooks, etc.). This reward system appeals to students who are

(A) intrinsically motivated.

(B) extrinsically motivated.

(C) reading below grade level.

(D) able to purchase their own school supplies.

73. The term "leveled books" refers to which of the following?

(A) Over-sized books

(B) Anthologies

(C) Trade books that match student reading levels

(D) Grade-level textbooks

74. Which of the following is the strongest rationale for reading aloud to young children as an effective part of literacy instruction?

(A) Reading aloud can strengthen writing, reading, and speaking skills.

(B) Reading aloud can strengthen listening skills.

(C) Reading aloud can entertain, inform, and inspire.

(D) Reading aloud can motivate the listener to read the book independently.

75. Which of the following sequences best describes the development of a young child?

(A) 1. Learning to trust others
    2. Developing independence
    3. Moral development

(B) 1. Learning to trust others
    2. Moral development
    3. Developing independence

(C) 1. Moral development
    2. Learning to trust others
    3. Developing independence

(D) 1. Developing independence
    2. Moral development
    3. Learning to trust others

76. Which of the following instructional approaches does the passage describe?

This approach attempts to facilitate students' language development through the use of experiences, rather than with printed material alone. After participating in an event or experience, the students, with assistance from the teacher, make a written record of it as a group.

(A) Sight word

(B) Whole language

(C) Think aloud

(D) Language experience

77. Which grade level does the following objective, from the national standards in mathematics, most likely address?

All students should identify and use relationships between operations, such as division as the inverse of multiplication, to solve problems.

(A) Kindergarten

(B) Second

(C) Fourth

(D) First

78. What is one important feature of classroom management?

(A) Speaking in a loud voice

(B) Developing a conduct code during the first half of the year

(C) Carefully stating expectations at the beginning of the year

(D) Ignoring minor infractions

79. A fourth-grade teacher includes the following question on a quiz about the planets: *How many moons does Jupiter have?* This is an example of which of the following types of questions?

(A) Comprehension
(B) Knowledge
(C) Evaluation
(D) Synthesis

80. A teacher tells her class that 1 meter equals 39.37 inches or 3.28 feet or 1.09 yard. The teacher has

(A) taught her class the principle of cause and effect.
(B) provided her class with a stated principle or law.
(C) connected cause-and-effect principles.
(D) provided applications of a law.

81. A major theme in the theoretical framework of many of today's educators is constructivist theory. Which of the following is true of this theory?

(A) Constructivist theory recognizes that most new ideas and learning cannot be based on current or past knowledge.
(B) The task of the instructor is to learn along with the student.
(C) Constructivist theory recognizes that it is more time economical to "tell" rather than to have the student "discover."
(D) None of the above

82. Which of the following is NOT an example of a closed question?

(A) Which bear's bed was too soft?
(B) What was the name of the girl who went to the three bears' house?

(C) Why did the girl go to the three bears' house?
(D) What happened when the girl sat in Little Bear's chair?

83. A first-grade teacher has the students explore with containers of different volumes of water. The teacher is most likely focusing on

(A) capacity.
(B) object permanence.
(C) force.
(D) conservation.

84. Miss Bailey teaches fifth-grade social studies in a self-contained classroom with 25 students of various achievement levels. She is starting a unit on the history of their local community and wants to stimulate the students' thinking. She also wants to encourage students to develop a project as a result of their study. Which type of project would encourage the highest level of thinking by the students?

(A) Giving students a list of questions about people, dates, and events, and then having them put the answers on a poster, with appropriate pictures, to display in class.
(B) Giving students questions to use to interview older members of the community, and then having them write articles based on the interviews and publish them in a booklet.
(C) Discussing the influence of the past on the present community, and then asking students to project what the community might be like in 100 years.
(D) Using archived newspapers to collect data, then having them draw a timeline that includes the major events of the community from its beginning to the current date.

85. Mr. Roberts' sixth-grade social studies class has developed a research project to survey student use of various types of video games. The class designed a questionnaire and then administered it to all fourth-, fifth-, and sixth-

grade students on their campus. The students plan to analyze their data, and then develop a presentation to show at the next parent–teacher meeting. Which types of computer software would be helpful during this class project?

I.   Word processing
II. Database
III. Simulation
IV. Graph or chart

(A) I, II, III, and IV
(B) I, II, and IV
(C) I and III only
(D) III and IV only

86. What might Mrs. Walker, a sixth-grade teacher of world history, include in her planning to keep gifted students challenged?

(A) Assign the students to write an extra report on the history of the Greeks.
(B) Let them tutor the students who are unmotivated.
(C) Encourage students to plan learning activities of their own.
(D) Create for the students a tightly organized and well-designed unit.

87. Which of the following is a national mathematics standard in the area of measurement?

(A) All students should carry out simple unit conversions, such as from centimeters to meters.
(B) All students should explore congruence and similarity.
(C) All students should recognize the differences in representing categorical and numerical data.
(D) All students should represent and analyze patterns and functions, using words, tables, and graphs.

88. Mr. Bates is a second-year early childhood teacher in an urban school. Because so many of his students have language deficits, he uses songs and gestures to call them together, line them up, and accomplish other organizational procedures. This practice indicates that Mr. Bates understands the

(A) importance of continuous monitoring of instructional effectiveness.
(B) developmental characteristics of young children.
(C) importance of communicating enthusiasm for learning.
(D) importance of adjusting communication to ensure that directions and explanations are understood.

89. At the end of each week, Ms. Axtel takes a few minutes to write in her journal. She makes written comments about the lessons she taught that week, as well as the students' responses to those lessons. She also includes comments about how to change or revise the lessons in the future. This practice indicates that Ms. Axtel is

(A) concerned about process writing.
(B) a reflective practitioner.
(C) keeping notes for her formal evaluation.
(D) is a habitual journal writer.

90. An upper elementary class is studying early explorers. The teacher plans to have the students read three different articles. All students are given one of the articles to read for homework. At class time the teacher has the students meet in groups to discuss what they read. The first group read about Columbus, the second about Magellan, and the third about Cortez. The "expert" groups discuss the main points of their article. Then the teacher has the students meet in mixed groups with classmates who have read the different articles. The students will teach each other about what they have read about the explorer. This strategy is known as a

(A) jigsaw.
(B) collaboration.

(C) think-pair-share.

(D) carousel.

91. Students in Pygmalion Primary School have studied the home and family, the school and community, and the state and nation, and are now studying regions of the world. The approach being used is probably which of the following?

(A) Expanding horizon approach

(B) Spiral curriculum

(C) Learning centers

(D) Open classroom

92. If a teacher is considered to be "with it," that teacher

(A) is always aware of what is going on in the classroom.

(B) wears modern clothes.

(C) understands student trends.

(D) uses language that the students relate to easily.

93. Mrs. Gerig, a second-grade teacher, is worried about a new student, Roseanna Jimenez, who will probably be tested for limited English proficiency (LEP) soon. Roseanna does not speak in class. She watches what the other children do and follows suit. She nods for "yes" and shakes her head for "no." She laughs at silly things she sees, but she rarely utters a word at school. When she is asked to read with Mrs. Gerig, she hunches over and cries. When she is asked to write, she copies words from the word wall or writes her ABC's. After a few days, Mrs. Gerig checks the student records and sees that the parents have listed English as the home language. What should Mrs. Gerig do?

(A) Demand that Roseanne speak, read, and write in English.

(B) Request a meeting with the parents, the campus designee for LEP, and a campus administrator as soon as possible to dis-

cuss Roseanna's academic progress and the benefits of the LEP program.

(C) File a concern with the district office regarding the likelihood of the inaccuracy of the parent information reported on the home-language survey.

(D) Say nothing and do the best she can to teach Roseanna to read and write in English.

94. Mrs. Gettler realizes that a student's preferred learning style contributes to his or her success as a student. Mrs. Gettler wants to accommodate as many of her students' individual learning styles as possible. Which of the following describes the way to identify baseline information about the students' learning styles?

(A) Mrs. Gettler should record her observations of individual student's behaviors over a period of several weeks.

(B) Each of the students should be tested by the school psychologist.

(C) Mrs. Gettler should administer a group screening test for identifying learning styles.

(D) Mrs. Gettler should review the permanent file of each student and compare the individual's previous test scores with classroom performance.

95. As the school year progresses, Mrs. Gettler includes discussions of holidays of many cultures. She introduces each holiday prior to the actual day of celebration. The children prepare decorations, learn songs, and read stories about children in the countries where the holiday is celebrated. Which of the following best describes the most likely purpose of this activity?

(A) Celebrating holidays of many cultures is one way to teach appreciation of human diversity.

(B) Celebrating holidays of many cultures is one way to satisfy the demands of political action groups.

(C) Celebrating holidays is one way to encourage students to read aloud to one another.

(D) Celebrating holidays is one way to encourage students to participate in class activities.

96. The students in a dual-grade class have written stories following the "Brown Bear, Brown Bear" format. The stories have been revised and edited by the teacher, Ms. Sanchez. For the next several days, students will enter their stories into the computer using a special software package that allows the addition of graphics and animation. Ms. Sanchez scaffolds each student's work on an as-needed basis. Which of the following criteria should guide her decision-making as she designs an evaluation rubric for the publishing task?

(A) The local, state, and national standards and the prior experience of her students regarding technology use

(B) Information from the parent survey regarding student interests

(C) Roles and responsibilities of support staff in the building

(D) The stages of play development in young children and the correlation to computer readiness

97. Third-grade students observe the characteristics of unknown substances. They write the color, smell, and texture of each unknown with their lab partner. Then they compare their findings with other partners in the class. They are most likely practicing

(A) drawing conclusions.

(B) observing properties.

(C) developing hypotheses.

(D) cooperative learning.

98. In a sixth-grade class students have been learning about the human impact on global warming. To best assess student learning, the teacher should have students complete a/an

(A) performance assessment.

(B) multiple-choice test.

(C) oral presentation with a partner.

(D) essay.

99. Human body temperature regulation via the skin involves

(A) respiration.

(B) transpiration.

(C) perspiration.

(D) sensation.

100. Which of the following vitamins is NOT fat soluble?

(A) Vitamin D

(B) Vitamin C

(C) Vitamin E

(D) Vitamin K

101. Of the following, which test does NOT measure muscular strength and endurance in children?

(A) Pull-ups

(B) Flexed-arm hang

(C) Grip strength test

(D) Sit-and-reach test

102. Dance can reflect the religion of a culture by

I. offering adoration and worship to the deity.

II. appealing to the deity for survival in war.

III. asking the deity for success in the hunt.

IV. miming the actions of planting and harvesting crops.

(A) I and II only

(B) I and III only

(C) II, III, and IV only

(D) I, II, III, and IV

103. Which of the following is NOT a characteristic of cholesterol?

(A) Cholesterol plays a role in the function of the brain.

(B) Cholesterol is a component in the creation of certain hormones.

(C) Cholesterol is produced in the liver.

(D) Excess cholesterol found in the blood of many people usually comes from internal production.

104. A table tennis game is scored to

(A) 15 points.

(B) 15 points, with a margin of 2.

(C) 21 points, with a margin of 2.

(D) 21 points.

105. Harmony results when a melody is accompanied by

I. a rhythm instrument.

II. a guitar.

III. another instrument or singer playing or singing the melody.

IV. another instrument playing chords.

(A) I and II only

(B) I and III only

(C) II and III only

(D) II and IV only

106. Reading and then dramatizing a story, using that story as the basis of a puppet play, scripting that story and performing it in the classroom, and then attending a performance of that story done as a play by a theatre company illustrates which of the following concepts?

(A) Teachers should work with material until they find the correct way to use it with students.

(B) There are multiple ways to express and interpret the same material.

(C) Plays are more interesting than classroom dramatizations.

(D) Students learn less as audience members than as participants in drama activities.

107. Which one of the following statements is most true regarding the materials of visual art?

(A) Industrial innovations in art-making materials have improved art in the past 150 years.

(B) The use of uncommon materials in art making has improved art in the past 150 years.

(C) The use of unusual materials in art making has changed the standards by which we view art.

(D) Industrial innovations in art-making materials have had little influence on visual art.

108. Which of the following is an important reason why music should be included in every child's daily classroom activities?

(A) The imagination, creativity, and aesthetic awareness of a child can be developed through music for more creative living in our mechanized society.

(B) Students need an opportunity to stay current with today's popular music culture.

(C) Making and listening to music is part of our cultural experience and provides opportunities for personal aesthetic growth.

(D) Participating in creatively planned musical activities helps build a child's self-esteem and understanding of others.

109. Which of the following is true for both jazz dance and tap dance?

(A) The technique is based upon isolation of body parts.

(B) The technique is primarily based upon intricate rhythms in the feet.

(C) The technique is based upon lightness and denial of gravity.

(D) The technique emerged from a blending of African and European cultures.

110. Which of the following is NOT true about the act of creating dances?

(A) It involves creative problem solving.

(B) It must happen outside of the classroom within a special time.

(C) It can express ideas and explore feelings.

(D) It can teach math or science.

Detailed Explanations of
Answers for Practice Test 1

PRAXIS 0011

1. (B)	23. (A)	45. (D)	67. (B)	89. (B)
2. (B)	24. (D)	46. (B)	68. (B)	90. (A)
3. (C)	25. (D)	47. (D)	69. (B)	91. (A)
4. (B)	26. (C)	48. (B)	70. (D)	92. (A)
5. (A)	27. (A)	49. (C)	71. (C)	93. (B)
6. (D)	28. (B)	50. (B)	72. (B)	94. (A)
7. (B)	29. (C)	51. (A)	73. (C)	95. (A)
8. (B)	30. (D)	52. (B)	74. (A)	96. (A)
9. (C)	31. (D)	53. (B)	75. (A)	97. (B)
10. (A)	32. (B)	54. (C)	76. (D)	98. (D)
11. (B)	33. (C)	55. (B)	77. (C)	99. (C)
12. (C)	34. (C)	56. (C)	78. (C)	100. (B)
13. (D)	35. (B)	57. (B)	79. (B)	101. (D)
14. (D)	36. (D)	58. (C)	80. (B)	102. (D)
15. (C)	37. (B)	59. (C)	81. (D)	103. (D)
16. (D)	38. (A)	60. (A)	82. (C)	104. (C)
17. (A)	39. (A)	61. (D)	83. (D)	105. (D)
18. (B)	40. (C)	62. (C)	84. (C)	106. (B)
19. (C)	41. (D)	63. (C)	85. (B)	107. (C)
20. (A)	42. (A)	64. (A)	86. (C)	108. (C)
21. (C)	43. (A)	65. (D)	87. (A)	109. (D)
22. (A)	44. (B)	66. (C)	88. (D)	110. (B)

PRACTICE TEST 1 PROGRESS CHART

Arts and Physical Education Curriculum, Instruction, and Assessment ____/13

88	99	100	101	102	103	104	105	106	107	108	109	110

General Information Curriculum, Instruction, and Assessment ____/25

1	5	6	7	9	10	12	16	36	37	43	51	55

56	60	71	72	75	78	81	82	89	91	92	93

Mathematics Curriculum, Instruction, and Assessment ____/16

8	11	25	26	27	33	34	35

61	67	68	69	70	77	80	87

Reading and Language Arts Curriculum, Instruction, and Assessment ____/34

2	13	14	15	17	18	19	28	29	30	31	32	38

39	40	41	42	44	45	46	47	48	53	54	57	58

59	62	63	73	74	76	94	96

Science Curriculum, Instruction, and Assessment ____/11

3	4	22	24	64	65	66	79	83	97	98

Social Studies Curriculum, Instruction, and Assessment ____/11

20	21	23	49	50	52	84	85	86	90	95

PRACTICE TEST 1
DETAILED EXPLANATIONS OF ANSWERS

1. (B)

Students are able to perform better on tests when their physical setting, which includes lighting, temperature, and seating, is favorable. When students feel anxious over a test (A), or when teachers threaten against poor performances (D), students do not perform as well. Outside disruptions (C) can break a student's concentration; this is especially true for younger children.

2. (B)

Cinquain, limerick and haiku are all forms of poetry. The teacher most likely read examples of each type of poem as part of a study of poetry. The correct answer is (B).

3. (C)

In this scenario the teacher is practicing interdisciplinary instruction. This requires the students to make a direct connection between what they are learning in different content areas. In this case the students are incorporating the information they are learning at science time with skills they are developing at math time. This is beneficial to student success in both areas of instruction.

4. (B)

The students are practicing classification when they sort cards that display different species of animals, such as mammals, reptiles, and amphibians. The

correct answer is (B). Hypothesizing and concluding are often parts of learning experiences in science; however, classifying best fits the task of the students in the scenario. While this task involves some organizational skills, this is not a scientific process.

5. (A)

As the decades change, so do the labels the school systems use to identify children who differ from the mainstream—and may have difficulty with mathematics and other subjects; the school systems of the twenty-first century tend to label children who differ from the mainstream as "at-risk" (A), not "culturally deprived" (B), "culturally different" (C), "slow learners" (D), "semi-lingual," or "limited-English speaking."

6. (D)

Individual goals for a student should be developed after reviewing both the student's history and assessing the student's motivation. This will ensure that the goals can be met by the student. Goals should not be based solely on the student's academic record (A) or created only from individual observations (C). They should also not be the same for all students (B) because students learn at different levels and aim for different goals.

7. (B)

Research has shown that it is favorable to provide feedback in test situations when the feedback is delayed by a day or so, rather than giving immediate feedback (A). Delaying the feedback session for a few weeks (C) is not beneficial to the students because too much time has elapsed. A class review of the test has been shown to be more beneficial in clearing up misunderstandings than handwritten notations (D).

8. (B)

While it is important for students to learn about budgets, it is not the objective of this learning experience for third graders. The correct answer is (B). Having students practice a skill such as maintaining a checkbook shows them how math is used in real life. Students will practice basic mathematical computations during this activity and may be reviewing concepts that have been previously taught; however, this is not the focus of the scenario.

9. (C)

Inclusion places the focus on ability and decreases the focus on disability and inability; choices (A) and (B) are incorrect. With inclusion, the neighborhood school accepts children as the first option and considers other educational placements only if that child, even with substantial support, cannot succeed in the class with age-appropriate peers. Choice (C) is the best option. The neighborhood school should not be the last option; (D) is not the best choice.

10. (A)

Praise has been shown to be the most effective when it is authentic and low-key. It should be used frequently; therefore, (B) is incorrect. It should consist of complex responses that provide information about the reasons for the quality of the student response; therefore, (C) is incorrect. It should be

used to provide all students with positive experiences; therefore, (D) is incorrect.

11. (B)

A fact family is a set of related addition and subtraction, or multiplication and division equations using the same numbers. The correct answer is (B), which includes multiplication and division equations using the numbers 3, 4, and 12 only.

12. (C)

Teachers/tutors who have "pulled out" students from an inclusive classroom situation for short-term instruction have found that these diverse learners seem to learn best with increased positive reinforcement (C). Skills should be emphasized; (A), therefore, is incorrect. The use of ONLY basic texts is not highly effective; (B) is not the best choice. Whole language instruction does not work with everyone; (D) is not the best choice.

13. (D)

Teachers and students must clarify the purposes for reading. These purposes—which may vary from passage to passage, student to student, and situation to situation—include aesthetics, fact attainment (efference), and a combination of factual and aesthetic purposes. Choice (D) is, therefore, the best answer. Neither the factual aspects (A) nor what the words suggest (B) are important alone. Both factual information and aesthetic purposes are important; (C) is not an adequate answer.

14. (D)

Letter grades and self-assessments will not provide specific feedback for students that would help further their development as writers. A rubric is most helpful in assessing student writing and promoting growth. The correct choice is (D). The rubric that takes descriptive language, content, sentence variety, and voice into account matches the lessons taught by the teacher. This is the best tool for assessing this writing assignment.

15. (C)

A word wall is composed of common words. It is also used to help build literacy; however, the words are usually listed together on a large piece of paper or hung clustered together like a quilt. Phonics instruction focuses on the letter sound symbol relationship. The correct answer is (C). The labeling of items, in the classroom in this example, is known as environmental print. Whole language refers to an approach to literacy instruction, which would support the inclusion of environmental print.

16. (D)

According to the operant model in behavioral theory, negative reinforcement is removing a stimulus in order to cause a behavior to increase. Reinforcement can be positive or negative in that is it applied or removed. All reinforcement, positive or negative, increases the likelihood that the behavior will occur again. Likewise, punishment can be positive or negative, but all punishment decreases the likelihood that the behavior will occur again.

17. (A)

In a balanced literacy approach the teacher uses a wide variety of resources and strategies aimed at developing skills in the area of language arts. Various types of authentic literature are used, as well as instructional techniques. Students work individually and in a range of groupings, depending on their needs, interests, and abilities.

18. (B)

A teacher keeps a running reading record by writing down what the student actually reads aloud. This helps the teacher in identifying and addressing what the student may need to do to increase reading skills. The record does not necessarily involve a tape recorder (A), testing (C), or noting the books that have been read (D).

19. (C)

During the publishing stage of the writing process, students often share their work with others; this would not be considering conferencing. Pre-writing or brainstorming is usually an independent activity, as is drafting or writing. The correct answer is (C). Peer editing is a common strategy that involves students conferring with one another regarding the content and mechanics of their writing.

20. (A)

A needs assessment will help students make the connection between their current skills and those that will be new to them. Choice (B) is wrong because a needs assessment focuses on the skills a student currently possesses. Choice (C) is incorrect because the needs assessment is designed to determine what needs to be taught that is not currently in the curriculum. Choice (D) is a false statement; a needs assessment is not designed to motivate students.

21. (C)

A positive environment must be created to minimize the effects of negative external factors. Choice (A) is inappropriate because changing the text but allowing the environment to remain the same only results in maintaining the status quo. Choice (B) is incorrect because relating the students' personal interests to the new material is only a part of creating a positive environment. Choice (D) is wrong because, again, it is only a small part of maximizing the effects of a positive learning environment.

22. (A)

When students are allowed to select their own problems for study, they become self-directed problem solvers. As such, they have the opportunity to structure their own learning experiences. Assessing students' needs in a naturalistic setting (B) is highly time-consuming and not an important benefit of having students select their own problem to investigate. There may not be a wide variety of instructional materials available to the students (C) as they engage in studying the temperature problem, so this is not likely to be a major benefit. Learning to appreciate opposing viewpoints (D) is a competency that would be better addressed in social studies and language arts rather than in an activity that deals with a natural empirical science.

23. (A)

People are more highly motivated to solve problems that they choose, rather than problems that are chosen for them. Choosing a problem for investigation does not increase student diversity (B). Problem selection has nothing to do with the structure of student groups (C). Although students may engage in more self-assessment (D), this is not the most important force at work.

24. (D)

When teaching a concept such as multiplication, it can be beneficial to students to begin with the more concrete tasks and lead up to the more abstract. Task I is the most concrete because it asks the students to physically manipulate the blocks. Task IV is more abstract because it requires students to visualize and illustrate the concept of grouping. Task III is even more abstract because it requires students to do problem solving by just using numbers and symbols. Task II is the most abstract because it asks students to solve the problem with an unknown. Therefore, (D) (I, IV, III, II) is the correct answer.

25. (D)

The student is multiplying the numbers on either side of the division symbol in the equations provided in the question. If the student continues to make this mistake it is likely that the answer to $12 \div 2$ would be 24. (D) is the correct choice.

26. (C)

If the students only estimate (A) the amount of supplies they need such as cups and plates, they may not end up having enough of the items. Probability (B) is not involved in calculating amounts. The correct answer is (C). The students will need to make sure that they have the exact amount of the supplies needed, so that there will be enough for everyone. Measurement (D) is not involved either.

27. (A)

Choice (A) depicts the best course of action for the teacher to take. Since several students do not understand the concept, the teacher needs to re-teach it using new materials and instructional approaches. Repeating past lessons without changing them would not be as helpful, nor would assigning additional computations or textbook readings.

28. (B)

Guided reading groups (A) are most often composed of students with similar ability levels and needs. The teacher facilitates their group meetings. The correct answer is (B). The groups described in the question are most likely to be considered literacy circles, since the students were grouped based on interest, the students have specific roles or jobs, and they work mostly independently from the teacher. Book clubs (C) is an informal name for readers who are grouped together for a variety of reasons, often outside of the school day. Homogenous groups (D) are comprised of students of the same skill level.

29. (C)

Mrs. Ratu's lack of competency is exhibited in her lack of understanding of her students and in her teaching at the elementary level. Mrs. Ratu was not teaching her students at the appropriate level (A). Although she may have desired to make reading easy for her students (B), she was not going about it correctly. When appropriate techniques are used, teaching ninth graders to read is no more difficult than teaching third graders to read.

30. (D)

Students who speak English as a second language (ESL) are a challenge to educators. Guidelines, however, are available to help both specialized and mainstream teachers who have not worked with ESL students in the past. Choice (D) is the best answer. Language-minority students have the right and the responsibility to learn to read and write in English. Response (B), which indicates that ESL students do not have the right to speak their native language, is incorrect and should not be a selection. ESL students do not have the obligation to speak their native language; therefore, (C) is not a good choice. ESL students do have the right in our country to speak their native language; therefore, (A) is not a good choice.

31. (D)

Activities that tend to combine reading, writing, listening, and speaking are more likely to enhance literacy and the development of orality for the language-minority student. Choice (D) suggests that this integration is advantageous. (D) is the best answer. Choices (A), (B), and (C) indicate a sequence in literacy instruction; none of these answers is appropriate.

32. (B)

Since the students are being asked to explain the actions of the character, they are working at the evaluation level of Bloom's Taxonomy. This level requires skills in reasoning, explaining, and assessing.

33. (C)

While some students may be uninterested in telling time or are unfocused during math time; that does not explain why most students are struggling. The correct answer is (C). Most second graders are six or seven years old in the beginning of the school year. It is likely that few to none of them are developmentally ready to understand sophisticated concepts such as elapsed time.

34. (C)

Scales (A) would be appropriate for teaching about weight. Rulers (B) would be a good tool for teaching about length and height. Tangrams (C) would be the LEAST appropriate tool for studying measurement. They are used primarily for geometry instruction. Therefore, (C) is the correct answer. Calendars (D) would be appropriate for learning about measurement of time.

35. (B)

By providing a variety of learning experiences that allow students to utilize different strengths and interests, the teacher is reaching many students. This shows an awareness of theories on learning styles. (B) is the correct answer.

36. (D)

The outcome or product of an instructional activity is to help students improve their work. Answers (A), (B), and (C) may be true statements, but they describe a teacher's priorities or expectations, rather than an instructional goal.

37. (B)

Focusing on process—not just content—is an important feature of inquiry learning. Inquiry learning creates a questioning environment, includes conferences, responds to issues, promotes individual and small-group inquiry, and is facilitated by guiding and encouraging teachers. Getting information mainly from a textbook (A), teacher lecture (C), and direct teaching (D) are not required components of inquiry learning.

38. (A)

Teaching multicultural students effectively should enable them to connect the curriculum to their own lives. Such teaching may not result in a standardized approach to the curriculum (B) but rather varying instructional approaches. Ideally, teachers may continue to examine their own beliefs

and those of their students; choices (C) and (D) are not the best answers.

39. (A)

Pat Conroy is a noted author; however, he has not written books for children. Beverly Cleary, Judy Blume, and Shel Silverstein are all esteemed writers of children's literature.

40. (C)

The correct answer is (C). Phonemes are the speech sounds. Graphemes (A) are the written symbols for the speech sounds. These voice-to-print relationships are important to reading. Phonetics (D) refers to the method of teaching reading that emphasizes the association between the grapheme and the phoneme. Semantics (B) refers to the study of the meaning of language.

41. (D)

Mnemonics are devices used to aid memorization, such as using ROY G. BIV to remember the colors of the rainbow (red, orange, yellow, green, blue, indigo, and violet). Choral responses (A) are the oral repetition (B) of skills or words, and codings (C) are making marks or taking shorthand.

42. (A)

The correct answer is (A). In the emerging literacy stage, children are making the transition from speaking to writing and reading with support from others. Their literacy skills are considered to be emergent. During the developing stage children are becoming more independent in their reading, their writing, and their speaking. They are usually on a middle-first to late-second-grade level. In the transitional reading stage, children usually have an instructional reading level of second grade or beyond. Ideally, these children should spend much of their time with independent-level and instructional-level materials. Mastery is not considered a stage in early literacy development.

43. (A)

The teacher is conducting an informal assessment by reviewing students work as they complete a task. Teachers are able to collect information on student progress by observing how students approach assignments, as well as their ability to complete them. This is an informal way to assess as opposed to tests, which are formal assessments.

44. (B)

Myths are stories written to explain things that the teller does not understand. (B) is the correct answer. Fairy tales (A) have the element of magic, often have a certain pattern, and may present an ideal to the reader. Legends (C) are usually exaggerated stories about real people, places, and things. A parable (D) is a story that is realistic and has a moral, which teaches a lesson.

45. (D)

Children learn more from a text if the teacher helps them figure out how the book was put together. It makes the text more understandable. It also helps them read the text critically, as part of the conversation can address the issue of what is missing in the text.

46. (B)

In using three different versions of this well-known story, Ms. Smith is creating an opportunity to bring a multicultural perspective to the drama ac-

tivity (I). In versions of *Cinderella* from around the world, the story of the mistreated but kindhearted protagonist is basically the same, but the characters, settings, and ways in which the plot unfolds are culturally centered. Furthermore, because Ms. Smith is using scripted versions of the story and staging these plays with costumes, scenery, and props, she is making theatrical elements integral to the performances (II). The students are engaging in formal dramatic activity that will result in a theatrical product, rather than informal, process-centered drama, so III is incorrect. Choice IV is incorrect because the students are not the ones who have adapted the story, and therefore, they are not having firsthand experience with that process. So the correct answer is (B), which includes only I and II.

47. (D)

Teachers must engage in ongoing self-evaluation of their own values, attitudes, disposition, and belief systems to teach diverse learners effectively and to invite and extend literacy forms, skills, and interests; these teachers must reflect on how their (1) literacy histories compare to those of other teachers and students, (2) peer experiences may have been privileged in school settings, and (3) literacy experiences are tied to their identities in order to extend literacy.

Choice (D) is the best answer. For this reason, choice (A) is incorrect because remembering one's past can help. Thinking back on one's school setting is applicable; (B) is a poor choice. Answer (C) suggests that school experiences have no effect on the learner's self-identity; this is false, so (C) is not a correct answer.

48. (B)

The best way to teach children to read, regardless of grade level, is to use a program of emergent literacy that includes pattern books and journal writing with invented spelling. Although an intensive phonics program that includes drill-and-practice work may be effective with some students, it is not the most effective way to teach all students to read, so (A) is incorrect. Choice (C) is clearly incorrect because none of the students read above the 2.0 grade level. An ESL program is intended to provide assistance to only those students who are learning English as a second language, so (D) is incorrect. Additionally, the learning resource teacher should provide assistance to only those students who have been identified as having a learning disability that qualifies them to receive services.

49. (C)

Careful planning (III), which includes checking on the availability of resources and materials (II) resulted in student involvement in the unit. Mrs. Doe did reflective thinking during the discussion (I); however, reflective thinking is only one component of communication and is included in careful planning and its correlation to success in the classroom. Resources and materials were available, but this is a result of careful planning. Personal acquaintance with a Native American (IV) would have helped shape the students' attitudes, but it is not necessary for student involvement. So the correct answer (C) includes II and III only.

50. (B)

Multiple strategies were planned for the motivation of the students (I), but a result of the strategies was that each student participated in some way regardless of ability (II) and the unit was integrated into other subjects (III)—for example, reading, writing—through library assignments. Ultimately, the unit will be integrated with the other subjects; however, this is not the only goal, so (A) and (C) are incorrect. Developing a foundation for teaching American history (IV) is not even a long-range goal, although the attitudes and beliefs developed

in the project may become the foundation upon which the students will build their philosophy of American history. Therefore, (D) is incorrect.

51. (A)

The external factors of the field trip could create a positive motivation and would allow the students to make the connection between their old skills and the new skills they were learning (I). The external factors involved in a field trip are positive; however, Mrs. Doe gave instructions that each student was to take notes on what he or she saw, heard, and experienced (II). The skill of note taking was founded upon the library assignment that had preceded the field trip, and the students were to make the connection. No mention is made of community involvement in the field trip; statement III is not relevant. The students did not take responsibility for their own learning (IV); they were given instructions concerning what they were to do before they left for the field trip. Choices (B), (C), and (D), which include incorrect statements (III and IV), are therefore incorrect.

52. (B)

Respect was shown to the children by allowing them a choice of field trips (II). It is an example of the array of instructional strategies (IV) used by Mrs. Doe. Choice (A) is incomplete and therefore incorrect. Enhancing students' self-concept and fostering the view of learning as a purposeful pursuit [(C) and (D)] are both incorporated in II, respecting differences and understanding the society in which we live.

53. (B)

Choice (B) is the correct answer. The purpose of persuasive writing is to convince the reader that the perspective or course of action suggested by the writer is valid. The purpose of expository writing (A) is to explain and clarify ideas. The purpose of descriptive writing (C) is to provide information about a person, place, or thing. A narrative (D) is a story or an account of an incident or a series of incidents.

54. (C)

Requiring both a cognitive and a performance objective makes the student show that he or she not only had the knowledge but could also apply that knowledge to a life situation, so (C) is the correct response. Although statement (A) is true, it is not the foundation for developing specific objectives. Statement (B), again, is an assumption and not relevant to the setting of certain objectives. Teaching style and learning styles (D) are not relevant to the behavioral objectives.

55. (B)

This question is designed to demonstrate an understanding that the performance objective should directly tie into the assessment. Students need to know what the expectation is for them to complete the necessary assignments. Students do not understand what assessment tools are; they need clear directions and a list of explanations, so (A) is incorrect. Although the unit may have many new vocabulary words, students need to learn them within the context of the unit rather than from a random list; they should not feel threatened when learning to prepare for a test, so (C) is incorrect. There is no connection between notebooks and learning, so (D) is incorrect.

56. (C)

Rubrics are designed to help teachers assess each student's achievement and the quality of his or her responses (I). Therefore, each criterion needs to

have quality points (II), such as outstanding (5–4), good (3–2), and/or fair (1–0). Rubrics need to cover a number of subject areas to allow for a fair assessment of the student's work, in contrast to option III. Students may rate themselves (IV); however, the teacher needs to work with them as they complete the ratings. Therefore, only I and II—option (C)—are correct.

57. (B)

Students often disclose more personal information when writing in journals than when speaking in class. The teacher can also check for comprehension of content and the success or failure of class objectives. Journals typically are not graded with consideration to standard usage or grammatical constructions; therefore, (A) is incorrect. The assignment has no direct bearing on time-management skills; therefore, (C) is incorrect. Choice (D) is irrelevant: no mention is made of giving daily grades on the journal writing.

58. (C)

The language experience approach (LEA) is a proven method of increasing students' reading and writing proficiency and their overall language competency. It requires that students write about what they know. Choices (A), (B), and (D) are irrelevant. Choice (A) superficially addresses that Ms. Johnson is an English teacher, and choice (B) refers to autobiographies, something that is not mentioned in the preceding information. Choice (D) foreshadows the library project, but it has not yet been introduced into the context of these questions.

59. (C)

A basic principle in providing students with appropriate feedback is to first note the student's strengths (or positive aspects of the student's work and/or performance) and then to note specific ways the student can improve his or her work and/or performance. Therefore, the best approach for a teacher to take in providing students with feedback on written work is to first note the good things about students' writings and then to suggest ways to improve. Choices (A) and (B) are in essence the same; both choices indicate that only students' strengths would be acknowledged, omitting the important aspect of addressing ways students can improve. Neither action would enhance students' cognitive skills nor their metacognitive skills (or self-awareness). Choice (D) is unacceptable because it denigrates the teacher's responsibility to evaluate students' performances on the basis of individual merit against the standards established by particular disciplines.

60. (A)

Option (A) is the best answer of the four options for the following reasons. First, learning-style information acknowledges that although learners acquire knowledge in different ways, those differences can lead to effective learning when students are taught cognitive strategies that complement their natural learning tendencies; basically, teaching students about learning styles (and especially about their own learning styles) is a recognition of human diversity. Second, beyond mere recognition of human diversity is the legitimacy of different approaches to learning. Every student can perform at a level of proficiency, although not every student will attain that level in the same manner; in other words, learning styles validate students as learners and promote high standards for academic achievement. Third, when students are taught not only about learning styles in general but also about their own learning styles in particular, they are empowered to take responsibility for their own learning. Fourth, of the four options, only choices (A) and (D) are tasks actively engaging the student. Choices (B) and (C) are both passive activities, and are therefore poor

choices. Choice (D) requires that students perform a task without any help (direct instruction) for accomplishing the task; simply asking students to name additional strengths without giving them an opportunity to self-examine, self-assess, and explore their strengths will not produce the desired outcome. Only choice (A) gives students the information they need to accomplish the task the teacher has identified as being important.

61. (D)

The question relates to appropriate sequencing of activities. Choice (D) is the best introductory activity in order to generate student interest in this new field of mathematics and to get students thinking about how to produce fractals. It would stimulate students to use higher-level thinking skills to make predictions by drawing on their knowledge of how to solve problems mathematically. Choice (A) would be the least appropriate to begin the study. Students who want to learn more could research this topic after they have developed an interest in fractals. Choice (B) would be appropriate as a later step, after students are interested in the process and are ready to learn how to produce fractals. Choice (C) would be appropriate as a subsequent step in the process of learning how to produce fractals. Choice (B) requires students to use preplanned formulas; choice (C) allows them to develop their own formulas, a very high-level activity.

62. (C)

During the pre-communication stage the student randomly uses letters. During the pre-phonetic stage (A) the student begins to use some letters correctly. (C) is the correct answer. During the phonetic stage (C) the student spells the words the way that they sound. During the transitional stage (D) the student uses both correct spelling and phonetic spelling.

63. (C)

Behavioral observation is the examination of what the student does during class time. A teacher should be interested in how much time a student spends on task and how much time is spent off task. Teachers generally observe a student for a limited period of time and mark the activities in which the student is engaged. If a particular activity, such as talking, appears frequently, the teacher notes it. Behavioral observation alone is not the best way to determine comprehension [(A) and (B)] or verbal skills (D).

64. (A)

While it may be important to provide a fact-based worksheet that can be used for a study guide for the end of the unit test, it is not an effective way to increase student motivation and interest at the beginning of a new science unit about mammals. (A) is the correct answer. Cards with actual photos and facts about mammals, nonfiction picture books, and videos are all more effective and interesting resources.

65. (D)

(D) is the correct answer. A performance task such as having the student label actual rock and mineral samples as a demonstration for the teacher is the best choice as an assignment of student understanding. It is most similar to how the student learned the information. A paper-and-pencil test and written description are very different formats than the students have been working in. Work that is completed at home is often a poor assessment of student learning as the students may receive varying levels of help with the assignment.

66. (C)

While the teacher does include hands-on activities, inquiry-based learning, and reflective prac-

tice, the scenario gives three examples of using literacy skills in the content area of science. Therefore, (C) is the best answer.

67. (B)

1,643 (A) is written in standard numeric form. The correct answer is (B). $1,000 + 600 + 40 + 3$ is written in expanded notation. Choices (C) and (D) represent the number through words.

68. (B)

The correct answer is (B). Differentiated instruction is aimed at teaching students at their current level in order to facilitate their growth to the next. With the range of students described in the scenario, the teacher will best meet the needs of all students by implementing this strategy. Whole class instruction (A) is appropriate when most to all students need to learn specific content or skills at the same time. Small group instruction (C) can be a part of differentiated instruction; however, it would need to be done with homogeneous groups. The choice did not specify this.

69. (B)

It is not best practice to avoid using manipulatives at math time. (B) is the correct answer. The best approach is for the teacher to give all students time to explore the manipulatives before the lesson. This allows students to freely explore the objects before they need to use them as the teacher directs. It would be unfair to the growth and development of the students to not allow everyone to use manipulatives at math time.

70. (D)

Having the students who finish early help classmates who are still working may be appropriate occasionally; however, it is unfair for a teacher to make this common practice. Having the students who finish early read quietly at their desks takes the focus away from math time and does not extend the students' learning in this area. Giving the students who finish early additional practice problems may not solve the issue, as they will likely quickly complete these. The correct answer is (D). By giving the students who finish early a challenging extension activity, the teacher keeps the focus on math and provides a productive learning experience.

71. (C)

A quiet classroom may be appropriate for some learning activities and inappropriate for others. It is not necessarily a good or bad learning environment, nor does it demonstrate that the teacher has appropriate control of the students (e.g., the students might all be asleep).

72. (B)

Providing external rewards (such as tokens and prizes) for reading appeals to students who are extrinsically motivated. Intrinsically motivated students (A) read for the pleasure and self-satisfaction of reading. Students who read below, at, and above grade level may be motivated extrinsically or intrinsically, so (C) is too exclusive. Some students may not be interested in earning tokens to acquire school supplies, whether or not they are able to purchase their own supplies (D).

73. (C)

Choice (C) is the correct answer. The term trade books refers to the authentic literature selections found in a classroom library. These are often chapter books of either fiction or nonfiction genres. Teachers and literacy experts "level" trade books by assigning letters to match the range of student reading levels. This helps teachers and students pick books that are right for them.

74. (A)

All of the choices present a rationale for reading aloud to students; however, (A) is the best answer. The strongest rationale for reading aloud as an effective part of literacy instruction is that it can strengthen writing, reading, and speaking skills.

75. (A)

The first thing children learn is to trust others. Moral development cannot occur without independence, as both independent judgment and maturation through interactions in social settings contribute to the development of a conscience. The correct order is (1) learning to trust others, (2) developing independence, and (3) moral development.

76. (D)

The sight word method (A) to reading instruction involves exposing students to lists or cards with words commonly found in beginning reader books. Whole language (B) refers to an approach to literacy instruction, which values holistic and authentic experiences with literature. During a think aloud (C) the teacher models, explains, and describes how to apply a literacy strategy successfully. The correct answer is (D), language experience.

77. (C)

The correct answer is (C). "All students should identify and use relationships between operations, such as division as the inverse of multiplication, to solve problems" is an objective for students in grades 3–5.

78. (C)

It has been shown that it is very important for a teacher to carefully explain the objectives and procedures of the classroom from the beginning. These objectives and procedures should then be consistently enforced throughout the year. Speaking in a loud voice (A) may intimidate the students and is not an effective method of classroom management. Developing a conduct code during the first half of the year (B) is not effective because students need to know what is expected of them from the beginning. Ignoring minor infractions (D) is not a feature of classroom management.

79. (B)

How many moons does Jupiter have? This question requires students to recall facts about the planet and to demonstrate this knowledge. The correct answer is (B).

80. (B)

By telling her students about equivalent measurements, she has stated a principle or law. She has not taught cause and effect [(A), (C)] or provided applications of the principle (D).

81. (D)

Choice (D) is the best answer because all of the other answers are incorrect, according to Jerome Bruner's constructivist theory. Bruner stresses that teachers must base new learning/ideas/concepts on the current or past knowledge of the learners, so (A) is incorrect. Bruner believes that the instructor should try to encourage students to discover principles on their own and to translate this new information into a format that is appropriate to the learner, so (B) is incorrect because Bruner does not stress that the instructor must learn with the students. A

major theme in Bruner's theoretical framework is that learning is an active (not a passive) process; because the students discover (ideally) on their own, (C) is incorrect.

82. (C)

This is not a closed question, but an open question, requiring some thoughtful reflecting and speculation to answer. Answers (A), (B), and (D) are examples of closed questions, requiring a simple statement of recall as an answer.

83. (D)

It is unlikely that a teacher would address capacity or force with students as young as first grade. Object permanence refers to a young child's developing understanding that objects remain in existence when they are out of sight. The correct answer is (D). The teacher is most likely focusing on conservation by having the students pour water into various containers. The concept of conservation is the understanding that certain things remain the same (such as the amount of water) despite changes in other features (such as the size and shape of the container).

84. (C)

Project (C) calls for work involving analysis, synthesis, and evaluation levels. Choice (C) is the best choice because it asks the students to analyze how past causes have produced current effects, then to predict what future effects might be based on what they have learned about cause–effect relationships. It requires students to put information together in a new way. Choice (A) may involve some creativity in putting the information on a poster, but in general, answering factual questions calls for lower-level (knowledge or comprehension) thinking. Choice (B) may involve some degree of creativity, but giving students prepared questions requires thinking at a lower level than having students develop their own questions, and then determining which answers to write about. Choice (D) also is a lower-level activity, although there may be a great deal of research for factual information. All options may be good learning activities, but (A), (B), and (D) do not require as much deep thinking as choice (C). Depending on the depth of the study, a teacher may want to include several of these activities.

85. (B)

This question asks for an evaluation of which software programs will help the students achieve their goals of analyzing data and presenting the results. Item I, word processing, would be used in developing and printing the questionnaire, as well as writing a report on the results. Item II, a database, would be used to sort and print out information in various categories so students could organize and analyze their data. Item III, a simulation, would not be appropriate here because the students' basic purpose is to collect data and analyze it. The project does not call for a program to simulate a situation or event. Item IV, graph or chart, would be very useful in analyzing information and in presenting it to others.

86. (C)

People are more highly motivated to solve problems that they choose than to solve problems that are chosen for them. Assigning an additional report (A) may seem like punishment. Although some students may enjoy teaching the unmotivated students (B) and may learn from the experience, the gifted students must always increase their level and must never take over the role of the teacher. Worksheets and many tasks (busywork activities?) are not the best way to help students; (D) is not the best answer.

87. (A)

The correct answer is (A). This is a grade 3–5 objective in the area of measurement. Choice (B) is a geometry objective. Choice (C) is an objective in data analysis and probability. Choice (D) is an algebra objective.

88. (D)

Songs, rhymes, and hand and arm signals resonate with young children as play. When procedural instructions are prompted in this way, young children have connections on cognitive, emotional, and physical levels. Choices (A), (B), and (C) are incorrect because they do not focus on communicating directions for organizational procedures.

89. (B)

Maintaining a written journal about events in the classroom as well as student responses is a technique used by reflective practitioners to review and evaluate their personal growth as professionals. Choice (A) is incorrect because journal writing may or may not indicate a concern about process writing. In addition, journal writing alone is not the same as process writing. Choice (C) is incorrect because the purpose of the journal is much broader, even though the instructor may use some of her journal entries in her formal evaluation. Choice (D) is incorrect because it is too simplistic. If Ms. Axtel were a habitual journal writer, she would be writing about a variety of topics, not just emphasizing those related to teaching.

90. (A)

The cooperative learning technique described in the scenario is known as a jigsaw. It involves students learning about a concept, place, or person and then meeting with classmates who learned or read the same thing. These "experts" determine the main ideas and then meet with classmates who studied or read something different to teach each other about the concepts. All students are then held accountable for all information.

91. (A)

The scope and sequence of social studies given here is a direct example of the expanding horizon or widening horizon approach developed originally in the 1920s and still used by many textbook companies, school systems, and teachers. The spiral curriculum (B) enables the children to build progressively on information learned previously, and it does not fit the sequence described. Learning centers (C) is a type of classroom organization; however, the sequence described seems to relate more to the vertical organization of the school than to the horizontal organization suggested by learning centers. The open classroom (D) is based on the British primary schools and involves a lot of pupil freedom and choice. Like learning centers, the open classroom relates to horizontal school organization whereas the question concerns vertical organization.

92. (A)

A teacher's "with it"-ness relates to the ability to observe and manage disruptions quickly, quietly, and at all times. For example, a "with-it" teacher who is helping a student with deskwork would be able to detect and distinguish any disruptive behavior in a different part of the room.

93. (B)

Response (B) is respectful of the learner and her parents while providing an opportunity to discuss the student's needs and the teacher's instructional goals. Parents who do not speak English often opt out of the LEP services because they want their children to speak English. They may not understand that the foundation of reading and writing is oral language, and therefore the LEP program would offer the strongest academic program for learning to read and write as well as to speak English. Choice (A) is incorrect because it is not centered around the student and would force inappropriate instructional cycles for this student. Choice (C) is incorrect because it dismisses the option of a campus-level solution with the parents and moves it to a policy-level issue. Choice (D) is wrong because it is not student centered and very likely is out of compliance with district policy and procedure.

94. (A)

One of the most reliable ways to identify individual learning styles is to observe students over a period of time and to make informal notes about their work habits and their choices within the classroom. Choice (B) is incorrect because although a school psychologist could provide information about each student's learning style, teachers can identify this information on their own. Choice (C) is incorrect because although administering a group screening test will identify learning styles, such a test may be difficult to obtain, and the teacher could gain the same knowledge through simple observation. Choice (D) is incorrect because a student's permanent file may not contain this information. An individual student's learning style may have changed over the years, and there is no guarantee that this change will be noted in the permanent record.

95. (A)

Celebrating holidays of different cultures teaches appreciation for human diversity. Even though celebrating different cultures has become a political issue, this should not influence a teacher when planning such a lesson, so (B) is incorrect.

Choice (C) is incorrect because although celebrating holidays is one way to encourage students to read, this may or may not be related to encouraging students to read aloud. Celebrating holidays may encourage all students to participate in class activities (D), but teaching an appreciation for human diversity is a more accurate statement of the most significant reason for the activity.

96. (A)

The evaluation rubric should be based on current technology standards. Because this is a dual-grade classroom, the rubric should include competencies from both grade levels. Choice (B) is incorrect because a parent survey will not provide the information needed to design a rubric. Choice (C) is incorrect because knowing the job expectations for colleagues is not relevant to this problem. Choice (D) is incorrect because stages of play development and computer readiness do not relate to the issue of rubric design.

97. (B)

During a science lab students are likely to practice drawing conclusions and developing hypotheses; however, these practices are not described in this scenario. By noting the color, smell, and texture of each unknown, the students are observing properties. The correct answer is (B). While the students are working with a partner and other classmates, the formal elements of cooperative learning are not mentioned.

98. (D)

The best way to assess students' understanding of a complex concept such as the human impact on global warming would be to have them write an essay. Performance assessments would be better used to assess demonstrated skills. Multiple-choice tests are best for fact-based concepts. While an oral presentation would allow students to discuss a range of understandings, presenting with a partner may not allow each student to best show individual understanding.

99. (C)

The body regulates water and heat through perspiration. Transpiration describes a process not involving humans; thus (B) is not correct. Respiration (A) is breathing in humans and will cause some water loss, but the question asks how the body regulates substances through the skin. Sensation (D) is the ability to process or perceive. Although the skin does have nerve endings that can sense, this does not involve temperature or water regulation.

100. (B)

Vitamin C is water-soluble—the remaining choices are fat soluble.

101. (D)

The grip strength test (C), pull-ups (A) for boys, and flexed-arm hang (B) for girls are all tests to measure muscular strength and endurance. The sit-and-reach test measures flexibility.

102. (D)

Statements I, II, III, and IV are all true, so (D) is the best choice. Dance can reflect the religion of a culture in many ways due to its deep historical roots in religious tradition.

103. (D)

Excess cholesterol found in the blood typically comes from cholesterol in a diet rather than internal production. Cholesterol, which is produced in the liver (C), plays a vital role in brain function (A) and is important for creating certain hormones (B).

104. (C)

Table tennis is scored to 21 and must be won by a margin of 2 points. In doubles play for badminton, the winner must score 15 points (A). Singles badminton is also scored to 21 points with a margin of 2 points needed for victory.

105. (D)

This question focuses on a basic musical concept, "harmony." Harmony is the performance of two or more different pitches simultaneously. Therefore, when looking at the answers provided, it is good to begin by eliminating answers that have nothing to do with pitch. A rhythm instrument is a nonpitched instrument in almost all cases, so choice I is not pitch related and that means that answers (A) and (B) are eliminated because they both include choice I. Two or more different pitches must be performed simultaneously to have harmony, so choice III can also be eliminated because there are two performers, but not two different pitches. That eliminates answer (C) and leaves answer (D) as the best and correct answer.

106. (B)

One of the virtues of using drama/theatre with young people is that it challenges them to think independently and creatively. Often, there is not one right answer or interpretation. Using the same material in a variety of theatrical formats offers the following advantages: (1) information is presented through multiple channels, thereby increasing opportunities for knowing; (2) using different types of dramatic activities broadens both the appeal of and the learning opportunities inherent in the material; (3) multiple formats increase opportunities to engage students and to address their learning styles; and (4) students can see that there are various ways of creating meaning and expressing ideas. Answer (A) is incorrect because there may not be only one correct way to use material. As the rationale for the correct answer implies, exploring content is one way to move students beyond the obvious and encourage them to use higher-level thinking skills. Answer (C) is incorrect because it requires a value judgment based upon personal preference; it is not grounded in fact. Likewise, (D) is incorrect because it reflects a value judgment that is without substance. Some students may learn more by directly participating in activities; others may learn more by watching a performance. Both creative drama activities and theatre performances are educationally sound undertakings.

107. (C)

The use of uncommon materials has dramatically changed the criteria by which one assesses visual art.

108. (C)

Choice (C) is the best answer because it covers all three of the objectives in at least a minimal way. Choice (A) is the second best answer because it deals with several of the objectives, but the focus on creativity keeps it from being the best answer. Answers (B) and (D) are not good answers because they do not deal with the objectives.

109. (D)

The technique for both jazz dance and tap dance emerged from a blending of African and European cultures.

110. (B)

It is not true of creating dances that "it must happen outside of the classroom within a special time," so (B) is the correct answer. In fact, dance should have a place in the classroom, where the focus should be placed on creative movement.

Practice Test 2

PRAXIS 0011

ANSWER SHEET FOR PRACTICE TEST 2

1. Ⓐ Ⓑ Ⓒ Ⓓ
2. Ⓐ Ⓑ Ⓒ Ⓓ
3. Ⓐ Ⓑ Ⓒ Ⓓ
4. Ⓐ Ⓑ Ⓒ Ⓓ
5. Ⓐ Ⓑ Ⓒ Ⓓ
6. Ⓐ Ⓑ Ⓒ Ⓓ
7. Ⓐ Ⓑ Ⓒ Ⓓ
8. Ⓐ Ⓑ Ⓒ Ⓓ
9. Ⓐ Ⓑ Ⓒ Ⓓ
10. Ⓐ Ⓑ Ⓒ Ⓓ
11. Ⓐ Ⓑ Ⓒ Ⓓ
12. Ⓐ Ⓑ Ⓒ Ⓓ
13. Ⓐ Ⓑ Ⓒ Ⓓ
14. Ⓐ Ⓑ Ⓒ Ⓓ
15. Ⓐ Ⓑ Ⓒ Ⓓ
16. Ⓐ Ⓑ Ⓒ Ⓓ
17. Ⓐ Ⓑ Ⓒ Ⓓ
18. Ⓐ Ⓑ Ⓒ Ⓓ
19. Ⓐ Ⓑ Ⓒ Ⓓ
20. Ⓐ Ⓑ Ⓒ Ⓓ
21. Ⓐ Ⓑ Ⓒ Ⓓ
22. Ⓐ Ⓑ Ⓒ Ⓓ
23. Ⓐ Ⓑ Ⓒ Ⓓ
24. Ⓐ Ⓑ Ⓒ Ⓓ
25. Ⓐ Ⓑ Ⓒ Ⓓ
26. Ⓐ Ⓑ Ⓒ Ⓓ
27. Ⓐ Ⓑ Ⓒ Ⓓ
28. Ⓐ Ⓑ Ⓒ Ⓓ

29. Ⓐ Ⓑ Ⓒ Ⓓ
30. Ⓐ Ⓑ Ⓒ Ⓓ
31. Ⓐ Ⓑ Ⓒ Ⓓ
32. Ⓐ Ⓑ Ⓒ Ⓓ
33. Ⓐ Ⓑ Ⓒ Ⓓ
34. Ⓐ Ⓑ Ⓒ Ⓓ
35. Ⓐ Ⓑ Ⓒ Ⓓ
36. Ⓐ Ⓑ Ⓒ Ⓓ
37. Ⓐ Ⓑ Ⓒ Ⓓ
38. Ⓐ Ⓑ Ⓒ Ⓓ
39. Ⓐ Ⓑ Ⓒ Ⓓ
40. Ⓐ Ⓑ Ⓒ Ⓓ
41. Ⓐ Ⓑ Ⓒ Ⓓ
42. Ⓐ Ⓑ Ⓒ Ⓓ
43. Ⓐ Ⓑ Ⓒ Ⓓ
44. Ⓐ Ⓑ Ⓒ Ⓓ
45. Ⓐ Ⓑ Ⓒ Ⓓ
46. Ⓐ Ⓑ Ⓒ Ⓓ
47. Ⓐ Ⓑ Ⓒ Ⓓ
48. Ⓐ Ⓑ Ⓒ Ⓓ
49. Ⓐ Ⓑ Ⓒ Ⓓ
50. Ⓐ Ⓑ Ⓒ Ⓓ
51. Ⓐ Ⓑ Ⓒ Ⓓ
52. Ⓐ Ⓑ Ⓒ Ⓓ
53. Ⓐ Ⓑ Ⓒ Ⓓ
54. Ⓐ Ⓑ Ⓒ Ⓓ
55. Ⓐ Ⓑ Ⓒ Ⓓ
56. Ⓐ Ⓑ Ⓒ Ⓓ

57. Ⓐ Ⓑ Ⓒ Ⓓ
58. Ⓐ Ⓑ Ⓒ Ⓓ
59. Ⓐ Ⓑ Ⓒ Ⓓ
60. Ⓐ Ⓑ Ⓒ Ⓓ
61. Ⓐ Ⓑ Ⓒ Ⓓ
62. Ⓐ Ⓑ Ⓒ Ⓓ
63. Ⓐ Ⓑ Ⓒ Ⓓ
64. Ⓐ Ⓑ Ⓒ Ⓓ
65. Ⓐ Ⓑ Ⓒ Ⓓ
66. Ⓐ Ⓑ Ⓒ Ⓓ
67. Ⓐ Ⓑ Ⓒ Ⓓ
68. Ⓐ Ⓑ Ⓒ Ⓓ
69. Ⓐ Ⓑ Ⓒ Ⓓ
70. Ⓐ Ⓑ Ⓒ Ⓓ
71. Ⓐ Ⓑ Ⓒ Ⓓ
72. Ⓐ Ⓑ Ⓒ Ⓓ
73. Ⓐ Ⓑ Ⓒ Ⓓ
74. Ⓐ Ⓑ Ⓒ Ⓓ
75. Ⓐ Ⓑ Ⓒ Ⓓ
76. Ⓐ Ⓑ Ⓒ Ⓓ
77. Ⓐ Ⓑ Ⓒ Ⓓ
78. Ⓐ Ⓑ Ⓒ Ⓓ
79. Ⓐ Ⓑ Ⓒ Ⓓ
80. Ⓐ Ⓑ Ⓒ Ⓓ
81. Ⓐ Ⓑ Ⓒ Ⓓ
82. Ⓐ Ⓑ Ⓒ Ⓓ
83. Ⓐ Ⓑ Ⓒ Ⓓ
84. Ⓐ Ⓑ Ⓒ Ⓓ

85. Ⓐ Ⓑ Ⓒ Ⓓ
86. Ⓐ Ⓑ Ⓒ Ⓓ
87. Ⓐ Ⓑ Ⓒ Ⓓ
88. Ⓐ Ⓑ Ⓒ Ⓓ
89. Ⓐ Ⓑ Ⓒ Ⓓ
90. Ⓐ Ⓑ Ⓒ Ⓓ
91. Ⓐ Ⓑ Ⓒ Ⓓ
92. Ⓐ Ⓑ Ⓒ Ⓓ
93. Ⓐ Ⓑ Ⓒ Ⓓ
94. Ⓐ Ⓑ Ⓒ Ⓓ
95. Ⓐ Ⓑ Ⓒ Ⓓ
96. Ⓐ Ⓑ Ⓒ Ⓓ
97. Ⓐ Ⓑ Ⓒ Ⓓ
98. Ⓐ Ⓑ Ⓒ Ⓓ
99. Ⓐ Ⓑ Ⓒ Ⓓ
100. Ⓐ Ⓑ Ⓒ Ⓓ
101. Ⓐ Ⓑ Ⓒ Ⓓ
102. Ⓐ Ⓑ Ⓒ Ⓓ
103. Ⓐ Ⓑ Ⓒ Ⓓ
104. Ⓐ Ⓑ Ⓒ Ⓓ
105. Ⓐ Ⓑ Ⓒ Ⓓ
106. Ⓐ Ⓑ Ⓒ Ⓓ
107. Ⓐ Ⓑ Ⓒ Ⓓ
108. Ⓐ Ⓑ Ⓒ Ⓓ
109. Ⓐ Ⓑ Ⓒ Ⓓ
110. Ⓐ Ⓑ Ⓒ Ⓓ

TIME: 120 minutes
110 questions

1. Before working with mathematical word problems, a teacher needs to determine that

   (A) the student can complete the math unit.
   (B) the student is at a high enough reading level to understand the problems.
   (C) the math textbook mirrors the skills used in the word problems.
   (D) the class will be on task for the problems.

2. A student describes an analysis of a recent presidential address for the class. The teacher replies, "You have provided us with a most interesting way of looking at this issue!" The teacher is using

   (A) simple positive response.
   (B) negative response.
   (C) redirect.
   (D) academic praise.

3. When a teacher leads choral chants, the teacher is

   (A) practicing aural skills.
   (B) practicing vocal exercises.
   (C) having students repeat basic skills orally.
   (D) repeating what the students answer.

4. A lesson for which students are given a tankful of water and various objects and are asked to order the objects by weight would be considered a(n)

   (A) science lesson.
   (B) discovery-learning lesson.

   (C) inductive-reasoning lesson.
   (D) eg-rule lesson.

5. Mr. Drake is a first-grade teacher who is using the whole language method while teaching about animals. Before reading a story to the students, Mr. Drake tells the students what he is expecting them to learn from reading the story. What is his reason for doing this?

   (A) The students should know why the instructor chose this text over any other.
   (B) It is important for teachers to share personal ideas with their students in order to foster an environment of confidence and understanding.
   (C) Mr. Drake wants to verify that all students are on task before he begins the story.
   (D) Mr. Drake is modeling a vital prereading skill in order to teach it to the young readers.

6. Mr. Drake wants to ensure that the class will have a quality discussion on the needs of house pets. In response to a student who said that her family abandoned their cat in a field because it ate too much, Mr. Drake asks, "What is one way to save pets that are no longer wanted?" This exercise involves what level of questioning?

   (A) Evaluation
   (B) Analysis
   (C) Comprehension
   (D) Synthesis

7. Mr. Drake has a heterogeneously grouped reading class. He has placed the students in groups of two—one skilled reader and one remedial reader—and asked that they read the selected story and question each other until they feel that they both understand the story. By planning the lesson this way, Mr. Drake has

(A) set a goal for his students.
(B) condensed the number of observations necessary, thereby creating more time for class instruction.
(C) made it possible for another teacher to utilize the limited materials.
(D) utilized the students' strengths and weaknesses to maximize time, materials, and the learning environment.

8. Mr. Drake is continuing his lesson on the animal kingdom. He wants to ensure that the students learn as much as they can about animals, so he incorporates information familiar to the students into the new information. Knowing that these are first-grade learners, what should Mr. Drake consider when contemplating their learning experience?

(A) The students will know how much information they can retrieve from memory.
(B) The students will overestimate how much information they can retrieve from memory.
(C) The students will be able to pick out the information they need to study and the information they do not need to study due to prior mastery.
(D) The students will estimate how much they can learn in one time period.

9. Before reading a story about a veterinary hospital, Mr. Drake constructs a semantic map of related words and terms using the students' input. What is his main intention for doing this?

(A) To demonstrate a meaningful relationship between the concepts of the story and the prior knowledge of the students
(B) To serve as a visual means of learning
(C) To determine the level of understanding the students will have at the conclusion of the topic being covered
(D) To model proper writing using whole words

10. Student data such as scores on tests and assignments would be the best criteria for determining which of the following?

(A) Only the students' academic grades
(B) Behavior assessment
(C) Student grades and the teacher's quality of instruction
(D) Student grades and behavior assessment

11. Results of a standardized test indicate that a teacher's students did poorly on the mathematics problem-solving section; students in another classroom in the same school did much better. What would be the best action to take for the teacher of the students who did poorly?

(A) Look at the students' scores from last year to justify their poor achievement.
(B) Tell future students to study more because that section is more difficult.
(C) Suggest that parents hire a math tutor.
(D) Ask the other teacher to share the strategies used to help make the other students successful.

12. A kindergartner is using first and last letters to write words. This student "reads" simple books that have been memorized through listening to them multiple times. The student can identify a few common sight words as well. This student's skills are known as

(A) mastery skills.
(B) literacy skills.

(C) emergent literacy skills.

(D) developmental skills.

13. The question "What was the name of Hamlet's father?" is

(A) a high-order question of evaluation.

(B) a low-order question that can be used to begin a discussion.

(C) a transition.

(D) a skills-assessment question.

14. Mr. Owen, a third-grade teacher, has been teaching in a small rural district for three years. He enjoys the slow pace of the community and the fact that he knows most of his students' families relatively well. He is a member of the Evening Lions Club, plays on the church basketball team, and volunteers at the animal shelter. His class this year is made up of 21 eight- and nine-year-olds. Most of the students are of average ability, two receive special services for learning disabilities, and one receives speech therapy. Mr. Owen works hard at making his classroom an exciting place to learn, with lots of hands-on, problem-based cooperative group projects. In the past, students have had difficulty grasping relationships between math concepts and economics. Mr. Owen has decided to offer a savings program with the help of local banks. Once a week, students will make deposits into their savings accounts. Periodically, they will use their accounts to figure interest at different rates, class totals saved, and so forth. As part of the social studies curriculum, he encourages them to do chores at home and in their neighborhoods to earn the money for their savings. This approach is evidence that Mr. Owen understands the importance of

(A) authenticity in planning instructional activities for students.

(B) integrating curriculum concepts across disciplines that support learning.

(C) saving money.

(D) all of the above.

15. Students are presented with the following problem: "Bill is taller than Ann, but Ann is taller than Grace. Is Ann the tallest child or is Bill the tallest?" This question requires students to use

(A) inductive reasoning.

(B) deductive reasoning.

(C) hypothesis formation.

(D) pattern identification.

16. Ms. Carter is a second-grade social studies teacher at a small rural school. Several times during the semester, she has found herself in conversations with colleagues in the school and various community members regarding concerns about a program initiated by the school librarian who is active in the wildlife refuge program in the county. The librarian often brings hurt or orphaned animals to the library to care for them during the day. Several parents are concerned about issues of hygiene and students with allergies. As a member of the site-based decision-making (SBDM) committee, Ms. Carter's best course of action is to

(A) tell the librarian to remove the animals at once.

(B) submit an agenda item to the principal to discuss the concerns at the next meeting.

(C) call the health department for a surprise inspection.

(D) support the librarian and praise her efforts to expose students to the issues of wildlife preservation.

17. The math curriculum states that all students will be able to solve problems in a variety of ways. Which of the following lesson objectives best matches this standard?

(A) Students will show all steps in the computation of problems.

(B) Students will provide multiple solutions to given problems.

(C) Students will correctly label their answers.

(D) Students will write regularly in math journals.

Read the following passage and answer question 18.

Mr. Shahid wants his students to understand how water is formed from the two elements of hydrogen and oxygen. He uses a manipulative of two blue balls labeled *hydrogen* and one white ball labeled *oxygen*. The balls are connected with wooden rods. Mr. Shahid briefly uses this manipulative but then continues his explanation with an in-depth description of how water is formed and the theoretical underpinnings for this scientific discovery.

18. In order for students to understand this science lesson, they must be at which one of Piaget's stages of development?

(A) Concrete operational
(B) Formal operational
(C) Preoperational
(D) Sensorimotor

Read the following passage and answer questions 19 through 21.

The social studies teachers of an inner city school wanted to change to a more relevant curriculum, with units on economics throughout the world instead of only regions of the United States. Ms. Dunn was asked to submit a proposal for the new curriculum, related activities, sequencing, themes, and materials. In consultation with the other teachers in the department, a needs assessment was planned.

19. The teachers believed that the needs assessment would

(A) help the students make a connection between their current skills and those that will be new to them.

(B) reveal community problems that may affect the students' lives and their performance in school.

(C) foster a view of learning as a purposeful pursuit, promoting a sense of responsibility for one's own learning.

(D) engage students in learning activities and help them to develop the motivation to achieve.

20. When the needs assessment was evaluated, it revealed an ethnically diverse community. Student interests and parental expectations varied, different language backgrounds existed, student exceptionalities were common, and academic motivation was low. The question confronting the teachers was how to bridge the gap from where the students were to where they should have been. The available choices were to

(A) change the textbook only.

(B) relate the lessons to the students' personal interests.

(C) create a positive environment to minimize the effects of the negative external factors.

(D) help students to learn and to monitor their own performance.

21. At the end of a question-and-answer period, the group of teachers, headed by Ms. Dunn, set a goal of having the students gain an awareness of the correlation between their skills or lack of skills and their expected salaries. A parent/guardian support group would be established to enhance the students' motivation to master new skills. Strategies to use at home and in the classroom would be developed. Ms. Dunn felt

that, with the aid of parents, this plan would enable her to

(A) promote her own professional growth as she worked cooperatively with professionals to create a school culture that would enhance learning and result in positive change.

(B) meet the expectations associated with teaching.

(C) foster strong home relationships that support student achievement of desired outcomes.

(D) exhibit her understanding of the principles of conducting parent–teacher conferences and working cooperatively with parents.

22. A teacher asks her eighth-grade English students to select a career they would enjoy when they grow up and then to find three sources on the Internet with information about that career. She tells the students that they must find out how much education is required for this career. If the career requires postsecondary education, then the student must find a school or college that provides this education and find out how long it will take to be educated or trained for this career. Through this assignment, the teacher is helping her students to

(A) explore short-term personal and academic goals.

(B) explore long-term personal and academic goals.

(C) evaluate short-term personal and academic goals.

(D) synthesize long-term personal and academic goals.

23. A teacher asks a student, "When you were studying for your spelling test, did you remember the mnemonic we talked about in class for spelling *principal* that 'a principal is your pal'?" The teacher is

(A) leading the student in a divergent thinking exercise.

(B) teaching the student mnemonics, or memory devices.

(C) asking a question to guide the student in correcting an error.

(D) modeling inductive-reasoning skills for the student.

24. When working with English as a second language (ESL) students, the teacher should be aware that

(A) students should speak only English in class.

(B) an accepting classroom and encouraging lessons will foster learning.

(C) such students should be referred to a specialist.

(D) limiting the number of resources available is beneficial to the students.

25. Ms. Borders, a second-year third-grade teacher, is preparing a theme study on water and the related concepts of conservation, ecology, and human needs. One of her instructional outcomes deals with students' abilities to demonstrate their new learning in a variety of ways. As she plans her unit of study, Ms. Borders first needs to consider

(A) the strengths and needs of the diverse learners in her classroom.

(B) the amount of reading material she assigns.

(C) how the theme connects to other academic disciplines.

(D) inviting guest speakers to the classroom.

26. Sequential language acquisition occurs when students

(A) learn a second language after mastery of the first.

(B) learn a second language at the same time as the first.

(C) learn two languages in parts.

(D) develop language skills.

27. Teachers should provide a variety of experiences and concrete examples for children with reading difficulties because some children

(A) come from environments with limited language exposure.

(B) have poor learning habits.

(C) have trouble distinguishing letters.

(D) can speak well but have difficulty reading.

28. A teacher writes "All men are created equal" on the board and asks each student to explain the meaning of the statement. One student says that it means that all people are equal, but another student says that it just applies to men. A third student says that it is a lie because not all people are equally good at all things, and that, for example, some people can run faster than others and some can sing better than others. The teacher's instructional aim is to

(A) see whether students can reach consensus on the meaning of the statement.

(B) see how well students can defend their beliefs.

(C) provoke the students to disagree with the statement.

(D) engage the students in critical thinking and to allow them to express their opinions.

29. Students in a first-grade class are learning how to recognize and continue patterns. Which of the following tools is most likely to help in their learning?

(A) Calendars

(B) Fraction tiles

(C) Multi-colored counters

(D) Base-ten blocks

30. The first life forms to appear on Earth were most likely

(A) complex single-celled organisms.

(B) complex multicellular organisms.

(C) simple multicellular organisms.

(D) simple single-celled organisms

31. Using student ideas and interests in a lesson

(A) takes students off task.

(B) detracts from the subject content.

(C) does not allow for evaluation of students' prior knowledge.

(D) increases learning and student motivation.

32. Before Ms. Chin's class goes to the library, she asks her students to predict how they will find the information they will need for the assignment. By doing this, Ms. Chin is

(A) engaging the students in hypothetical thinking and inductive reasoning.

(B) saving time so that the students will be able to go straight to work once they get to the library.

(C) helping her students acquire good self-management skills.

(D) assisting the librarian by covering important information in class.

33. The term *trade books* refers to which of these items found in a classroom library?

(A) Over-sized books

(B) Anthologies

(C) Authentic literature

(D) Textbooks

34. An English for speakers of other languages (ESOL) student is proficient in oral language; however, he continues to experience difficulty with academic language used in science and social studies classes. The teacher believes academic proficiency correlates with oral language proficiency. What has the teacher failed

to acknowledge in her analysis of the student's language proficiency?

(A) Both basic interpersonal communication skills and cognitive academic language proficiency are needed for successful academic performance.

(B) Basic interpersonal communication skills develop equally with cognitive academic language proficiency.

(C) Basic interpersonal communication skills are criteria for successful academic performance.

(D) Cognitive academic language proficiency is primary to basic interpersonal communication skills.

35. A student making top grades in class has received a percentile score of 63 on a nationally standardized math test. The best explanation of the student's score is

(A) a percentile score of 63 means that on a scale of 1 to 100, the student is 37 points from the top.

(B) a percentile score of 63 means that out of a group of 100 students, 37 would score higher and 62 would score lower, and the student has done well by scoring in the top half of all students taking the test.

(C) a percentile score of 63 is just like a grade of 63 on a test; it means that the student earned a low D on the test.

(D) a percentile score of 63 means that out of a group of 100 students, 37 would score higher and 62 would score lower, showing a big difference between the student's performance on the standardized test and in class.

36. Many students in a second-grade class consistently spell the same commonly used words incorrectly. Which of the following would be the most appropriate instructional technique for their teacher to implement?

(A) Have the students write the misspelled words ten times each.

(B) Add the misspelled words to a weekly spelling test.

(C) Have the students use the misspelled words in sentences for homework.

(D) Add the misspelled words to a "word wall" that hangs in the classroom.

37. Rueben Stein is a middle school teacher who wants to teach his class about the classification system in the animal kingdom. He decides to introduce this unit to his class by having the students engage in general classification activities. He brings to class a paper bag filled with 30 household items. He dumps the contents of the bag onto a table and then asks the students, in groups of three or four, to put like items into piles and then to justify or explain why they placed certain items into a particular pile. By assigning this task to his students, Mr. Stein is providing his students with a developmentally appropriate task because

(A) middle school students like to work in groups.

(B) the items in the bag are household items with which most students will be familiar.

(C) the assignment gives students the opportunity to practice their skills at categorizing.

(D) the assignment will give students a task to perform while the teacher finishes grading papers.

38. In the middle of a unit of study a teacher gives second-grade students plastic replications of quarters, dimes, nickels, and pennies to use to solve computation problems involving money. The teacher is most likely

(A) testing the students knowledge of coins.

(B) accessing students' prior knowledge of coins.

(C) incorporating authentic materials into instruction.

(D) teaching students how to add and subtract monetary amounts.

39. Elva Rodriguez teaches fourth grade. She has structured her class so that students can spend 30 minutes daily, after lunch, in sustained silent reading activities with books and reading materials of their own choosing. In order to maximize this reading opportunity and to recognize differences among learners, Ms. Rodriguez

(A) allows some students to sit quietly at their desks while others are allowed to move to a reading area where they sit on floor cushions or recline on floor mats.

(B) makes sure that all students have selected appropriate reading materials.

(C) plays classical music on a CD player to enhance student learning.

(D) dims the lights in the classroom in order to increase students' reading comprehension.

40. Karla Dixon is a second-grade teacher who has selected a book to read to her class after lunch. She shows the students the picture on the cover of the book and reads the title of the book to them. She then asks, "What do you think this book is about?" By asking this question, Ms. Dixon is

(A) learning which students are interested in reading strategies.

(B) trying to keep the students awake because she knows they usually get sleepy after lunch.

(C) encouraging students to make a prediction, a precursor of hypothetical thinking.

(D) finding out which students are good readers.

41. Mrs. Johnson teaches sixth-grade reading. She teaches reading skills and comprehension through workbooks and through reading and class discussion of specific plays, short stories, and novels. She also allows students to make some selections according to their own interests. Because she believes there is a strong connection between reading and writing, her students write their responses to literature in a variety of ways. Some of her students have heard their high school brothers and sisters discuss portfolios, and they have asked Mrs. Johnson if they can use them also. Which of the following statements are appropriate for Mrs. Johnson to consider in deciding whether to agree to the students' request?

I. Portfolios will develop skills her students can use in high school.

II. Portfolios will make Mrs. Johnson's students feel more mature because they would be making the same product as their older brothers and sisters.

III. Portfolios will assist her students in meeting course outcomes relating to reading and writing.

IV. Portfolios will make grading easier because there will be fewer papers and projects to evaluate.

(A) I, II, and IV
(B) I and III only
(C) II and III only
(D) II and IV only

42. Reading aloud is a strategy that should be used with what types of students?

(A) Any age or level of student
(B) Students in kindergarten through grade 3
(C) Native language speakers
(D) Students with language-processing problems

43. The teacher has her first graders read out loud individually to her from a passage. As each

child reads, the teacher notes any mispronunciations, pauses, missed punctuation, and expression on a copy of the passage. The teacher is likely to be assessing the student's reading through which technique?

(A) Informal observation
(B) Running record
(C) Reading inventory
(D) Tracking

44. Which of the following is the last step of the writer's workshop approach to writing instruction?

(A) Revising
(B) Peer editing
(C) Publishing
(D) Brainstorming

45. Ms. Thompson wants to teach her students about methods of collecting data in science. This is an important skill for first graders. Which of the following describes the most appropriate method of teaching students about collecting data in science?

(A) Ms. Thompson should arrange the students into groups of four. She should then have each group observe the class's pet mouse while she gently touches it with a feather. The students should record how many times out of 10 the pet mouse moves away from the feather. Then, she should gently touch the class's philodendron 10 times with a feather. The students should record how many out of 10 times the philodendron moves away from the feather.

(B) Ms. Thompson should arrange the students into groups of four. She should give each group five solid balls made of materials that will float and five solid balls made of materials that will not float. She should have the students drop the balls into a bowl of water and record how many float and how many do not.

(C) Ms. Thompson should show the students a video about scientific methods of gathering data.

(D) Ms. Thompson should have a scientist come and talk to the class about methods of collecting data. If she cannot get a scientist, she should have a science teacher from the high school come and speak about scientific methods of data collection.

46. A fourth-grade teacher is introducing the concept of two-digit by two-digit multiplication. One goal of the teacher is for students to successfully use the algorithm. A second goal is for students to understand the process. Which of the following teacher assignments is most likely to address both goals?

(A) Have each student complete a worksheet of several two-digit by two-digit multiplication problems.

(B) Have each student write the steps to solving two-digit by two-digit multiplication problems in a math journal.

(C) Have each student study for a math test with two-digit by two-digit multiplication problems.

(D) Have each student solve two-digit by two-digit multiplication problems and write the steps to solving two-digit by two-digit multiplication problems in a math journal.

47. The following examples are representative of a student's work in math class:

$$72 - 49 = 37$$
$$56 - 28 = 32$$
$$84 - 55 = 31$$

If the error continues, the student's answer to the problem $43 - 26$ will most likely be which of the following?

(A) 69
(B) 23

(C) 17
(D) 29

48. A teacher gives the students the following mathematics problem:

> Cindy has one blue skirt and one green skirt. She has one red shirt, one blue shirt, one white shirt, and one black shirt. How many different outfits of a skirt and a shirt can she make?

Which of the following student responses best answers the question?

(A) Sahil: 6
(B) Aimee: 5
(C) Clara: 9
(D) Bryant: 8

49. Which of the following materials would NOT be considered "math manipulatives"?

(A) Cuisenaire rods
(B) Journals
(C) Base-10 blocks
(D) Calculators

Read the following passage and answer questions 50 through 53.

> The issue of adult literacy has finally received recognition in the media as a major social problem. It is more important that the politicians themselves recognize the seriousness of the problem and support increased funding for literacy programs.
>
> Literacy education programs need to be directed at two different groups of people with very different needs. The first group is composed of people who have very limited reading and writing skills. These people are completely illiterate. A second group is composed of people who can read and write but whose skills are not sufficient to meet their needs. This second group is called functionally illiterate. Successful literacy programs must meet the needs of both groups.
>
> Instructors in literacy programs have three main responsibilities. First, they must meet the educational needs of both the illiterate and the functionally illiterate. Second, the instructors must approach the participants in the program with empathy, not sympathy. Third, all participants must experience success in the program and must perceive their efforts as worthwhile.

50. What is the difference between illiteracy and functional illiteracy?

(A) There is no difference.
(B) A person who is functionally illiterate is enrolled in a literacy education program, but one who is illiterate is not.
(C) A person who is illiterate cannot read or write, and one who is functionally illiterate can read and write but not at a very high skill level.
(D) There are more illiterate than functionally illiterate people in the United States today.

51. What is the purpose of the passage?

(A) To discuss the characteristics of successful literacy programs
(B) To discuss the manner in which literacy programs are viewed by the media
(C) To discuss some of the reasons for increased attention to literacy as a social issue
(D) All of the above

52. According to the passage, which of the following is NOT a characteristic of successful literacy programs?

(A) Participants should receive free transportation.

(B) Participants should experience success in the program.

(C) Instructors must have empathy, not sympathy.

(D) Programs must meet the educational needs of those who are illiterate.

53. What is the author's opinion of the funding for literacy programs?

(A) Too much

(B) Too little

(C) About right

(D) Too much for those who are illiterate and not enough for those who are functionally illiterate

Read the following passage and answer questions 54 and 55.

Mr. Dobson teaches fifth-grade mathematics at Valverde Elementary. He encourages students to work in groups of two or three as they begin homework assignments so they can answer questions for each other. Mr. Dobson notices immediately that some of his students choose to work alone even though they had been asked to work in groups. He also notices that some students are easily distracted even though the other members of their group are working on the assignment as directed.

54. Which of the following is the most likely explanation for the students' different types of behavior?

(A) Fifth-grade students are not physically or mentally capable of working in small groups; small groups are more suitable for older students.

(B) Fifth-grade students vary greatly in their physical development and maturity; this

variance influences the students' interests and attitudes.

(C) Fifth-grade students lack the ability for internal control and therefore learn best in structured settings. It is usually best to seat fifth-graders in single rows.

(D) Mr. Dobson needs to be more specific in his expectations for student behavior.

55. Mr. Dobson wants to encourage all of his students to participate in discussions related to the use of math in the real world. Five students in one class are very shy and introverted. Which of the following would most likely be the best way to encourage these students to participate in the discussion?

(A) Mr. Dobson should call on these students by name at least once each day and give participation grades.

(B) Mr. Dobson should not be concerned about these students because they will become less shy and introverted as they mature during the year.

(C) Mr. Dobson should divide the class into small groups for discussion so these students will not be overwhelmed by speaking in front of the whole class.

(D) Mr. Dobson should speak with these students individually and encourage them to participate more in class discussions.

Read the following passage and answer question 56.

Mrs. Kresmeier teaches sixth-grade language arts classes. One of her curriculum goals is to help students improve their spelling. As one of her techniques, she has developed a number of special mnemonic devices that she uses with the students, getting the idea from the old teaching rhymes like "*I* before *E* except after *C* or when sounding like *A* as in *neighbor* or *weigh*." Her own memory tricks—"The moose can't get loose from the noose" or "Spell rhyme? Why me?"—have caught the interest of her students. Now, besides Mrs. Kresmeier's memory tricks for better spelling, her students are developing and sharing their own creative ways to memorize more effectively.

56. To improve her students' spelling, Mrs. Kresmeier's method has been successful primarily because of which of the following factors related to student achievement?

(A) The students are not relying on phonics or sight words to spell difficult words.
(B) Mrs. Kresmeier has impressed her students with the need to learn to spell.
(C) The ideas are effective with many students and help to create a learning environment that is open to student interaction.
(D) Mrs. Kresmeier teaches spelling using only words that can be adapted to mnemonic clues.

Read the following passage and answer questions 57 through 59.

Mr. Freeman is preparing a year-long unit on process writing for his fifth-grade class. He plans for each student to write about a series of topics over each six-week grading period. At the end of each grading period, students will select three completed writing assignments that reflect their best work. Mr. Freeman will review the assignments and conference with each student. During the conference, Mr. Freeman will assist the students with preparing a list of writing goals for the next grading term.

57. Which of the following best describes Mr. Freeman's plan for reviewing student writing assignments, conferencing with each student, and helping each student set specific goals for writing to be accomplished during the next grading period?

(A) Summative evaluation
(B) Summative assessment
(C) Formative assessment
(D) Peer evaluation

58. Mr. Freeman's goal in planning to conference with each student about the student's writing could be described as

(A) creating a climate of trust and encouraging a positive attitude toward writing.
(B) an efficient process for grading student writing assignments.
(C) an opportunity to stress the importance of careful editing of completed writing assignments.
(D) an opportunity to stress the value of pre-writing in producing a final product.

59. Philip, a student in Mr. Freeman's class, receives services from a resource teacher for a learning disability that affects his reading and writing. Which of the following is the most appropriate request that Mr. Freeman should make of the resource teacher to help Philip complete the writing unit?

(A) Mr. Freeman should ask the resource teacher to provide writing instruction for Philip.
(B) Mr. Freeman should excuse Philip from writing assignments.
(C) Mr. Freeman should ask the resource teacher for help in modifying the writing unit to match Philip's abilities.
(D) Mr. Freeman should ask the resource teacher to schedule extra tutoring ses-

sions to help Philip with the writing assignments.

60. Mr. Liu, a math teacher, and Mr. Lowery, a science teacher, are planning a celebration of Galileo's birthday. The students will research Galileo's discoveries, draw posters of those discoveries, and prepare short plays depicting important events in his life. They will present the plays and display the posters for grades 1 through 4. This is an example of

(A) an end-of-the-year project.
(B) problem solving and inquiry teaching.
(C) working with other teachers to plan instructions.
(D) teachers preparing to ask the Parent–Teacher Association (PTA) for science lab equipment.

61. The principal asks Mr. Liu and Ms. Gonzalez, another fifth-grade math teacher in the school, to visit the math classes and the computer lab in the middle school that most of the students at Valverde Elementary will attend. By asking Mr. Liu and Ms. Gonzalez to visit the middle school, the principal is most likely encouraging

(A) collaboration among the math teachers at Valverde and the middle school.
(B) Mr. Liu and Ms. Gonzalez to consider applying for a job at the middle school.
(C) the use of computers in math classes at Valverde.
(D) the use of the middle school math curriculum in the fifth-grade classes.

62. A fifth-grade teacher wants the students to master long division. The teacher is planning class work to help the students achieve this goal. Which instructional strategies are likely to be most effective in reaching this goal?

(A) Unit tests and practice-problem drills

(B) Practice-problem drills and quizzes
(C) Games, practice-problem drills, quizzes, and writing in math journals
(D) Games, lectures, and writing in math journals

63. A teacher will be conducting a unit on rocks and minerals with a third-grade class. At what point in the unit would it be most effective to have students complete the parts of a K-W-L chart?

(A) All parts of the K-W-L chart at the start of the unit
(B) All parts of the K-W-L chart at the end of the unit
(C) A K-W-L chart should not be used as part of a science unit.
(D) The K and the W at the beginning of the unit and the L at the end

64. The teacher is concerned that the ESL and inclusion students in the class will have difficulty with the terminology involved with the third-grade science unit on rocks and minerals. What is the LEAST effective way of addressing this issue?

(A) Assign the science work for homework.
(B) Introduce the vocabulary in advance of the start of the unit.
(C) Involve ESL and special education teachers in assisting the students.
(D) Create vocabulary cards with photographs for the students to use.

65. Which of the following depicts the correct order of the scientific method?

(A) Question, hypothesis, experiment, conclusion
(B) Hypothesis, question, experiment, conclusion
(C) Question, hypothesis, conclusion, experiment

(D) Hypothesis, experiment, questions, conclusion

66. The teacher collects student journals at the end of a science unit. A few students have all the labs completed, including labeled drawings and written reflections on the work. The content is accurate; however, the spelling and other elements of writing show many errors. Which is the most appropriate way for the teacher to address this situation?

(A) Give the students a high mark for content, then take off points for writing errors.
(B) Give the students a lower grade overall.
(C) Give the students a high mark for content and ignore the writing errors.
(D) Give the students a high mark for content and conference with the students regarding the errors in writing.

67. A fourth-grade class is taking a field trip to a local museum as part of their study of the history of their community. The teacher wants to make sure that the students remember important elements of the trip. Once they return to school the teacher will have the students write about their experience in a journal and then share this with a partner. What cooperative strategy is the teacher using?

(A) Jigsaw
(B) Buddy learning
(C) Think-pair-share
(D) Guided discovery

68. The state standards require that a middle school social studies teacher address the Revolutionary War with the students. The teacher wants to plan a unit of study to address key aspects of the war, but does not know how to get started. Which of the following is the best task for the teacher to complete FIRST in order to plan the unit?

(A) Write guiding questions.
(B) Create learning activities.
(C) Survey the students for prior knowledge.
(D) Ask last year's teachers what the students know.

69. Which of the following is NOT a primary source?

(A) Journal
(B) Biography
(C) Letter
(D) Photograph

70. A teacher asks the students to place the following presidents in order from the MOST recent to the least recent:

George H. Bush	William J. Clinton
Jimmy Carter	
Ronald Reagan	Gerald Ford

Which of the following students placed the presidents in order correctly?

(A) Will: William J. Clinton, George H. Bush, Ronald Reagan, Jimmy Carter, Gerald Ford
(B) Ann: George H. Bush, William J. Clinton, Ronald Reagan, Jimmy Carter, Gerald Ford
(C) Nate: William J. Clinton, Ronald Reagan, George H. Bush, Gerald Ford, Jimmy Carter
(D) Ajay: Gerald Ford, Jimmy Carter, Ronald Reagan, George H. Bush, William J. Clinton

71. A physical education teacher is beginning a unit on floor hockey with an elementary class. Before the students begin to play, it is LEAST important for them to

(A) understand the rules of the sport.
(B) understand the roles of each position on the field.

(C) understand how to use the equipment properly.

(D) understand how to score a goal.

72. Which of the following is NOT a part of a curriculum for arts instruction?

(A) Design
(B) Timbre
(C) Art history
(D) Technique

73. Which one of the following statements is most true regarding the materials of visual art?

(A) Industrial innovations in art-making materials have improved art in the past 150 years.
(B) The use of uncommon materials in art making has improved art in the past 150 years.
(C) The use of unusual materials in art making has changed the standards by which we view art.
(D) Industrial innovations in art-making materials have had little influence on visual art.

74. Which artistic movement saw an important revival in recent centuries?

(A) Classical
(B) Baroque
(C) Gothic
(D) (A) and (C)

75. How can a teacher elicit a high-order response from a student who provides simple responses?

(A) Ask follow-up questions.
(B) Repeat the questions.
(C) Ask the same questions of a different student.
(D) Ask another student to elaborate on the original response.

76. Why should children be taught to use graphic organizers as a method of organizing data during an inquiry?

(A) It discourages the practice of copying paragraphs out of the source book.
(B) It helps children to see similarities and differences across sources.
(C) Graphic organizers look good to parents.
(D) It provides the students an opportunity to use a word processor.

77. What is one way of incorporating nonperformers into a discussion?

(A) Ask a student to respond to a previous student's statement.
(B) Name a student to answer a question.
(C) Call only on students who have their hands raised.
(D) Allow off-topic conversations.

78. A third-grade teacher gives students the following problems:

$$37 \div 9 \qquad 41 \div 5 \qquad 73 \div 8$$

The teacher is most likely focusing on

(A) Inverse multiplication
(B) Long division
(C) Division with a remainder of one
(D) Fact families

79. Piaget's theory of cognitive development states that

(A) children should be able to understand complex directions.
(B) younger children are unable to understand complex language.
(C) younger children will be unable to understand directions, even in simple language.
(D) directions should not be given to young children.

80. Of the following individuals, who is most likely to find difficulty in establishing good interpersonal relationships outside her own community?

    (A) Consuela enjoys listening and finding out about other people.
    (B) Katy always tries to keep an open mind in social situations.
    (C) Aimee is a good verbal communicator but is not always aware of her body language.
    (D) Viveka always tries to live by the "golden rule."

81. Inductive thinking can be fostered through which activity?

    (A) Choral chanting of skill tables
    (B) Computer experience
    (C) Multiple-choice questions
    (D) Personal-discovery activities

82. Who of the following is NOT associated with cognitive development and learning theories?

    (A) Vygotsky
    (B) Piaget
    (C) Erikson
    (D) Mager

83. A teacher uses a picture book about a child who has a nightmare about seeing number problems everywhere. This teacher most likely chose this book to

    (A) Address math anxiety
    (B) Point out that math is all around
    (C) Make a real-life connection to math
    (D) Encourage students to study math facts

84. The pose of the horse in the sculpture pictured below serves to express

    (A) physical aging and decay.
    (B) massiveness and stability.
    (C) lightness and motion.
    (D) military prowess.

    Flying Horse. 2nd Century Han.
    Wuwie Tomb, Gansu.

85. In the lines below, what does the stage direction "(*Aside*)" mean?

    King: Take thy fair hour, Laertes; time be thine,

    And thy best graces spend it at thy will! But now, my cousin Hamlet, and my son,—

    Hamlet: (*Aside*) A little more than kin, and less than kind.

    (A) The actor steps aside to make room for other action on stage.
    (B) The actor directly addresses only one particular actor on stage.
    (C) The actor directly addresses the audience, while out of hearing of the other actors.
    (D) The previous speaker steps aside to make room for this actor.

86. Who is the central focus in the picture *The Death of Socrates* shown below, and why?

The Death of Socrates, Jacques-Louis David, 1789

Source: Metropolitan Museum of Art, New York

(A) The man on the left, with his hands and face pressed against the wall, because he is separate and thus draws the viewer's attention

(B) The man sitting at the foot of the bed, because he is at the lowest elevation

(C) The man standing beside the bed, because he is standing alone

(D) The man sitting on the bed, because the other men are focused on him

87. Which of the following seems most true of the sculpture *David* pictured below?

(A) The statue is conceived as a decorative work without a narrative function.

(B) The figure seems to be static, passive, and introverted.

(C) The figure is depicted as though frozen in a moment of action.

(D) The figure's garments indicate that he is a soldier or warrior.

David, Gianlorenzo Bernini, 1623

Source: Galleria Borghese, Rome

88. A third-grade student is still using invented spelling often when writing independently. The best action for the teacher to take is

(A) allow the use of invented spelling so the student can write freely.

(B) contact the Child Study Team immediately to test the student for a learning disability.

(C) advise the parents of the student to hire a tutor to work on spelling at home.

(D) model the correct spelling of misspelled words in the student's writing and provide specific strategies for learning conventional spelling.

89. Physical education goals for children include all of the following EXCEPT

(A) aerobic conditioning.

(B) sportsmanship.

(C) joining a sports team.

(D) strength training.

90. Which of the following is the most important artistic device in the example shown below?

Tawaraya Sotatsu and Hon-Ami Koetsu,
***Deer Scroll*, Early Edo period**

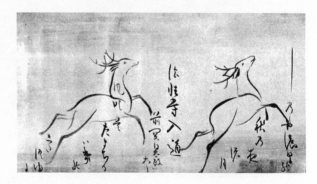

Source: Seattle Art Museum, Seattle

(A) Line
(B) Tone
(C) Color
(D) Volume

91. Which is the national professional organization that represents teachers of students who speak another language?

(A) IRA
(B) NATM
(C) NASDTEC
(D) TESOL

92. A teacher plans and implements a mini-lesson on the use of quotation marks in the writing of dialogue. The teacher's perceived need for this lesson most likely stemmed from

(A) recognizing the misuse of quotation marks in the students' writing.
(B) a staff development workshop on the writing process.
(C) poor standardized test scores in writing on a state assessment.
(D) a district mandate.

93. A fourth-grade teacher is reviewing probability with the class. Which of the following approaches would be most effective in encouraging student interest and skill building?

(A) Have students roll dice and keep track of the results
(B) Have students flip a coin and keep track of the results
(C) Have students practice examples in a textbook
(D) Have students participate in rotating learning centers with a variety of hands-on activities

94. Students often have difficulty with the concept of regrouping ones, tens and hundreds. Which of the following is LEAST likely to help?

(A) Calculators
(B) Base-ten blocks
(C) Coins and bills
(D) Place value cards

95. As a part of a geometry unit involving basic plane figures, kindergarten students have been working with one-dimensional squares, circles, triangles, and rectangle manipulatives. Which of the following means of assessing student knowledge would be most effective?

(A) Have students identify shapes depicted on a worksheet
(B) Have students identify shape manipulatives individually
(C) Have students identify shape manipulatives in a small group
(D) Have students match shape word cards to shape manipulatives

96. Listening is a process students use to extract meaning out of oral speech. Activities in which teachers can engage to assist students in becoming more effective listeners include

I. clearly setting a purpose for listening.
II. allowing children to relax by chewing gum during listening.
III. asking questions about the selection.

IV. encouraging students to forge links between the new information and knowledge already in place.

(A) I and II only
(B) II, III, and IV
(C) I, III, and IV
(D) I, II, III, and IV

97. The following graph shows the distribution of test scores in Ms. Alvarez's class. Based on the graph, which of the following statements do you know to be true?

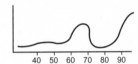

I. The majority of students scored higher than 60.
II. The test was a fair measure of ability.
III. The mean score is probably higher than the median.
IV. The test divided the class into distinct groups.

(A) I and II only
(B) I and IV only
(C) I, III, and IV
(D) IV only

98. Mrs. Johnson, a language arts teacher, is considering having her students use the Internet to help them with their essay writing. The librarian tells her that certain rules and regulations must accompany the use of the Internet in schools and libraries. These rules and regulations do NOT include

(A) the use of blocking or filtering technology to protect students against access to certain visual depictions on all school and library computers with Internet access.
(B) the filtering of text.
(C) disclosing personal identification about minors.

(D) unauthorized access, including so-called "hacking," by minors online.

99. A language arts teacher is considering copying some writings to supplement the textbook. Certain copyright laws govern the use of materials in the classroom. Which of the following is NOT true?

(A) The "fair use" doctrine prohibits even limited reproduction of copyrighted works for educational and research purposes.
(B) A teacher can copy a chapter from a book; an article from a periodical or newspaper; and/or a chart, graph, diagram, drawing, cartoon, or picture from a book, periodical, or newspaper.
(C) A teacher can make copies of a short story, a short essay, or a short poem, whether or not from a collective work.
(D) For a classroom, a teacher can make multiple copies (not to exceed the number of students in the class) as long as the copying meets the tests of brevity, spontaneity, and cumulative effect, and each copy includes a notice of copyright.

100. Students in a reading class decide that they would like to read about an American they admire. Asking the members of the class to work together in pairs, Ms. Johnson requests that the students select and find a magazine article about the person they have chosen. In order to form pairs so that students can work together in the library, Ms. Johnson decides that the approach that will allow students to be most productive is to assign students to work together so as to ensure that learning preferences and learner characteristics are compatible for the pair of students. In choosing this approach, Ms. Johnson

(A) avoids having students form their own groups so that the students simply end up working with someone they like.

(B) takes advantage of the information she has about students' individual learning styles so as to maximize student learning effectiveness and efficiency.

(C) avoids randomly assigning students to pairs.

(D) risks having incompatible students working together in pairs.

101. Which of these painters are considered Impressionists?

I. Monet
II. Rembrandt
III. Da Vinci

(A) I only
(B) II only
(C) I and II only
(D) I, II, and III

102. Using student ideas and interests in a lesson

(A) takes students off task.
(B) detracts from the subject content.
(C) does not allow for the evaluation of students' prior knowledge.
(D) increases learning and student motivation.

103. The tango, samba, cha-cha, and bossa nova are all examples of

(A) African dance.
(B) Middle Eastern dance.
(C) Latin American dance.
(D) Indian dance.

104. Ms. Woods has come to the conclusion that her students are having trouble assessing their own writing strengths and weaknesses. Which of the following would be appropriate ways of monitoring and improving the students' writing?

I. Have students each day submit for a grade an original work on a topic they choose.

II. Have students identify, with the help of the teacher, one area of writing in which they feel they need improvement; they will then focus on this area until they have reached their goal and are ready to identify a new area.

III. Keep all draft and final copies in a portfolio; the student will pick a piece to discuss with the teacher at a teacher–student conference.

IV. Once a week the teacher will read a quality composition written by a class member.

(A) II and III only
(B) I and III only
(C) I, III, and IV only
(D) II, III, and IV only

105. Andy Warhol's portrait of Marilyn Monroe was done in which genre?

(A) Impressionism
(B) Cubism
(C) Pop art
(D) Dadaism

106. What concepts are always present in cooperative learning?

I. Team rewards
II. Individual accountability
III. Equal opportunities
IV. Rules
V. Specific tasks

(A) I, III, and IV only
(B) I, II, and III only
(C) II, III, and IV only
(D) I, II, III, and V only

107. Which of the following is the LEAST likely reason for a teacher to give a pretest?

(A) To inform the planning of the unit

(B) To access students' prior knowledge

(C) To have information to calculate student gains at the end of the unit

(D) To have a test grade to calculate student report card grades

108. Some teachers have their students perform Reader's Theater activities, which involve reading a scripted part of a play for classmates or other small audiences. Which of the following is the best rationale for using Reader's Theater plays?

(A) They motivate the students who enjoy acting more than reading.

(B) They encourage students to build fluency and expression while reading

(C) They help students build decoding skills.

(D) They encourage students in the audience to build listening skills.

109. Which of the following forms of exercise emphasizes breathing techniques, stretching, and relaxation?

(A) Yoga

(B) Pilates

(C) Aerobic conditioning

(D) Spinning

110. BMI represents

(A) body movement index.

(B) body mass index.

(C) binary motion index.

(D) bilingual maturational index.

Detailed Explanations of
Answers for Practice Test 2

PRAXIS 0011

1. (B)	23. (C)	45. (B)	67. (C)	89. (C)
2. (D)	24. (B)	46. (D)	68. (C)	90. (A)
3. (C)	25. (A)	47. (B)	69. (B)	91. (D)
4. (B)	26. (A)	48. (D)	70. (A)	92. (A)
5. (D)	27. (A)	49. (B)	71. (D)	93. (D)
6. (D)	28. (D)	50. (C)	72. (B)	94. (A)
7. (D)	29. (C)	51. (D)	73. (C)	95. (B)
8. (B)	30. (D)	52. (A)	74. (D)	96. (C)
9. (A)	31. (D)	53. (B)	75. (A)	97. (B)
10. (C)	32. (A)	54. (B)	76. (B)	98. (B)
11. (D)	33. (C)	55. (C)	77. (A)	99. (A)
12. (C)	34. (D)	56. (C)	78. (C)	100. (B)
13. (B)	35. (D)	57. (C)	79. (B)	101. (A)
14. (D)	36. (D)	58. (A)	80. (C)	102. (D)
15. (B)	37. (C)	59. (C)	81. (D)	103. (C)
16. (B)	38. (D)	60. (C)	82. (D)	104. (D)
17. (B)	39. (A)	61. (A)	83. (A)	105. (C)
18. (B)	40. (C)	62. (C)	84. (C)	106. (B)
19. (A)	41. (B)	63. (D)	85. (C)	107. (D)
20. (C)	42. (A)	64. (A)	86. (D)	108. (B)
21. (C)	43. (B)	65. (A)	87. (C)	109. (A)
22. (B)	44. (C)	66. (D)	88. (D)	110. (B)

PRACTICE TEST 2 PROGRESS CHART

Arts and Physical Education Curriculum, Instruction, and Assessment ____/17

3	71	72	73	74	84	85	86	87	89

90	101	103	105	108	109	110

General Information Curriculum, Instruction, and Assessment ____/19

4	6	10	14	15	20	21	31	43	59

75	76	77	79	80	82	102	106	107

Mathematics Curriculum, Instruction, and Assessment ____/18

11	17	29	38	46	47	48	49	54

55	61	62	78	83	93	94	95	97

Reading and Language Arts Curriculum, Instruction, and Assessment ____/36

1	5	7	12	13	22	23	24	26	27	32	33	34

35	36	39	40	41	42	44	50	51	52	53	56	57

58	81	88	91	92	96	98	99	100	104

Science Curriculum, Instruction, and Assessment ____/12

8	9	18	25	30	37	45	60	63	64	65	66

Social Studies Curriculum, Instruction, and Assessment ____/8

2	16	19	28	67	68	69	70

1. (B)

It is important to ensure that the word problems given to students are at their reading level; otherwise, a teacher will be unable to evaluate their successes with these problems accurately. Choices (A), (C), and (D) are not the best answers to the question.

2. (D)

Academic praise comprises specific statements that give information about the value of the object or about its implications. A simple positive response (A), such as, "That's a good answer!" does not provide any information other than the praise. There is nothing negative (B) about the teacher's response. A redirect (C) occurs when a teacher asks a student to react to the response of another student.

3. (C)

Choral chant is the term used for students' repeating basic facts, spellings, and laws.

4. (B)

A discovery-learning lesson is one in which the class is organized to learn through the students' own active involvement in the lesson. In inductive-reasoning lessons (C), the students are provided with examples and nonexamples and are expected to derive definitions from this information. The egrule method (D) moves from specific examples to general rules or definitions. Even though the lesson may take place in a science class (A), the type of learning is discovery.

5. (D)

Comprehension is shown when the reader questions his or her intent for reading. For example, one may be reading a story to find out what terrible things may befall the main character. The rationale for choosing a book (A) may be an interesting bit of information, but it is not a major topic of discussion with the students. Sharing personal information (B) creates a certain bond, but this is not directly relevant to the question. It is also important that all students are on task before the beginning of a lesson (C), but this is a smaller part of the skill modeled in response (D).

6. (D)

A question testing whether a student can synthesize information will include the need to make predictions or solve problems. An evaluation question (A) will require a judgment of the quality of an idea or solution. In order to be a real analysis (B), the question would have to ask students to analyze given information to draw a conclusion or find support for a given idea. Comprehension questions (C) may require the rephrasing of an idea in the students' own words, and then using this for comparison.

7.   (D)

By having a mixed-level pair read together, the remedial student receives instruction and the skilled student receives reinforcement. This method uses alternate teaching resources, the students themselves, to enhance the learning environment. A certain goal, comprehension, has been set (A), but this is not the most important outcome. The teacher will need to observe fewer groups (B), but it is unlikely that this will change the time needed to work with all groups as long as quality is to be maintained. Even though they are reading in pairs, each student should have a book, and it would be impractical to permit another teacher to utilize the books (C) while one teacher is using them.

8.   (B)

Students at this age do not have the cognitive skills to realize how much they have actually learned or how much they will actually be able to retain. For this reason, choice (A) must be incorrect. At this stage in their intellectual development, students cannot differentiate material that is completely understood from material they have not completely comprehended (C). Students will generally feel that they are capable of learning much more than they will actually retain (D).

9.   (A)

By mapping out previous knowledge, information already known can be transferred to support new information. Although words on the board are visual (B), this is not the underlying motive. Semantic mapping done at the beginning of a story tests how much knowledge the students have about the topic at the outset, not the conclusion (C). Although this method does model proper use of words (D), this is not the main intent of the exercise.

10.   (C)

Data gathered within the learning environment resulting from day-to-day activities could also provide a means for reflection and discussion. This includes using student scores in class not only for their most recognized use, student academic grades (A), but also using the success of students to guide a teacher's professional development plan. Looking for inconsistencies in grading can be a basis for teachers to explore their teaching practices while looking for new and more effective methods. Student academic grades should never be used in behavior assessment [(B) and (D)].

11.   (D)

All teachers have different strengths and weaknesses. By working collaboratively, they can share their abilities to create more strengths and fewer weaknesses. If a teacher has found a method of teaching a concept that is successful, it is worth trying. Viewing the students' scores from the previous year would assist in assessing whether they had made any progress since their last test, but the students' previous scores should not be used to justify their current poor scores (A). This does nothing to assist students in improving their academic achievement. Telling future students to study more (B) or suggesting math tutors (C) may be good advice but should not be the only course of helping students improve in a certain area.

12.   (C)

The correct answer is (C). The early literacy skills described in the scenario are characterized as emergent or emerging. This includes pre-reading and pre-writing skills demonstrated by young children who are beginning to read and write independently.

13. (B)

The question presented here is a low-order question that ensures that a student is focused on the task at hand; it can be used to develop into higher questioning. A high-order question (A) tests the student's ability to apply information, evaluate information, create new information, and so on, rather than to recall simple content. Transitions (C) are used to connect different ideas and tasks. The information that the question is looking for is one of content, not skill (D).

14. (D)

The integrated, real-life nature of this project builds deeper understandings of the economic concept of work and wages, saving versus spending, and banking. While providing the authentic experience of working and saving, the project also builds the class's capacity to complete mathematical functions such as figuring interest rates and compounding interest. In addition, the idea of the value of saving money has been communicated.

15. (B)

The example illustrates a deductive-reasoning task. Inductive reasoning (A) would be giving the class some information and asking them to form a rule or generalization. Choices (C) and (D) are simply examples of inductive tasks.

16. (B)

Choice (B) describes the procedure in place at the campus level to deal with this type of issue. It respects the processes and oversight authority of the committee while addressing the concern of faculty and community. Choice (A) is incorrect because Ms. Carter does not have the authority to enforce the removal of the animals.

Choice (C) is incorrect because the issue should remain at the campus until the committee and the principal have an opportunity to consider the concerns. Choice (D) is incorrect because even though Ms. Carter may appreciate the librarian's efforts, the health concerns are legitimate. Ms. Carter should remain neutral until the campus can act on the issue.

17. (B)

While choices (A), (C) and (D) are all important objectives for students in the area of mathematics, the correct answer is (B). Students will provide multiple solutions to given problems best matches the standard that all students will be able to solve problems in a variety of ways

18. (B)

Students at the formal operational stage can understand complex theoretical descriptions with little or no direct observation. Students at the concrete operational stage (A) must have direct observation to reach understanding and generally have trouble with complex theoretical descriptions. The sensorimotor stage (D) applies to infants, and the preoperational stage (C) applies to children ages 2 to 7.

19. (A)

A needs assessment will help students make the connection between their current skills and those that will be new to them. Choice (B) is incorrect because a needs assessment focuses on the skills a student currently possesses. Choice (C) is incorrect because the needs assessment is designed to determine what needs to be taught that is not currently in the curriculum. Choice (D) is a false statement; a needs assessment is not designed to motivate students.

20. (C)

A positive environment must be created to minimize the effects of negative external factors. Choice (A) is inappropriate because changing the textbook but allowing the environment to remain the same only results in maintaining the status quo. Choice (B) is incorrect because relating the students' personal interests to the new material is only part of creating a positive environment. Choice (D) is incorrect because, again, it is only a small part of maximizing the effects of a positive learning environment.

21. (C)

The teacher would be fostering strong home relationships that support student achievement of desired outcomes. Choice (A) is a result of choice (C); as the teacher interacts with professionals in the community, her own professional growth would be promoted. Choice (B) is also the result of choice (C); all teachers are expected to interact with the community to help meet the expectations associated with teaching. Choice (D) is incomplete, because strong home relationships are developed through the principles of conferences, trust, and cooperation.

22. (B)

This assignment asks students to gather information or explore long-term goals—goals many years in the future. Short-term goals [(A) and (C)] are those that can be achieved in days, weeks, or maybe months. Answer (D), synthesize, is a more complicated process than merely gathering information.

23. (C)

The teacher is asking the student questions to allow the student to correct a spelling error. Spelling does not allow for divergent or creative think-

ing (A). Although the teacher reminds the student of a mnemonic, the teacher is not teaching the mnemonic (B). Finally, applying spelling rules or guides to improve spelling would be an example of deductive reasoning, not inductive reasoning (D).

24. (B)

It is very important that all students feel welcome, but it is especially effective for ESL students to feel comfortable and welcome in the classroom. Students should be able to use many resources to help them so (D) is incorrect. Most schools will not have a specialist to whom the teacher can refer the student; (C) is not an acceptable choice. A teacher should never deprive a student of the student's language or culture; (A) is not an appropriate answer.

25. (A)

Ms. Borders must consider the learning preferences and emotional factors of her learners as she constructs learning activities for the study. Considering cooperative group projects versus independent work is one aspect of her preparation. Another would be the range of products deemed acceptable as demonstrations of knowledge (written or spoken, visual or performed art, technology based, etc.). Choices (B), (C), and (D) might be considered once she plans the study, but they are unrelated to the issue of preparing for the stated instructional outcomes.

26. (A)

Students learn to speak two languages in one of two ways: sequentially, in which one language is mastered before the study of the second language has begun (A), or simultaneously, in which both languages are learned concurrently (B). Sequential language acquisition does not mean a student learns two languages in parts (C) or that the student develops language skills (D).

27. (A)

Some students may not speak English at home or may have limited exposure to the vocabulary of the classroom. It is important to be aware of these factors and provide the materials appropriate to help guide mastery. Answers that say negative things about the students are never the best choice; for that reason, one should not choose answer (B), (C), or (D).

28. (D)

The teacher hopes to engage the students in critical thinking by allowing them to express their opinions; the teacher realizes that students will have different interpretations of the statement. Choices (A), (B), and (C) are possible outcomes, but (D) is the best answer because it relates specifically to the teacher's aim.

29. (C)

All of the manipulatives listed are good math resources. While students may be able to notice patterns when using calendars it is not the best tool for first graders. Fraction tiles are beneficial for students of any age who are studying fractions. The correct answer is (C). Multi-colored counters are the best choice for students who are recognizing and building patterns. They are easy for young children to manipulate and come in many interesting shapes and sizes. Base-ten blocks are a good resource for students studying place value and regrouping.

30. (D)

The first life forms would be the simplest, so simple single-celled organisms, choice (D) is correct.

31. (D)

Students are more likely to be more enthusiastic when something that they enjoy is the subject or focus of a lesson, which, in turn, helps to build the academic success of the lesson.

32. (A)

Only choice (A) recognizes the cognitive principle underlying the teacher's assignment. Choices (B) and (D) are essentially the same; although the assignment may result in these time-saving features, they are not the instructional principle guiding the teacher's practice. Choice (C) is irrelevant. Asking students to hypothesize is not directly related to inculcating self-management skills in learners.

33. (C)

The term *trade books* refers to the authentic literature selections found in a classroom library. These are often chapter books of either fiction or nonfiction genres. What makes a trade book authentic is that it is a complete literary work written by an author for a variety of purposes.

34. (D)

In general, teachers believe that oral language proficiency correlates with academic proficiency. Research indicates, however, that oral language proficiency is easily acquired through daily living experiences, whereas academic language proficiency requires an academic setting with context-related activities.

35. (D)

Choice (D) is the best answer because it contains information that is technically correct and expresses a concern about the difference in the student's standardized test score and about the usual performance in math class. Choice (A) is technically correct; however, it does not really provide as complete an answer as (D). Choice (B) tends to provide the student with a false impression; although the student scored in the top half, as one of the best students in class, the student could have been expected to have scored perhaps in the top 10 percent or at least the top quartile. Choice (C) is simply a false statement.

36. (D)

Word walls are commonly found in elementary classrooms. They are sometimes referred to as "word banks" as well. It is an alphabetical listing of words that is generated by the teacher and students and is hung in the classroom to use as a spelling reference tool. Correctly using words on a spelling test or on homework does not necessarily mean students will apply this knowledge while writing in the classroom.

37. (C)

According to Piaget's theory of cognitive development, students in middle school would be at the stage of concrete operational thought. Students at this stage of cognitive development would be able to categorize items. Choice (A) is a false statement. Although some students do like to work in groups, other students prefer to work alone—at this and at any age group or cognitive stage. Preferring to learn in groups (or socially) or to learn alone (or independently) is a characteristic of learning style or pref-

erence, not a characteristic of cognitive or affective development. Choice (B) is irrelevant to the teacher's intent in assigning the task. Students could just as easily work with unfamiliar items, grouping them by observable features independent of their use or function. Choice (D) is not a good choice under any circumstances. Teachers should assiduously avoid giving students any assignments merely to keep them busy while they do something else. All assignments should have an instructional purpose.

38. (D)

Although a teacher should provide students with coins to use during testing (end) and pre-testing (beginning) situations, the scenario specifies that it is the middle of a money unit. If the teacher is intending to incorporate authentic materials, then real coins should be used. The correct answer is (D). The teacher is most likely in the process of teaching students how to add and subtract monetary amounts.

39. (A)

Only Choice (A) takes into account differences among learners by giving them options as to how and where they will read. Choice (B) violates the students' freedom to select reading materials they find interesting and wish to read. When students are allowed to choose their own reading materials, it may seem that some students select materials beyond their present reading comprehension. However, reading research indicates that students can comprehend more difficult material when their interest level is high. Therefore, any efforts by the teacher to interfere with students' selection of their own reading material would be ill-advised. Choices (C) and (D) are equally poor in that they both describe a concession to only one group of learners. For example, with choice (C), even though some students may prefer to read with music playing in the background, other students may find the music distracting. The best action for the teacher to take would be to allow some students to listen to music on earphones while others read in quiet. In regard to choice (D), some students will prefer bright illumination just as some students will read better with the lights dimmed. Ms. Rodriguez would do well to attempt to accommodate various learner needs by having one area of the room more brightly illuminated than the other.

40. (C)

The teacher is encouraging students to become engaged in the learning process by making a prediction based on limited information given in the book title and cover illustration. When students can generate their own predictions or formulate hypotheses about possible outcomes on the basis of available (although limited) data, they are gaining preparatory skills for formal operations (or abstract thinking). Although second-grade students would not be expected to be at the level of cognitive development characterized by formal operations, Piagetian theory would indicate that teachers who model appropriate behaviors and who give students opportunities to reach or stretch for new cognitive skills are fostering students' cognitive growth. Choice (A) is a poor choice because students' responses to this one question posed by the teacher cannot be used to assess adequately their interest in reading activities. Choice (B), likewise, is a poor choice in that it implies no instructional intent for asking the question. Choice (D) is incorrect because students' responses to a single question cannot allow the instructor to determine which students are good readers and which ones are not.

41. (B)

The question asks for appropriate statements for Mrs. Johnson to consider in making an instructional decision. Option I is a valid reason

for teaching students how to develop portfolios. Teachers teach students skills that will be useful in school and in their careers. Although option II may produce positive affective results, feeling mature because students are imitating older siblings is not a sufficient reason to choose portfolios. Option III is the most appropriate reason for using portfolios. Most activities and projects that promote achievement of course outcomes would be considered appropriate strategies. Option IV is not necessarily true; portfolio assessment can result in more written work, which can be more time-consuming. Even if option IV were true, emphasizing student achievement is more important than easing the workload of teachers. Options I and III (B) are appropriate.

42. (A)

Reading aloud to children has been found to be one of the most effective means of fostering literacy in students. Choice (A) is the best answer. Students of any age or ability level can enjoy and learn from a read aloud experience. This technique is used for a variety of reasons including the teaching of vocabulary, fluency, and reading comprehension skills, as well as motivating students to read independently.

43. (B)

A running record is a technique used for assessing a student's reading ability. The teacher and student have the same passage in front of them. The teacher keeps track of the student's reading by making marks on the passage as the student reads it aloud. This enables the teacher to analyze any miscues, as well as noting strengths and weaknesses the student may have.

44. (C)

Of the listed steps, publishing is the last step of the writer's workshop approach. Choice (C) is the best answer. A teacher may not choose to have the students reach this step each time they embark on a writing project. However, publishing allows the students to complete the process and have a finished product to share. Sometimes teachers add an additional step of sharing or celebrating the student's work after it has been published in the classroom.

45. (B)

A hands-on activity will best help the students learn about data collection. Choice (B) is the only choice that employs a hands-on activity, so this is the best answer. The students would learn about direct observation by watching Ms. Thompson tickle the mouse and the philodendron (A); however, this method would not be as effective as allowing the students to conduct their own data collection. Research suggests that viewing a video (C) is an inefficient method of learning. Having a guest speaker tell the students about data collection (D) is not a good choice for first graders.

46. (D)

Having each student solve two-digit by two-digit multiplication problems and write the steps to solving two-digit by two-digit multiplication problems in a math journal best addresses the goals set by the teacher. It is important that students are able to explain their thought processes through writing, as well as to be able to solve mathematical problems through computation. Having the students perform each task during the course of the unit is most likely to address this goal.

47. (B)

The student in the example is subtracting the top number in the ones column from the bottom number in the ones column. The student should be regrouping from the tens column since the top number in each example is greater than the bottom number. If the student continued this method, he would subtract three from six in the ones column, and 2 from four in the tens column for the erroneous answer of 23.

48. (D)

Bryant gave an answer of 8, which reflects the number of outfit combinations that can be made from the items listed. The blue skirt can be worn with each of the four shirts for a total of four outfits. The green skirt can be worn with each of the four shirts for a total of four outfits. Therefore, there are eight different outfits of a skirt and a shirt.

49. (B)

Manipulatives specifically refers to the hand-held objects used to solve problems by students in a math class. There are varieties of manipulatives available including blocks, rods, tiles, counters, tangrams, chips, and other items used to build numeracy. Choice (B) is the correct answer: while journals are an integral part of math instruction, they would not be considered a manipulative.

50. (C)

Choice (C) restates the definition of *illiterate* and *functionally illiterate* given in the second paragraph of the passage. Choice (A) cannot be correct because the passage clearly distinguishes between those who are illiterate and those who are functionally illiterate. Choice (B) is not correct because the definition stated is not related to participation in a program. The relative number of illiterate and functional illiterate people is not discussed; Choice (D) is incorrect. .

51. (D)

This passage has several purposes. First, the author presents some complaints concerning the way literacy issues are presented in the media (B). The author also discusses the increased attention given to literacy by society (C). Third, the author discusses many aspects of successful literacy programs (A). Therefore, choice (D), which includes all of these purposes, is correct.

52. (A)

This question must be answered using the process of elimination. You are asked to select a statement that names a possible program component that is *not* characteristic of successful literacy programs. Choice (A) is correct because choices (B), (C), and (D) are specifically mentioned in the passage.

53. (B)

Choice (B) is correct because the author specifically states that politicians should support increased funding for literacy programs. Choices (A) and (C) are incorrect because the author states that funding should be increased. There is no discussion of funding for different programs, so choice (D) is incorrect.

54. (B)

The variance in fifth-graders' physical size and development has a direct influence on their interests and attitudes, including their willingness to work with others and a possible preference for working alone. Choice (A) is incorrect because

fifth graders do have the physical and mental maturity to work in small groups. Choice (C) is incorrect because not all fifth-grade students lack the ability for internal control. Choice (D) is incorrect; although Mr. Dobson might need to be more specific in his directions to the students, this is not the main reason for their behavior.

55. (C)

Students who are shy are usually more willing to participate in small groups than in discussions involving the entire class. Choice (A) is incorrect because calling on each student once per day will not necessarily assist shy students to participate in class discussions, even if participation grades are assigned. Choice (B) is incorrect because although students may become less shy as the year progresses, the teacher still has a responsibility to encourage students to participate. Choice (D) is incorrect because although speaking to students individually may help some to participate; it is likely more students will participate if the procedure outlined in choice (C) is implemented.

56. (C)

Mrs. Kresmeier uses effective communication strategies to teach students and encourages them to interact for the same purposes. Mnemonic devices are apparently a new technique for most of the students; in addition, the teacher's own creative spelling clues are often new ones matching the age level, interests, and patterns of humor enjoyed by her students. The most success is probably derived from her encouragement to examine the words to find a feature that can be turned into a mnemonic device. Choice (A) is incorrect because there has been no attempt to rule out other techniques of learning to spell. Choice (B) is incorrect because certainly other teachers have also impressed upon the students that spelling is important. The creative methodology is probably the major difference between Mrs. Kresmeier's method and those that students have encountered in the past. Choice (D) is incorrect because no evidence exists to show that Mrs. Kresmeier is especially selective in choosing her spelling lessons.

57. (C)

Formative assessment (C) is continuous and is intended to serve as a guide to future learning and instruction. Summative evaluation (A) and summative assessment (B) are both used to put a final critique or grade on an activity or assignment with no real link to the future. Peer evaluation (D) would require students to critique each other.

58. (A)

Meeting one-to-one to discuss a student's strengths and weaknesses creates a feeling of trust and confidence between the student and the teacher. Grading papers solely on the content of a conference (B) is not an efficient means of grading. The student–teacher conference should not focus on only one part of the writing process, such as careful editing (C) or prewriting (D).

59. (C)

The role of the resource teacher is to provide individual instruction for students who qualify for services and, through collaborative consultation, work with the classroom teacher to adapt instruction to match each student's needs. A resource teacher should not be entirely responsible for teaching a learning-disabled student (A) and is also not responsible for tutoring outside of the scheduled class meetings (D). A learning-disabled student should not be totally excused from assignments (B).

60. (C)

This is an example of working with other teachers to plan instruction. Response (A) is incorrect because it is incomplete. This activity may complete the school year, but this activity is not necessarily an end-of-the-year project. Choice (B) is incorrect because problem solving and inquiry teaching are only small components of the activity. Choice (D) is incorrect because asking students to research Galileo and asking the PTA to buy science equipment are not necessarily related.

61. (A)

Visiting other teachers in other schools will promote collaboration and cooperation. Choice (B) is incorrect because there is no reason to believe that the principal is encouraging these teachers to apply for a job in the middle school. Choice (C) is incorrect because, although using computers in science classes may be a topic on which teachers choose to collaborate, choice (A) is more complete. Choice (D) is incorrect because the middle school math curriculum is not intended for use in the fifth grade.

62. (C)

Including games, practice-problem drills, quizzes, and writing in math journals is an effective approach. Using the greatest variety of instructional techniques is the most helpful way to assist students in mastery of any skill. Choice (C) is the best answer. A teacher increases the chance that each student will learn by including tasks that touch on a variety of learning styles and intelligences.

63. (D)

A K-W-L is an effective instructional tool. It is an acronym for *What I **K**now, What I **W**ant to* *know, What I Learned*. The K and the W are completed before the unit begins. Teachers can set lesson objectives and develop big ideas based on what the students already know about a topic, as well as what they want to know. The L is completed by students at the end to demonstrate what they have learned from the unit of study.

64. (A)

ESL students and inclusion students benefit from a variety of strategies. Introducing the vocabulary ahead of time (B) is an effective method, as is making vocabulary cards with photographs for the students to use (D). It is also beneficial to include specialists such as ESL and special education teachers (C) who may work with the students outside or inside the classroom. Assigning the work for homework (A), however, may be of no assistance to the students, as parents and guardians should not be relied on to support academic tasks.

65. (A)

The scientific method is used for problem solving in a scientific environment. First student scientists are asked to pose or state a question for experimentation. Second, students develop hypotheses that potentially answer the question. Next, students conduct an experiment based on the question. Last, students draw conclusions based on the evidence gathered through experimentation.

66. (D)

It is most appropriate to recognize the high-quality content with a high mark and to speak with students regarding their writing errors. The content in students' journals reflects their understanding of the subject studied. While spelling and other mechanics of writing are important conventions for students to learn, they are not the focus of a science

journal and should not be used to penalize students. Receiving low grades based on mechanics may discourage students from writing in the content areas.

67. (C)

The cooperative learning strategy described is called a think-pair-share. Students are asked to think about an idea or experience, turn to a peer, and share their ideas. This facilitates risk taking, peer learning, and social development.

68. (C)

Choice (C) is the best answer. It is important to access students' prior knowledge of a topic in order to plan a unit of study. While writing guiding questions (A) and creating learning activities (B) are also important steps, finding out what students have already learned is the first step.

69. (B)

A primary source is a firsthand or inside account. Journals, letters, and photographs are all original documents from this perspective. A biography, choice (B), involves a person or people researching and writing about another individual from an outside or secondhand perspective.

70. (A)

Will has placed the former presidents in order from the most recent, in this case William J. Clinton, to the least recent, Gerald Ford.

71. (D)

In order to play any game or sport, students must understand the rules (A), the roles of the positions (B), and proper use of the equipment to ensure safety and success (C). While it is essential to understand how to score a goal in hockey, it is the least important in this learning environment.

72. (B)

Timbre is a musical term that describes the aspects of a sound other than pitch, loudness, or length. The difference in sound between two distinct instruments playing the same note is in the timbre of the sounds. Design, technique, and art history are all parts of an art curriculum.

73. (C)

The use of unusual materials has dramatically changed the criteria by which one assesses visual art.

74. (D)

During the nineteenth century, there was a revival of interest in Classical and Gothic styles.

75. (A)

A teacher can guide a student to a higher-level answer through questioning. Repeating the question (B) would probably elicit the same response, and asking a different student [(C) and (D)] would not help the student who provided the simple response.

76. (B)

Asking children to complete a graphic organizer as they research an issue helps them stay organized, see connections, and pull together what they can then use in some interesting and meaningful way.

77. (A)

Nonperformers are students who are not involved in the class discussion at that particular moment. Asking a student to respond to another student's statement (A) is one way of incorporating nonperformers into a class discussion. Therefore, (B), (C), and (D) are incorrect.

78. (C)

Choice (C) is the correct answer. All of the problems included in the question require students to use division, which results in an answer that includes a remainder of one.

79. (B)

Piaget identified four stages of cognitive development. As children go through each stage, they will develop new abilities, but they will be unable to exhibit this ability until they reach that particular stage. Children under the age of eight do not have the understanding of language that grasps complexities (A). Accordingly, teachers should use simple language when working with these children [(C) and (D)].

80. (C)

Although verbal communication skills are very important in establishing and maintaining interpersonal relationships, being aware of—and controlling—one's body language is at least equally important. Choices (A), (B), and (D) are statements of necessary, and teachable/learnable, traits for successful social interaction.

81. (D)

In inductive thinking, students derive concepts and definitions based upon the information provided to them, which can be fostered through personal-discovery activities (D), by which students try to determine the relationships among the objects given to them. Choral chanting (A) practices skills, multiple-choice questions (C) usually test objective knowledge, and general computer experience (B) fosters computer knowledge.

82. (D)

Robert F. Mager is the name most frequently associated with objectives. Lev Vygotsky, Erik Erikson, and Jean Piaget are all associated with cognitive development and learning theories.

83. (A)

The correct answer is (A). The teacher most likely chose a book in which a child has a nightmare involving math to address math anxiety in students. The book may also point out that math is all around and make a real-life connection to math; however, these are not the strongest reasons. A book with a number-based nightmare is as likely to discourage students to study math facts as it is to encourage this.

84. (C)

The horse shows lightness and motion. You should notice, for instance, that the tail and feet seem to imply movement. The horse is young and spry; (A) could not be true. The horse does not suggest warlike attitudes; (D) is not appropriate. The horse is light on its feet; massiveness (B) is not acceptable.

85. (C)

An *aside* is a comment spoken directly to the audience that the other actors on stage are supposedly unable to hear.

86. (D)

This question tests one's ability to determine the central focus in a staged dramatic production and to explain why there is such a focus. The central attraction in this picture is the man on the bed (D). Many eyes are turned to him, and he appears to be speaking. The other men in the picture are turned away from the viewers, and many are directing their attention toward the man on the bed. Since this character is in a full-front position, he will draw more attention than those in profile or full back, which are weaker positions.

87. (C)

Gianlorenzo Bernini's *David* of 1623 is a perfect example of the Baroque sculptor's wish to express movement and action and to capture a fleeting moment of time. Here, the figure's twisting posture and intense facial expression create a dynamic, not a static, character, as David begins the violent twisting motion with which he will hurl the stone from his sling; (B) is incorrect. His gaze is directed outward at an unseen adversary, implying interaction with another character and denying any purely ornamental conception behind this work (A). The figure's meager garments, far from identifying him as a warrior (D), emphasize both his physical vulnerability and his idealized, heroic beauty.

88. (D)

While it is important to allow young students to write with inventive spelling in order to encourage early attempts at writing, a third grader should be writing primarily using conventional spellings. The Child Study Team should be consulted if a teacher has serious concerns about a student, after other strategies are explored in the classroom. Parents may decide to hire a tutor on their own to help their child's progress; however, it is inappropriate for a teacher to suggest this instead of attempting to assist the child in the classroom. (D) is the correct answer. The teacher should help the student become aware of the correct spelling of misspelled words and should instruct the student on spelling strategies.

89. (C)

The physical education curriculum is designed to promote healthful living in students and to introduce them to a variety of physical activities. Thus aerobic conditioning helps train their hearts, strength training works on muscle groups, and sportsmanship teaches children how to behave toward one another. Joining a team is an optional activity for children, not a goal of physical education.

90. (A)

The seventeenth-century Japanese ink-on-paper scroll painting shown in the example relies almost exclusively on the qualities of line to convey the graceful forms of two leaping deer. In this painting, called *Deer Scroll*, both the animals and the scripted characters share the same quality of fluid, rhythmic, spontaneous "writing." Gradations of tone (B) and color (C) are unimportant here because the images are defined by black lines on white. Volume (D), too, is absent because these forms show no shading or modulation of tone.

91. (D)

Among all of the nationally recognized professional organizations, Teachers of English to Speakers of Other Languages, Inc. (TESOL) is identified as the organization that provides professional support for educators; (D) is the best answer. *IRA* stands for the International Reading Association; (A) is not the best choice. NATM is the National Association of Teachers of Mathematics; (B)

is incorrect. NASDTEC is the abbreviation for the National Association of State Directors of Teacher Education and Certification; (C) is not the best choice.

92. (A)

The students' writing is the best resource to inform a teacher when a skill should be taught or reinforced. While teachers are often influenced by factors such as staff development, standardized tests, and district mandates, they most often have the autonomy to decide what and when to teach based on their students' needs. Therefore, (D) is the best answer.

93. (D)

Having students roll dice or flip a coin and keep a record of the results, and practicing examples in a textbook are all appropriate tasks for reviewing probability. They may not, however, keep students interested for long. Having students participate in rotating learning centers with a variety of hands-on activities would be the best way to encourage interest and skill building.

94. (A)

The correct answer is (A). Calculators will be of little help to students who are having difficulty conceptualizing regrouping. Base-ten blocks, coins and bills, and place value cards may all be beneficial tools for struggling students.

95. (B)

Since students have been working directly with shape manipulatives, allowing students to identify the shapes using the manipulatives would be the most effective form of assessment. It is the most similar experience for them. Having the students do this individually rather than in a small group would be a better measure of each student's understanding. The correct answer is (B).

96. (C)

Clearly setting a purpose for listening (I), asking questions about the selection (III), and encouraging students to forge links between the new information and knowledge already in place (IV) are all supported by research as effective strategies.

97. (B)

Just from looking at the graph, it is clear that most of the space under the curve is past the 60 mark on the x-axis, and there are clearly two groups. Answer (D) is eliminated because it doesn't include statement I. Statement II cannot be answered by what the graph shows. It appears possible that certain questions were too difficult for many in the class and that there were not enough questions to differentiate students in the 70 to 90 range, but perhaps the class performed exactly as it should have, given the students' ability and Ms. Alvarez's teaching. The distribution can give Ms. Alvarez many clues about the test and the students and even herself, but by itself tells her nothing about the fairness of the test. Thus, answer (A) can be eliminated. Also, without specific data, we cannot determine whether the mean is higher than the median, so (C) is incorrect.

98. (B)

Rules and regulations for schools and libraries that make the use of the Internet available to students do *not* currently include the filtering of text (B). However, these computers must provide the use of blocking or filtering technology to protect students against access to certain visual depictions (A). The rules also require that personal information about the students must not be disclosed (C) and prohibit the use of the computers for "hacking" (D).

99. (A)

Choice (A) is not true; the "fair use" doctrine *does* allow limited reproduction of copyrighted works for educational and research purposes. Teachers can copy chapters, articles, charts, graphs, diagrams, or cartoons for the classroom, so (B) is legally possible and is *not* the correct answer. Regardless of whether the copy is from a collective work, an educator may make copies of a short story, essay, or poem for the classroom; so (C) is true and is not the answer to the question. Because teachers can make multiple copies for the class (not to exceed the number of students in the class) as long as the copying meets the tests of brevity and spontaneity, (D) is not the best choice.

100. (B)

Although (A), (C), and (D) are possible choices, the best answer to the question is (B). Choices (A), (C), and (D) are basically restatements of the idea that the teacher forms the groups instead of the students; this was specified in the context of the question. The only option which gives a rationale for the teacher's action is answer (B).

101. (A)

The Impressionists were a group of painters who wanted to show their view of reality, not necessarily a photographic image of what appeared. They often used a pointillist style of painting, in which the painting consisted of dots of colors. Claude Monet is an acclaimed painter of this style. Rembrandt, a sixteenth-century Dutch artist, is famous for his use of chiaroscuro, or light and dark, to evoke emotions and scenes. Leonard Da Vinci is the artist famous for, among his many other talents, his painting of the Sistine Chapel in the Vatican.

102. (D)

Students are more likely to be more enthusiastic when something they enjoy is the subject or focus of a lesson; this, in turn, helps to build the academic success of the lesson.

103. (C)

These dances all originated in South America, although they spread in popularity all over the world.

104. (D)

Choice (D) includes all of the techniques that would be useful in improving and monitoring writing. The students have set goals toward which they will strive (II) bit by bit until they reach them. The teacher and student have an opportunity to discuss good and bad points of the student's writing in a nonthreatening atmosphere (III). It is always helpful to have a model of good writing (IV), and by choosing students' papers, the teacher enhances students' self-esteem. Thus, choice (A), which does not include IV, is incorrect. Forcing a student to write every night (I) will do little to create quality work; therefore, choices (B) and (C) are incorrect.

105. (C)

Andy Warhol made the genre of Pop art famous. Pop art uses typical cultural icons, such as Warhol's Campbell Soup cans or Marilyn Monroe, to make a statement about popular culture. Impressionism (A) was a nineteenth-century art

form used by such artists as Monet to create a dreamy, "impressionistic" view of reality. Cubism (B), which Picasso made famous, separated reality into geometric figures. Dadaism (D), an early twentieth-century movement, is exemplified in the work of Max Ernst and Marcel Duchamp. It was a rebellion against the times and preached that everyone had a right to his or her own interpretation of reality.

106. (B)

Team rewards (I), individual accountability (II), and equal opportunities for success (III) are always present in cooperative learning. Rules (IV) and specific tasks (V) may be part of the instructions given for cooperative learning groups, but are not required in cooperative learning situations; therefore, choices (A), (C), and (D) are incorrect.

107. (D)

Because they are given before the start of a unit, to have a test grade to calculate student report card grades is an unlikely reason to give a pretest. A pretest is used to inform unit planning since it demonstrates the students' prior knowledge. It is then compared to a corresponding post-test at the end of the unit to calculate students' gains in learning.

108. (B)

Reader's Theater activities are often enjoyable to many students; however this is not the strongest rationale. The correct answer is (B). They encourage students to build fluency and expression while reading because they require students to project their voices and embody a character. Reading plays aloud does not necessarily build decoding skills. While listening to a performance can encourage the improvement of listening skills, it is not the strongest rationale.

109. (A)

Yoga, a form of exercise brought from the Far East, emphasizes correct breathing, stretching exercises, and relaxation techniques. Pilates (B) is a method of strengthening one's "core," or abdominal and back muscles. While both aerobic conditioning (C) and spinning (D) require correct breathing, neither exercise emphasizes all three: correct breathing, stretching exercises, and relaxation techniques.

110. (B)

BMI, or body mass index, is a tool for indicating weight status. It is a measure of weight for height and helps determine whether an individual is overweight, underweight, or at a normal weight.

Index

PRAXIS 0011

Index

H

Harmonic instruments, 193

Harmony, 190

HDL (high-density lipoprotein), 204

Health risks, 207–209

Heckleman, R. G., 67–68

Heterogeneous groups, 32–33

Hexagons, 119

Higher-order thinking skills, 26–29

Hollingsworth, Paul, 68

Homogeneous groups, 32–33

Homogeneous mixtures, 159

Hue, 183

Human body, 163–165

Human-environmental interaction, 137, 140–143

Humans, early, 141–142

Hydration, 203

Hypothesis, 151

I

Identity element of addition/ multiplication, 112

"I" messages, 45

Immune system, 164

Important ideas, 76

Individual appropriateness, 66

Inductive reasoning, 100–101, 155

Industry, vs. inferiority, 17

Inferences, 76, 150–151

Inferential questions, 78–79

Inferiority, industry vs., 17

Informal assessment, 49, 92–94, 145

Informal checks, 49

Initiative, vs. guilt, 17

Inquiry lessons, 101, 154–155

"Instant word" lists, 93

Instruction. See also Technology

academic learning time, 35–36

checking for understanding, 80–81

classroom management, 41–48

inquiry lessons, 101, 154–155

learning activities, 32–33, 37–38

mathematics, 128–130

motivation, 43–44, 213–218

organization, 39–40

physical education, 209–213

physical environment, 34–35, 210–211

procedures for learning success, 36–41

questions, wait time for, 38

reading comprehension, 87–89

science, 154–155

social and emotional climate, 35

social sciences, 132–136

suitability of, 33–34

time management, 38–39

vocabulary, 85

Instruments, 190, 192–194

Integers, 113

Interior angles, 116

International Reading Association (IRA), 72

Internet, 129, 134, 175, 178–181

Interoceptors, 164

Interpretation, of experimental results, 152

Interpretive level of comprehension, 78–79

Intersecting lines, 117

Invented spellings, 71

Inverse, 108, 110

Investigations, designing and conduction, 132

Iron, 206

Irrational numbers, 114

J

Jigsaws, 33

Johnson, Spencer, 31, 44

Jointly constructed meaning, 214–215

Joints, 163

Journals, 81

Judging, 79

Jung, Carl, 20–21

K

Key words, 127

Kidneys, 164

Kilometer (km), 123

Kinesthetic learners, 21–22

Klein, Robert, 90

Kohlberg, Lawrence, 17–19

K-W-L (know-want-learned) chart, 87–88

L

Language arts, 63, 89–94. See also Reading

Language experience approach (LEA), 69, 92

Latitude, 139

Lava, 157

LDL (low-density lipoprotein), 204

Learners, role of, 19–20

Learning activities, 32–33, 37–38, 215

Learning style inventories, 21

Learning styles, 20–23, 36–37, 38

Learning theories, 15–19

Left-to-right direction, 64–65

Legends, 138

Libraries, 129, 132–133, 180–181

Library of Congress, 136

Ligaments, 163

Installing REA's TEST*ware*®

SYSTEM REQUIREMENTS

Pentium 75 MHz (300 MHz recommended) or a higher or compatible processor; Microsoft Windows 98 or later; 64 MB available RAM; Internet Explorer 5.5 or higher.

INSTALLATION

1. Insert the PRAXIS Elementary Education 0011 CD-ROM into the CD-ROM drive.

2. If the installation doesn't begin automatically, from the Start Menu choose the RUN command. When the RUN dialog box appears, type d:\setup (where d is the letter of your CD-ROM drive) at the prompt and click OK.

3. The installation process will begin. A dialog box proposing the directory "C:\Program Files\REA\Praxis_ElEd\" will appear. If the name and location are suitable, click OK. If you wish to specify a different name or location, type it in and click OK.

4. Start the PRAXIS Elementary Education TEST*ware*® application by double-clicking on the icon.

REA's PRAXIS Elementary Education TEST*ware*® is **EASY** to **LEARN AND USE**. To achieve maximum benefits, we recommend that you take a few minutes to go through the on-screen tutorial on your computer. The "screen buttons" are also explained here to familiarize you with the program.

TECHNICAL SUPPORT

REA's TESTware® is backed by customer and technical support. For questions about **installation or operation of your software**, contact us at:

> **Research & Education Association**
> **Phone: (732) 819-8880 (9 a.m. to 5 p.m. ET, Monday–Friday)**
> **Fax: (732) 819-8808**
> **Website: *www.rea.com***
> **E-mail: info@rea.com**

Note to Windows XP Users: In order for the TEST*ware*® to function properly, please install and run the application under the same computer administrator-level user account. Installing the TEST*ware*® as one user and running it as another could cause file-access path conflicts.